Performing in Comedy

Comic acting is a distinct art form and as such, it demands a unique skill set. By exploring the ways in which performance choices and improvised moments can work in conjunction with texts themselves, *Performing in Comedy* offers an indispensable tool for enhancing comic performance.

Ian Angus Wilkie synthesises theories and principles of comedy with practical tips, and re-evaluates the ways in which these ideas can be used by the performer. Exercises, interviews and guides to further resources enhance this comprehensive exploration of comic acting.

Performing in Comedy makes the skills necessary to a comic actor – timing, focus, awareness – achievable and accessible. This volume is a must-read for any actors, directors or students who work with comic texts.

Ian Angus Wilkie is a lecturer in performance at the University of Salford. Formerly he was a tutor in post-compulsory education at the UCL Institute of Education, London, and a visiting lecturer at the Guildhall School of Music and Drama. He is an editor for the *Comedy Studies* journal and still works as a professional actor.

Performing in Comedy

A Student's Guide

Ian Angus Wilkie

Routledge
Taylor & Francis Group

LONDON AND NEW YORK

First published 2016
by Routledge
2 Park Square, Milton Park, Abingdon, Oxon OX14 4RN

and by Routledge
711 Third Avenue, New York, NY 10017

Routledge is an imprint of the Taylor & Francis Group, an informa business

British Library Cataloguing-in-Publication Data
A catalogue record for this book is available from the British Library

Library of Congress Cataloguing-in-Publication Data
Names: Wilkie, Ian Angus, author.
Title: Performing in comedy: a student's guide / Ian Angus Wilkie.
Description: Milton Park, Abingdon, Oxon; New York, NY; Routledge,
    2016. | Includes index.
Identifiers: LCCN 2015040531| ISBN 9781138913875 (hardback) |
    ISBN 9781138913882 (pbk.)
Subjects: LCSH: Acting. | Comedy—Technique.
Classification: LCC PN2071.C57 W66 2016 | DDC 792.2/3028—dc23
LC record available at http://lccn.loc.gov/2015040531

ISBN: 978-1-138-91387-5 (hbk)
ISBN: 978-1-138-91388-2 (pbk)
ISBN: 978-1-315-69116-9 (ebk)

Typeset in Sabon
by Book Now Ltd, London
Printed in Great Britain by Ashford Colour Press Ltd

To Denzil, Lynn, Carl, Mark, Jeffrey and
Stephen – who left us wanting more.

Contents

Preface

It is always difficult to assess the success of a comedy when it is greeted with stony silence.
(Eric Sykes, *If I Don't Write It, Nobody Will*, 2010: 368)

This book aims to provide a tool for performers working with textual comedy, whether in live theatre or with television or film scripts. It is primarily aimed at practitioners – actors, directors and students – who are interested in acting within (and through) comic text.

Performing in comedy is different to other forms of performance in that audience laughter (or, at least, their amusement) is the primary aim of the form. Performing in comedy, moreover, requires a set of extra craft skills, many of which are defined and discussed in this book.

You will be encouraged to become a 'reflective practitioner' (Schön, 1987), that is, to evaluate the effectiveness of your comic performance skills through interplay with your fellow performers and, crucially, with the audience. You will also be prompted to create comic performance that is truthful, original and, hopefully, above all else, funny.

Drawing on the reflections of performers, directors, scholars, critics (and a surprising weighty cast of philosophers – including Freud, Schopenhauer, Bergson, etc.) who have all expressed something on the topic of comedy, you will be guided through the development of your comic performance. Your craft and expertise skills will be discussed using the ideas and theories that they propose, placed in conjunction with practical exercises that can be done in the studio or rehearsal room. Blending the advice taken from theorists and practitioners alike, it is intended that this book will become a useful student's guide to comic performance.

It is also truly meant to be a 'student's guide', in that it has been put together by a life-long student of comedy and is intended for fellow students of performance. As an actor, I can make absolutely no claims to any expertise myself, having at best only attempted to put into practice what is being preached here. Now in my third decade of attempting to perform comedy, I am still firmly striving to get it right! I am grateful for all the thoughts, advice, examples and ways of thinking about comic performance that have come my way from people much better qualified to comment on the subject – many of whose ideas are referenced in this book.

I truly hope that this text will help you to think about 'doing' comedy in a different and informed way and will aid you to explore the means to produce effective comic performance. I also hope it will give you the chance to exercise your 'funny bones' while engaging with some of the theories on the mechanics of the performance of comedy.

Ian Angus Wilkie
Brighton 2016

Acknowledgements

With thanks to Alex Lord-Hardman and her performing arts students at Southgate College; the cast of Principal Theatre Co.'s *Twelfth Night*; the cast of the 2006 production of *The Underpants* (by Carl Sternheim, 1910, adapted by Steve Martin, 2002) at the Old Red Lion, Islington, London, and all the performers who have so generously talked to me both informally and formally about the 'doing' of comic performance over the years.

Chapter I

Overview of comic performance

You're not doing comedy if nobody laughs.

(John Wright, 2007: 5)

Introduction

So, you are performing in a comedy? Should you approach the performance of it any differently? From inside the acting profession the knee-jerk response is often a horrified 'no!' while theories on performance and acting theory tend to remain strangely non-committal on the matter. But dig a little deeper and it soon becomes clear that, due to the different formulations and expectations of non-comic and comic forms of drama, subtle differences in the manner of their performance are required. Do exactly the same received 'rules' and theories of performance really apply to the practice of comedy as pertain to 'serious', 'tragic', 'straight' or non-comic forms of drama? For the performer, as, for example, the actress Frances de la Tour explained in an interview, 'if you can do comedy, you can do tragedy. If you can do tragedy, you can't necessarily do comedy' (in Walsh, 2015: 27). Certainly, however, favoured traditional theories of acting and performance do not seem to differentiate the practice of performing comedy, and, from the perspectives of the performer or director, texts on how to approach the art of performance often disregard the doing of comedy completely. Those influential modern European performance gurus who have dominated Westernised thinking on the practice of drama (e.g. Constantin Stanislavski and his 'System', Lee Strasberg and 'The Method', Jerzi Grotowski and the 'Poor' Theatre, Bertold Brecht and the 'Epic' Theatre, or Peter Brook and the 'Empty Space') do not appear to draw any differences between the performance of comic and non-comic forms of drama. But accepted acting theory concepts such as the exploration of 'emotional memory', the uncovering of 'subtext', or the presentation of 'gestus' as a means of presenting emotional or intellectual truths in dramatic form do not quite fit the practice of doing comedy so satisfactorily. So, in short, the means to create the representation of comic and non-comic dramatic 'truths' are usually accepted to be the same. And that is the end of story.

And yet ... and yet ... performing comedy is different. By its very nature, comic performance has unique properties. For, basically, if what you, the actor or director, present to the audience is not funny, or it fails to provoke amusement, even actual laughter, in the audience, then that performance has not been effective. As Armando Iannucci, the creator of *The Thick of It* (BBC, 2005–) and the film *In the Loop* (Iannucci, 2009) observed in an interview, 'if it's not funny ... it's been a waste of time. There isn't a noise that you make during drama that says "I really like this drama". Whereas with comedy, it's instant' (in Patterson, 2009: 9).

Comic performance requires the provocation of amusement (the stimulation of a humorous response) in an audience. Other forms of dramatic presentation do not. So, in that one simple respect, comic performance must take a unique form and requires the practice of specific, pertinent skills from the performer (and director) to create the required effects. Indeed, practitioners themselves often concede that comedy is actually 'harder' to do. As the American actress Elaine Stritch noted, 'comedies are a lot harder and more stressful to play than serious parts. As Neil Simon says 'Dying is easy, comedy is hard' (in Luckhurst and Veltman, 2001: 141).

This book is, therefore, an attempt to place comic performance's special formulations at the centre of the actors' and directors' practice and to redress the neglect that comic performance, taken as a separate phenomenon, has traditionally experienced within performance studies. Too often the performers' contribution to the successful transmission of a comedy has been ignored or even denigrated. Indeed, the mistrust of 'acting' that pervades in modern performance culture (especially in film or television) means that you may well be told that the lines or situation are 'funny enough in themselves' and all that is required of you, the actor, is just to say them. The falsehood there is that the text will take care of itself and the actor's interpretation of the part is somehow secondary. The nonsense of such a statement is illustrated in film and TV 'remakes' where the same lines and situations do not necessarily always 'take care of themselves' when another performer interprets them. Any takers for, say, the 1970 remake of *Laughter in Paradise*? The 1996 UK remakes of the Hancock TV shows? The 2011 remake of *Arthur*? That the performances – the interpreters' playing of the role – provide a huge part in assuring the effectiveness of the comedy is, surely, indisputable.

Features that define comic performance will be suggested throughout this book, and these will be supplemented with exercises for the performer, director or facilitator to help you find – and practice the doing of – comic performance. A chapter on the role that audience 'interplay' takes within 'truthful' comic performance follows along with chapters on working as part of an ensemble; on the use of rhythm and timing; on working with comic text; on acting in film, television and sitcom formats, plus one containing advice from practitioners. All of these chapters will encourage you to become a reflective practitioner – that is, someone who:

- reviews their practice both during and after the event;
- applies potential improvements to their practice based on observation of the effect of their performance;
- in collaboration with their co-performers, applies changes as a result of witnessing the evolving effects;
- continues the cycle of practitioner doing, reviewing, redoing and re-reviewing throughout the performance process.

In this book, there is a difference made between acting and performance. The sociologist Erving Goffman (1959) used the term 'acting' for everything we do in everyday life, while the Theatre Workshop director Joan Littlewood (1994: 199) pronounced:

> Everybody can act ... aren't we all acting most of the time? Performing is something different. Our politicians, popes, barristers and rabble rousers are all actors, but con-men, spies, crooks and plain-clothes policemen are even better. What is a good actor? Part priest, part poet, part clown.

Theatre or television acting, therefore, is, at its most basic, simply the presentation of what people do – a representation of a state of being. You will find that television and film directors are, sometimes, suspicious of 'actors', as they fear any perceived 'theatricality', viewing this as mere overemphasis. They sometimes think that all that they crave is some form of simple representation of being – and would often prefer to hire an actual butcher, baker, candlestick-maker, criminal, mother or vicar, rather than employ a performer to play the role! Sometimes, anything that smacks of performance is simply an anathema to directors for the screen. However, where this comes unstuck for them is when the real butcher or baker is required to act anything other than their occupational role. Playing real feelings or emotions and prompting a reaction through representation of these (this includes inducing amusement or laughter) is the skilled job of the performer. The 'real' person cannot always reproduce the dramatic or comic moments that enliven any text in the way that the script requires, so performers are, albeit sometimes warily, employed to impersonate the characters required.

Acting, therefore, in its simplest sense of 'being' or 'impersonating' is something that everyone can do. It is something, indeed, that we all do all of the time.

Performance, however, is not something that everyone can do. It is, instead, a case of manifesting authentic states of more complex human 'being'. It is the ability to create interactions, reactions, provocations and responses. The performer must convey meanings, ones that are often hidden or sublimated, to other humans, through the media of screen or stage. Not everyone can do this.

Any worries about 'performance' in the media are also somewhat different in theatre where acting (in the sense of replicating behaviours) is more clearly needed to get the messages across. Here, both acting and performance are required.

Performance, then, for the purposes of this book, specifically means a professional mastery of those skills and expertise that will enhance a comic text. It means the conscious display of intercommunicative, representational skills which the actor can deploy to cause an effect, specifically, in this case, in the doing of comedy. Discussion of these skills will centre mainly round how they feature in live situations, that is, as in the theatre context. It will be argued that these skills need not be overt or made noticeable to the audience, and, indeed, some of the craft of the actor is in hiding these skills, making them appear innate and natural.

In short, what follows aims to illustrate the differences between comic and non-comic performance forms, how comic performance works in practice, and how the actor and director might develop the repertoire of acting skills that are required to produce effective comic performance. This chapter also provides a summary overview of the key themes involved in performing in comedy which will then be explored in more detail throughout the chapters that follow.

INDIVIDUAL EXERCISE

Textual clues

Try reading out different selected serious dramatic and comic speeches and extracts and contrasting them. See how much or how little 'performance' or acting is needed to make the text work and 'come alive'. Ask yourself which texts require the most extra performance skills to lift them off the page? For example, try firstly reading aloud – and without intonation – the dramatic text of Shakespeare's Macbeth speech:

> Tomorrow, and tomorrow, and tomorrow,
> Creeps in this petty pace from day to day
> To the last syllable of recorded time;
> And all our yesterdays have lighted fools
> The way to dusty death. Out, out, brief candle!
> Life's but a walking shadow, a poor player
> That struts and frets his hour upon the stage
> And then is heard no more. It is a tale
> Told by an idiot, full of sound and fury,
> Signifying nothing.
>
> (*Macbeth*, Act 5, Scene 5)

Now contrast this with the Porter's speech from the same play:

Knock, knock, knock! Who's there i'the name of Belzebub? Here's a farmer that hanged himself on the expectation of plenty. Come in time! Have napkins enow about you; here you'll sweat for't. (Knock).

Knock, knock! Who's there in the other devil's name? Faith, here's an equivocator that could swear in both the scales against either scale, who committed treason for God's sake, yet could not equivocate to heaven. O, come in, equivocator. (Knock).

Knock, knock, knock! Who's there? Faith, here's an English tailor come hither for stealing out of a French hose. Come in, tailor: here you may roast your goose. (Knock).

Knock, knock! Never at quiet! What are you? – But this place is too cold for hell. I'll devil-porter it no further. I had thought to have let in some of all professions that go the primrose way to the everlasting bonfire. (Knock).

Anon, anon! I pray you remember the porter.

(*Macbeth*, Act 2, Scene 3)

Experiment with adding extra performance layers, for example, vary your vocal intonation, add gestural touches, or try 'lightening' or 'darkening' the interpretation. Which type of text requires more 'performance' layers to be communicated effectively?

Try this experiment with other 'serious' and 'comic' excerpts from plays of different genres to test out whether comic text needs more performance to bring the script fully to life.

Amusing the audience

Firstly, it is perfectly true that comedy should be played as 'seriously' as any other form of drama. Comedy, as a performative art, is as 'real' in, and of, itself as any other form of theatre. In comedy, your performance must still serve the wider 'message' of the play, sitcom, radio drama or film. However, comic performance is an activity that, fundamentally, is intended to amuse an audience. It is an experience that is crafted to be something enjoyable that should make the spectators smile or laugh. In executing comic performance, a link between the player and the audience is formed. The audience provides both the expectation of and a response through laughter, while the performer must somehow be aware of this live interchange from the audience and respond, in turn, to their response. The actor's awareness of potential laughter is still necessary when acting in television or film, even where no live audience may be present. It is in the interchange between performer and spectator where comic performance most often comes fully to life. It is the audience's response to the stimulus created by the actor(s) that is the defining feature of comedy and is that which makes comic performance different to non-comic forms. Comedy works within a world of a mutual consciousness of the performers' attempts to inspire each audience's laughter. To create this cause and effect, to a large extent, the comic performer creates and relies on a peculiar form of interplay with the audience. As Peter Thomson notes, 'the comic actor is always in collusion with the spectators' (2002: 141). The performer operates within a unique state of permissible 'truth' within an accepted pretence. Laughter is the mutual reward and is also the indicator (to both performer and audience) of the effectiveness of the performance.

In the following chapter, we will investigate further how this form of complicity, empathy or interplay – 'the interchange between actor and audience' (Mamet, 1998: 56) – can be created and established while still maintaining the comic 'truth' of the situation or plot. On purely practical grounds, for you, the comedy performer, the ongoing assessment of audience laughter provides you with an instantaneous reflection of your practice. And, arguably, the audience's amusement (or relative lack thereof) is a much more reliable indicator of the effectiveness of your performance when you are being a comic actor than the perception of silence is when you are being a 'serious' actor. After all, you may be receiving nothing back from the audience when acting in serious drama, but what may you take for rapt attention might conceivably be the silence of utter boredom! The 'serious' actor cannot really tell how the audience is receiving their performance to nearly the same level of exactitude as the 'comic' can in live shows. Monitoring the audience's response – even in recorded performance formats, where the imagined audience's response must still be taken into account – is an essential part of the activity of comic performance. In live performance, moreover, the interplay created between the actor and the audience might very well even lead you to modify your performance. You might change your use of rhythm through, say, simply inserting or holding a pause or a look, or altering the timing of a line. As Brett Mills states, 'performers respond to the ways in which audiences react to the comedy which is performed for them' (2005: 89). This may take the form of the performer, in a live situation, creating a meaningful beat or exaggerating or reducing a reaction as an 'unacknowledged acknowledgement' to the audience.

However, the comic performer must scrupulously avoid indulging in any comic 'tricks' or cheap effects – what Howard Jacobson refers to as the worst of TV sitcom acting, that is, the 'gurning, knowing pauses, double takes, winks, nudges' (Jacobson, 2013). This kind of excessive, pantomimic performance is both what produces a mistrust of 'acting' (as those above mentioned screen directors can manifest) and what simultaneously destroys the fragile state of 'truth' which is necessary for effective transmission and reception of 'believable' comedy. This exchange between the Victorian dramatist and director W. S. Gilbert and his leading comedian George Grossmith indicates the self-defeating nature of such inauthentic comic performance behaviour:

> Grossmith, anxious to score a 'laugh' during one of his scenes, fell over and rolled on the floor.
> 'Kindly omit that', said Gilbert sternly.
> 'Certainly, if you wish it', replied Grossmith, 'but I get an enormous laugh by it'.
> 'So you would if you sat on a pork-pie', was Gilbert's comment.
>
> (Pearson, 1950: 111)

In interpreting comedy, it should also be borne in mind by the performer and director that not everything in a comedy is necessarily supposed to be laugh-out-loud funny or, indeed, in certain instances, funny at all. Laughter merely for laughter's sake is not always helpful for comic performance to retain its innate truthfulness. This was a point that was not lost on the comic playwright Ian Hay who wrote in his introduction to his 'Comedy in Three Acts' (*Housemaster* (1936)) that 'the humour of ... the characters is of the unconscious variety, and should not be forced upon the audience ... the parts should be played quite straight, without indulgence in extraneous "funny business"' (1938: 3). The role of the performer and director here is a matter of becoming thorough and rigorous reflective practitioners and discovering the most authentically truthful interpretation of the text, without losing any of the believable comedy potential from the overall process. In some ways, this will become an enormously subtle, nuanced and creative process of discovery for you.

However it might be defined, in this one important sense, comic performance actually requires a much more reflexive, outward-looking and interpersonal approach to be adopted by the performer. Rather than the introspective, internalising approach that characterises much Western 'method-based' performance theory, the audience must play a much bigger contributory part in completing the circle of evaluating the effectiveness of your performance.

GROUP EXERCISES

The humming exercise

In order to develop listening skills and working to the response of the audience, try the following:

One member of the group leaves the room. The remainder decides on an object (a watch, a pen) and the object is hidden from view. The outsider is then invited back in and has to find the hidden object.

The object of the game is to 'direct' the seeker through humming. Low humming means 'cold' – the seeker is far away from the object and its hiding place, while louder humming indicates 'hot' – that the seeker is nearing the object and is closer to uncovering its hiding place.

As well as developing the ensemble's concentration and encouraging team work, this exercise requires the individual – the outsider – to listen closely and to react to the audience's responses.

Principles of comedy

There are three major 'philosophies' regarding comedy which can help us think about what comedy actually 'is'. We will return to these three basic concepts throughout this book, as each of these can directly affect how you approach the performing of a comedy. The three principles – or mechanisms that impel comedy – have been identified as 'relief', 'superiority' and 'incongruity' (Double, 1997: 89; Morreall, 1987: 1). Each of these notions has variously been identified as an essential way of cueing laughter. Charles Darwin neatly summarised how the three major principles work in conjunction to prompt human laughter, as being 'something incongruous or unaccountable, exciting surprise and some sense of superiority in the laugher, who must be in a happy frame of mind, seems to be the commonest cause' (in Enck, 1872, 1960: 31).

Let us look at the three principles, briefly, in turn.

Relief

The relief theory (also interchangeably referred to as 'release') was originally seen by the ancient dramatists as a form of 'catharsis' – that is, an outlet for the expression of an emotion. Laughter was seen as one of the emotions to be 'purged'. Relief, through audience laughter, can best be seen as a purely physiological manifestation, that is, a biological, bodily response to comic presentations.

In comic performance, 'comic relief' can also appear as a form of escapism, that is, the presentation of a deviation from, and perhaps even a complete subversion of, the normal rules. In dramatic text, there is often a scene or character designed to be a 'tension-breaker.' Such instances of comic relief are sometimes deliberate insertions by the dramatist into non-comic or serious forms (e.g. the porter in Shakespeare's *Macbeth*, the Gravedigger in *Hamlet* or Private Mason, the cook in R. C Sherriff's *Journey's End* (1929)). All of these characters provide opportunities for the physical release of tension through laughter for the audience, by their juxtaposition with highly serious or dramatic scenes. Comedy itself, moreover, often offers escapism and is seen as a release from the tensions and norms of ordinary life. Comic performance can reflect this expression of liberation – sometimes through the depiction of the oddness, quirkiness, surprise or incongruity contained within its characters and situations.

GROUP EXERCISES

The concealed fart

Two actors from the group perform the following scenario.

Actor A reads out (or improvises) a serious speech. (This could be, say, a lament, an elegy, a funeral oration or a public apology.)

Actor B punctuates the speech with intermittent fart noises (preferably faked).

This broad and unsubtle exercise illustrates the workings of this principle of comedy. The undercutting of the seriousness of the speech by the timed ribaldry of the farting should provide the exercise of comic relief (and release)!

Staring/smiling competition

Performers take turns to sit opposite each other as, in, say, a bus or train carriage. One student remains in neutral while the other student must gradually stare, smile and/or grimace at their counterpart opposite until the first student smiles or laughs. The next student in line then takes over the role of trying to crack their colleague up.

Superiority

The superiority theory also originated in classical drama, where comedy was seen to require characters presented in positions of inferiority, appearing to be what Plato termed 'merely ridiculous' (in Morreall, 1987: 12). Plato believed that comedy mixes 'malice with laughter' (ibid.: 10), although his pupil, Aristotle, classified comedy as, 'an imitation of characters of a lower type, – not, however, in the full sense of the word bad, the Ludicrous being merely a subdivision of the ugly. It consists in some defect or ugliness which is not painful or destructive' (1997: 9). Later philosophers such as George Santayana expanded on Aristotle's notion that the cruelty of laughter through presentation of superiority play needed to be somewhat tempered – 'whether it be in the way of ingenuity, or oddity, or drollery, the humorous person must have an absurd side, or be placed in an absurd position' (in Morreall, 1987: 96).

Superiority often occurs in comic presentations. A clash occurs between the one who knows better (the audience) and the one who is unaware and whose vulnerability through the situation is being exploited for comic effect (the character). An audience for a comedy is often being invited to laugh at depictions of human folly, stupidity, loss of face or at other excessive behaviours. We revel in the characters' lack of awareness of the effects they are causing and, in doing so, tacitly celebrate our own superior knowledge of that which the characters themselves do not know.

GROUP EXERCISES

1. Master/servant mirroring

One actor is the master, the other the servant. As the master moves around the space, the servant should follow and try to copy the master's every move without the higher-status figure seeing. The servant should try to mock or 'send up' their master without being noticed or caught out.

Players can then swap over the roles and explore the comic potential that the different dynamics of the relationships afford.

The hierarchy of status play can be explored in this game. In terms of 'superiority' – which actor is actually 'in charge' in the performance, the master or servant?

2. The master/servant status swap

Players should be paired up – one in the essential 'master' role, the other as 'servant' and they play out different scenes. The scenarios given might be a diner and waiter in a restaurant; a teacher and student in a school; or a doctor and patient in a consulting room. The actors improvise a simple scene given the situation and typical characterisations within these scenarios. After a certain time the performers should be instructed to 'swap' instantly within the unfolding scene. Players swap roles but continue with the same character. Within the continuing scenario the actors should explore the incongruities that arise out of the altered superiority play – for example, with the waiter now sitting at the table; or the pupil in front of the class; or the doctor being examined by the patient. How does this affect the superiority play? Do the performances become more comical because of the unexpectedness of the situations?

Incongruity

The third major philosophy of comedy, incongruity, perhaps unsurprisingly, also has its roots in classical drama. Aristotle wrote that 'most jokes arise through transference and the arousal of false expectations' (2007: 33). The theme of comedy emerging from the confounding of expectation was also taken up by later comic theorists, such as William Hazlitt, who wrote in his *Lectures on the English Comic Writers* of the 'incongruous' being:

The ludicrous, or comic, is the unexpected loosening or relaxing of this stress below its usual pitch of intensity, by such an absurd transition of the order of our ideas, as taking the mind unawares, throwing it off guard, startling it into a lively sense of pleasure, and leaving no time for painful reflection.

(1885: 68)

Indeed, a surprisingly big-name cast of philosophers has attempted to explain the workings of comedy through incongruity over the centuries. Immanuel Kant wrote in his *Critique of Judgment*, 'in everything that is to excite a lively convulsive laugh there must be something absurd (in which the understanding, therefore, can find no satisfaction)' (1892: 54). Arthur Schopenhauer (1907: 54–55) noted,

The phenomenon of laughter always signifies the sudden apprehension of an incongruity between such a conception and the real object thought under it ... the greater and more unexpected, in the apprehension of the laugher, this incongruity is, the more violent will be his laughter.

Incongruity in comedy, then, is perhaps best summed up as 'the familiar as if it were strange' or as 'a "violation" of expectation' (Morreall, 1987: 2, 216). Even the most basic pieces of comedy 'business' – a man slipping on a banana skin; John Cleese's 'silly walk' (*Monty Python's Flying Circus*, BBC, 1969–1974); David Brent's dancing in *The Office* (BBC, 2001–2003) all contain the element of incongruity. A comic theme often contains an element of surprise that is present in the perception of any 'contradiction, and wherever there is contradiction, the comical is present' (Kierkegaard, 1941: 83). For the audience, recognising the incongruity provides a concurrent, subconscious sense of 'superiority', that is, in the 'getting' of the joke. The ensuing clash or mismatch (which nevertheless, as we will see below, must contain its own innate 'truth') leads, in turn, to relief, which triggers the physiological laughter response in the audience.

GROUP EXERCISES

Comic clock

In her book *Through the Body* (2001) Dymphna Callery describes a basic piece of physical comedy that demonstrates all three 'traditional' principles of comedy (above) in a simple comic routine:

Imagine the stage area as a clock with the 12 upstage and the 6 downstage nearest the audience. A player runs around the stage and at 3 o'clock on the second circuit makes brief eye contact with the audience. S/he continues running but at 9 o'clock trips up and falls. Upright again s/he runs around clockwise for a third time and trips up in the same place. S/he continues running round again but looks back at 9 o'clock and then back at the audience. As s/he approaches the 9 o'clock point once more, s/he jumps over the 'obstacle' and smiles. Then at 3 o'clock s/he trips, and falls – and looks at the audience in disbelief. This simple sequence invariably elicits laughter.

(2001: 108)

Superiority can be seen in the performer's look to the audience and her smile. We, the audience, know something that the performer, as yet, does not, that she has signalled a hubris that inevitably must result in some sort of failure. The look and smile also set up a sense of suspense for the fall that surely must follow as a consequence of such self-assuredness and pride. There is a feeling of relief fulfilled for the spectator in the inevitability of a sequence such as this that unfolds and duly comes to a satisfactory conclusion. We know all along that the pay-off will be that the 'clown' will somehow come to grief – what we do not know is quite how – or how convincingly – this will come about. There is incongruity present in the routine itself – why would anyone run in such a circle in the first place and what exactly are these invisible obstacles that we, the audience, are complicit in 'creating'?

The manner of the comic performance is also vital. The performer's expertise – that is, how well this comic mini-drama is interpreted and performed by the actor – is crucial to our enjoyment. Overdone, and the comic effect will fail. The performance requires a comic 'truth' in that, despite the incongruities, the audience must accept what the performer is doing as 'true', that is, plausible, realistic and well executed.

There is interplay with the audience. Here, the performer breaks the 'fourth wall' completely; her looks to the audience invite the spectators' participation, while the invisible obstacles require the audience to become complicit in the fictional world created.

Furthermore, the performer also uses comic rhythm. She must manufacture the repetitive build-up and execute the comic fall at the denouement with carefully controlled comic timing for the humour to work. The playfulness of the scene may encourage a feeling of 'likeability' in the audience towards the performer who, in common with many stock, clownish, comic figures, is portrayed as a harmless, naïve and potentially endearing character.

Maintaining comic 'truth' in performance

Modern, Westernised, Anglo-American cultural considerations of performance are almost always based on some sort of adherence to the notion of 'dramatic truth'. Since Aristotle's time, the conception of the dramatic ideal of tragedy was 'the depiction of a heroic action that arouses pity and fear in the spectators and brings about a catharsis of those emotions' (in Koss, 1997: 1). And, since then, performance, in Anglo-American culture, still means a 'mimesis' or stylised, structured representation of an imitated event intended to provoke some sort of cognitive or emotional response in the audience. In comic performance, of course, laughter is the overwhelming, intended response. In the West, moreover, a 'naturalistic' theatrical style and system has gradually evolved and become the preferred format over the centuries. The development of dramatic performance in the West demonstrates a more comprehensive subsuming of its earliest ritualistic origins than may be evident in other cultures, especially that of Africa, India, Japan, China and the Far East (Meyer-Dinkgrafe, 2001: 94–136). This can present particular problems for the performer in comic drama, as you still need to (inter) communicate directly to your audience in 'working' their laughter. There is, today, an almost exclusive preference for 'naturalistic' forms of theatrical expression in Western performance culture – and comedy can, generally, be a much less naturalistic form of theatre. The comic performer in drama (unlike the stand-up comedian), for example, usually has to operate from behind the artificial 'fourth wall'. But comic performance still needs to register as being 'true' despite comedy's reliance on a different set of rules as to what constitutes 'truth'! As Christian Metz states, 'each of the representative arts is based on a partial illusion of reality, which defines the rules of the game for that art' (1974: 12). Indeed, comic truth, at least in the UK, European and US tradition, relies on the audience's recognition of strongly established set of separate 'rules' that distinguish the game of comedy, such as vagaries in characterisation and plotting in, namely, the use of stock comic figures, romanticised plots and the occurrence, generally, of a happy resolution. In pursuit of performance, 'theatre acting is about finding a kind of artificial truth' (Merlin, 2010: 146).

Once again, Western comedy's roots are most obviously evident in the archetypal characterisations that evolved from the work of classical (particularly the Roman) comic authors, in the 'new comedy' formulae of, say, Plautus and Terence. The routines and status play that then emerged from the Commedia dell'arte, from the late sixteenth century onwards, were also hugely influential, taking root in Western theatre. R. A. Banks defines Commedia as 'the Italian professional comedy … with its emphasis on stereotyped characters (the lover, the braggart, the cunning politician) who used stock jokes, told by professional actors, each playing a single part such as Harlequin, Pantaleone or the Doctor' (1998: 101). Variations of these stock figures, the domineering woman, the bombastic politician, the embarrassing boss, the hapless suitor, and so on are all still evident in contemporary comic drama. Comic performance takes place in a world of heightened reality or 'distorted truth' (Seyler, 1943, 1990: 2) in which comic 'types' abound, the 'blustering soldiers, young men in love with unsuitable women, or [the] father figure who cannot follow his own advice' (Triezenberg in Raskin, 2008: 525).

Despite the incongruities and absurdities that abound in comedy, and the use of stock characters and plots, for it to work, it must still somehow register as 'truthful' to the audience. But comic truth is different to non-comic forms of dramatic 'truth'. And, for performers, finding and effectively expressing this 'comic truth' can actually be much harder than finding the 'serious' truth that non-comic forms require. Crudely put, it is easier to express, say, sadness, disappointment, anger, gullibility, naivety or jealousy 'seriously truthfully' than it is to portray these emotions 'comically truthfully' without running the danger of tipping the balance of the play, text or film into some other unwelcome area. Take the character of Egeon, in Shakespeare's *The Comedy of Errors*. As he informs us at the beginning of the play, he is an old man facing imminent death by execution, who has lost both his children and he has spent his life going from city to city desperately searching for them. In this, he is a truly tragic and heroic figure. Yet to play the full serious 'truthfulness' of this brave and piteous character's circumstances and to express only his tragic potential within the play could irrevocably pitch the play into a darker and more tragic area from which the comic truth might not be redeemable. The actor may have to find a comic truthfulness which also explores and expresses the possibilities of the comic situation. He may have to emphasise the light as well as the shade within the character, pointing up, in this case, say, Egeon's garrulousness, his innate goodness or his indomitability of spirit, rather than concentrating solely on the character's tragic internal scarring. Finding the (heightened) truth and playing the 'gap between the way the character sees himself and the way the audience sees him' (Callow, 1991: 36) can be difficult and demanding for the performer, but it is the essence of effective comic performance. In an interview, one actor I spoke to – Julian Protheroe – described the finding of a form of heightened comic truth:

> A director I worked with recently, who is very much based in a Stanislavskian approach to any type of performance, nevertheless would point out when a comic scene wasn't working and saying that it lacked a 'comic brightness' – it seems to me to describe an inexplicable truth – something about a lightness of touch and an instinctive sense that somehow thwarts expectation in the audience and so they are put off balance – recover and laugh.

Similarly, Georgie Glenn, another performer I spoke with, described it thus:

I love to be aware of its comic potential, establish the laughs, then play it in deadly earnest. I need to see it in all its comic glory before I can strip it down and make it serious, grounded and unaware.

It is worth remembering, as Susan Purdie puts it, that 'comic performers ... are seeking the laughter which is unknown or unwelcome to their character' (1993: 16), and comic 'truth' can involve the actor also finding and emphasising the lighter and more overtly amusing aspects of the character they are playing. Finding those features that can provoke laughter from the audience, sometimes despite the potentially serious circumstances or sad situations in which those characters may be placed, is a big part of the performer's job.

EXERCISE

Stock comedy characters

Make a note of how many stock comic figures are used in contemporary and classic TV comedy, for example:

- The master/servant – Frasier Crane and Daphne Moon in *Frasier* (NBC, 1993–2004); or Basil Fawlty and Manuel in *Fawlty Towers* (BBC, 1975, 1979).
- The boastful boss – *Frasier* again; David Brent in *The Office* (BBC, 2001–2003); or Captain Mainwaring in *Dad's Army* (BBC, 1968–1976).
- The domineering wife or mother-in-law – in *Fawlty Towers* again; or in *Everybody Loves Raymond* (CBS, 1996–2005).
- The hapless lover in just about every rom-com ever committed to the screen.
- Observe how the performers flesh out these stereotypes and make them seem like 'real' people.

Also note how many standard plots are used in comedies – that is, plans going astray, love becoming complicated, misunderstandings arising, characters getting 'above' themselves, happy resolutions – and try to work out, despite adhering to these 'rules of the game', how it is still, nonetheless, possible to convey comic truth in performance.

Conclusion: towards comedy acting?

It is argued in this book that comic and non-comic forms of drama are dissimilar in fundamental ways. Each form is intended to invoke different emotions and responses from the audience and each relies on modified approaches from you, the performer, when enacting the various scenarios in each form. The comic actor must be attuned to the audience's laughter response in a way that the 'serious' actor need not be. And, just as in non-comic forms of drama where someone else has written the lines and the situations, your job as a performer is still to bring that text to life. But in comedy there is the added expectation that you should get the laughs (wherever, of course, that audience laughter is what is intended within the play). Comedy acting requires you to be 'truthful' but the 'truth' that you will be playing is different. The comic world spins to a different set of truths. This is a world that operates within a heightened form of reality. The actor Vikki Michelle described it to me thus:

> The character has to be real. You shouldn't 'play' comedy ... just up the ante slightly ... make it slightly larger than life.

As another actor, Simon Callow, wrote, 'thinking, feeling, sensing, intuiting must (still) be present not imitation' (1984: 67) in your performance. As a performer of comedy, however, you still need to be adept at what the actress Athene Seyler in her book, *The Craft of Comedy* (itself a rare foray into the field of critical analysis of comic performance), called 'the craft of appearing to believe in the balance of a thing one knows is out of balance' (1943, 1990: 12).

These extra skills that you need for doing comedy can be developed by using some of the exercises in this book – and through reflecting on your practice. Note what works and what does not and experiment with making refinements to the process. Exposing your performance to live audiences and, in turn, evaluating its effectiveness is the only sure way to improve your comic performance.

In the next chapter we will consider how the comic performer maintains some form of interplay with the audience while performing in comic text. We will see how, through their laughter, your comic performance becomes shaped by the audience's reaction. We will consider how this audience interplay can shape your performance and discuss how to remain 'true' to your character and the situation within the parameters of the accepted fiction.

INDIVIDUAL OR GROUP EXERCISES

1. Mirror levels

This can be done at home with the performer looking in the mirror and acting as your own audience, or in the studio as a paired 'mirroring exercise'.

First loosen up by gently stretching and contorting your facial muscles. Make small, pinched faces and then stretch your facial expressions as far as they can go. Try out extremes of, say, dignity, shock, evil or greed.

(Continued)

(Continued)

The object of the exercise is to explore and find your own inner absurdity (and, don't forget, we are all fundamentally ridiculous)!

Look into the mirror or into your partner's eyes. Pull really grotesque, extreme faces. Try to catch your own eye or that of your partner during the extremes of the face-pulling. See if you can genuinely make yourself laugh when experimenting with these facial contortions. Then try the exercise again trying not to laugh (i.e. keeping a straight face while keeping a 'mobile' face).

Remember, it is easier in rehearsal to bring your performance and energy levels down to a 'truthful' level that registers properly than it is to build up to the correct level from too low an energy level. You may find that the pep and brio that are required in performing comedy are often higher and quicker than you think (or that you may initially feel comfortable working with). Comedy, however, generally requires the exploitation of a rhythm that is more, rather than less, energetic – see Chapter 4 for more detail on this).

2. Truth and lies

You can extend this exercise to experiment with expressing a 'true' dramatic emotion. Try sadness or, perhaps, anger. Cry, or rage, as in a serious

'Stanislavskian' way where you link in with the truthful core of the emotion and try to replicate the feeling, performing it in as real and actual a way as possible.

Now try and express exactly the same emotions for trivial reasons, for example, you have broken a pencil, there is no milk in the fridge, there is a fly in your soup.

When you attempt these exercises, be as inventive and as expressive as you like. The secret of this process is to learn (and know) that you can be funny. Of course, in actual performance, bear in mind that it is important never to show the audience that you know you are being funny!

Finding – and experimenting with extremes of intensity – means that communicating through your performance will be easier. You will be able to 'do' less, as necessary, in live performance, having explored the excesses and found where the outer limits lie in rehearsal. You should then feel more able to control your performance while still retaining the 'truthfulness' of the comic situation.

3. Using the audience directly

Improvise or describe a scene, for example, the making of a journey. Instruct the audience to become the scenery or props within the scene at points in your narrative. They might become the sea, form a mountain, become a table and chairs, impersonate an unruly mob or provide a chorus to boo or cheer, as appropriate.

This direct audience participation will develop your interplay skills with the audience.

Suggested further study

Reading

Callery, Dympnah (2001) *Through the Body: A Practical Guide to Physical Theatre*, London: Nick Hern Books. This book contains numerous expertly devised exercises to help develop the performer's expressive abilities and their creative physicality.

Comedy Studies published by Taylor & Francis. This is a journal in which current thinking and research into comedy in all its incarnations is published.

Morreall, John (ed.) (1987) *The Philosophy of Laughter and Humor*, New York: Albany. For the theories of laughter, humour and comedy, this is an excellent resource and contains summaries of much of the key thinking on the subject of comedy.

Seyler, Athene (1943, 1990) *The Craft of Comedy*, London: Nick Hern Books. This is a valuable, rare and reflective meditation on the subject of comic performance by the actress Athene Seyler. Originally written in 1943 as a series of letters, Seyler identifies Stanislavskian, subtextual factors as being crucial to the execution of comic performance.

Wright, John (2007) *Why Is That So Funny?* New York: Limelight. John Wright's
   book explores playing comedy predominantly from the perspective of clowning
   (a form that usually disregards the fourth wall). It contains a number of very
   useful exercises and games on developing and exploring funniness.

Example

The sketch *Dinner for One* (NDR, 1963) is worth studying for spotting
the principles of comedy, all within a 16-minute piece of vintage comedy
performance. *Dinner for One* is a British comedy skit, little known in the
UK that has become cult viewing in a large number of Nordic countries,
including Germany and the Netherlands, as a staple requirement of traditional New Year's Eve television scheduling. It is a single location sketch,
filmed in black and white, which makes no attempt to disguise its stage
origins. The skit stars the comedian Freddie Frinton as James, an increasingly drunken butler, serving his employer, Miss Sophie (May Warden),
dinner and drinks on the occasion of her ninetieth birthday party. The
incongruous premise of the comedy is that Frinton also serves four non-
existent guests (Sir Toby, Admiral Von Schneider, Mr Pomeroy and Mr
Winterbottom). These (literally) 'absent' friends are presumably Miss
Sophie's long-departed coterie – and from this situation springs the performance (the clowning, mime and vocal circumlocutions) that Frinton's
butler character employs during the pretence. The sketch assumes many of
the classic formulae of performed comedy – its master/slave dynamic harks
back to classic Roman comedy while the guests' titles hint at the kind of
names used in Restoration comedy (e.g. John Vanburgh's Sir Tunbelly
Clumsy in *The Relapse* (1697), or Charles Sedley's Harry Modish or
Widow Brightstone in *The Mulberry Garden* (1668)).

   Dinner for One is based on the incongruities of the situation – in the
butler maintaining the pretence of serving imaginary guests – and also in
Frinton's increasingly drunken attempts to negotiate the service of three
courses and the accompanying drinks (which he himself downs in re-
enacting each 'guest's' toast to 'Miss Sophie'). The comedy performance
is visual and verbal. Many repetitions are performed – verbal, as in the
exchanges of 'Same procedure as last year, Miss Sophie?' 'Same procedure as every year, James?' that recur between Frinton and Warden before
each course is served – and visual, as in Frinton's (ten) physical trips on
the head of the tiger skin rug as, each time, he completes a circuit of the
service routine. Frinton's comic expertise is also evident – his increasingly
drunken actions are skillfully performed and raise the laughter of release
as he displays increasingly sloshed behaviour. Superiority is also at play
here. The audience feels superiority over the characters within the situation, the folie de grandeur that is set up and then undercut by James'

increasingly absurd behaviour. Also, note Frinton's direct interplay with the non-present audience. At the punch line of the sketch, as he prepares to escort Miss Sophie up the stairs to her bedroom, the line 'same procedure as last year?' is repeated by James and accompanied by his comment 'I'll do my very best!' straight to camera and with a (literal) wink and a nod to the audience and a sign-off declaration of 'Goodnight'!

Audio visual

For YouTube clip, type 'Dinner for One complete sketch' into the search box.

Chapter 2

Interplay and the audience

Successful comedy cannot be done in a vacuum.

(Provine, 2000: 138–139)

Introduction

Let us now look in some more detail at the notion of interplay and working with the audience in comic performance. As the playwright David Mamet notes, 'doing the play [is] for the audience' (1998: 4). As a (reflective) performer in comedy, you will be more reliant on gauging how the audience's reaction to your effects provides a reliable measurement of their success or failure. You will be able to evaluate in real time whether what you are doing is working or not. Live comic performance relies on you, the actor, taking a more interactive approach, as the audience's signalling of their engagement through their laughter provides a useful and instant indicator of the effectiveness of the onstage activities. In this way, as Michael Chekhov notes, 'the audience is an active co-creator of the performance' (2002: 146), and in a comedy, no laughter definitively (and sometimes very uncomfortably) means that no comedy is taking place when it should be! Comedy performance, then, requires you to adopt a form of 'in-action reflection' (Schön, 1987: 14) where you will monitor the instantaneous reaction to the activities that are being played out.

Comic performers, in fact, have always deliberately pursued this type of audience interplay and complicity to measure their effects. Take this example of reflection on practice from the Scottish music hall comic Harry Lauder ('the world's first superstar'; Sclater, 2015) in 1919:

I've always learned from those that disapproved o' me ... I ha' to watch folk, and see from the way they clap, and the way they look when they're listening, whether I'm doing richt [sic] or wrong.

(1919, 2008: 119)

James Agee, meanwhile, noted that the early silent film comedians (clearly highly reflective practitioners) divided audience laughter 'into four categories in ascending order of hilarity; the titter, the yowl, the belly laugh, and the boffo' (in Palmer, 1987: 101).

Of course, it is true that this two-way processing between actor and audience is not merely confined to performing in comedy. As the actor Martin Jarvis states, 'communication between actor and audience is not unlike telepathy – your slightest vibes will be picked up' (1999: 54).

Interestingly, actor/audience inter-communication relies on the very same 'transactions' (Wright, 2007: 85) being made as are found in any basic communication activity:

> Communication consists of the 'sender' intending to cause the 'receiver' to think or do something, just by getting the 'receiver' to recognise that the 'sender' is trying to cause that thought or action.
>
> (Levinson, 1983: 16)

However, the peculiar form of communication that you make in live performance relies on an accepted agreement being made between the actor and the audience. Both parties enter into a state where the theatrical flow of 'to and fro' takes place. The mutually accepted rules of comic performance assume that there will be a cause-and-effect mechanism in play between the performer and their activities (i.e. a cause) and audience's reaction to those activities (i.e. an effect).

The flow between the two parties is what delineates the effectiveness, or otherwise, of this particular form of communication, and 'comedy is ... scarcely more than a game, which like all games depends on a previously accepted convention' (Bergson, 1900, 1960: 58). In any successful live comic performance, the overall message relies on the signals sent by you, the performer, being correctly cued and clearly received by the audience. In return, the signal of responsiveness given by the audience through their laughter also needs to be in place. Some recognition of the audience's part in the process needs to be made by the performer playing comedy. As the writer Dan Swimer notes of the process of trying out his comic material on fellow writers, 'I need to see the reaction. Comedy is meant to be quite visceral. I'll know instantly if I can see the reaction on their face and they're laughing, then that's the right tack. I can't imagine doing it without that interaction' (in Jones, 2015: 45).

Thus, you, the comic performer, need to be a very active and careful 'listener'. You need to hear, not only the responses and intercommunications made by your fellow players but also those made by the audience, in order to shape your performance. The audience's input into the dialogue makes the process of performing comedy more like a three-way process – effectively, making it a 'trialogue'.

GROUP EXERCISES

Frustrating objects

In front of the group, players individually attempt a basic clowning activity. Allocated activities include an action that appears simple and straightforward enough but which proves tricky in execution.

A simple prop can help the performer to improvise the clowning act – in the following cases a piece of material is suggested for students to use to physically mime:

- Changing behind a beach towel
- Putting up a deckchair
- Fighting an imaginary bull
- Laying a carpet
- Doing a catwalk
- Performing a magic act.

Alternatively, actors can use an example from their own experience to attempt a simple clowning action, using any simple prop of their choice to illustrate the action.

This exercise allows practise of basic performance skills while honing the skills of audience interplay, reaction and the performer's response to stimuli.

Audiences and laughter

In developing a reflective awareness of the audience's reactions – particularly recognising the *quality* of their laughter – the comic performer draws on the same set of interactive, performative tools that the stand-up comedian employs. Oliver Double defines the stand-up comedian as 'a single performer standing in front of an audience, talking to them with the specific intention of making them laugh' (1997: 4). For performers working in comic plays, the predominant, modern, Western fashion for acting behind a fourth wall makes any direct connection something of an impossibility. Unlike stand-up comedians, comic performers also, more usually, operate under the circumstances of collaborative peer interaction on stage, and the importance of building interplay with your fellow performers will be discussed in the next chapter. In live situations, like the stand-up comic, your interplay with the audience plays a vital part in the communication and the reception of comedy:

> A successful comedian must be attentive to audience cues that govern timing – the audience must be given an interval in which to laugh or applaud ... Audience feedback also influences pacing and the selection of improvised material – comedians go with what works.
>
> (Provine, 2000: 138–139)

In some circumstances, direct address, even audience participation, can become part of your comic theatre-making. Here, interplay becomes a key element in the 'discursive exchange' (Purdie, 1993: 6) of comic performance. This might take the extreme form of involving the audience to the extent where it too becomes part of the joke (as in the deliberate teasing of expectations of fourth wall convention indulged in by popular UK vaudevillian comics the 'Crazy Gang'):

> 'Sorry to disturb you, madam', Teddy Knox would say, dressed as an usherette and falling onto some woman's lap, 'I just wanted to see what the audience is laughing at. Don't tell me it's your hat'.
>
> (Owen, 1986: 8)

Inattentiveness to audience response when performing comedy can cause problem though. Put simply, 'squashing' the audience's laughter by ploughing on through a laugh response leads to a situation where the audience will become less inclined to laugh as the play goes on. Perceiving that they are not being treated as participants in the process, they feel that they might miss something and so consequently feel excluded and unlikely to be drawn any further into what is being performed for them.

In contrast to the work of stand-up comedians, however, as a comic performer you will be working through the medium of a written text which has, usually, been created by another. You will, most often, have to work within the convention of the fourth wall and will also (most likely) be working in collaboration with other performers. Despite these apparent barriers to achieving interplay with the audience, you should still, nonetheless, continue to strive to develop some complicity or rapport with the audience as part of your performance technique. As J. L. Styan notes, 'for the actor, comic business and dialogue are not a matter of memory but of imagination. So the comedy grows anew each night, and relevantly, for each new audience' (1975: 81).

GROUP EXERCISES

1. Playing with the fourth wall

Taking turns, imagine that a large glass, soundproof wall separates you from the audience. Mime trying to communicate something with the audience through the opaque wall. You might be a shopper outside a store trying to get a window dresser's attention (or vice versa) or a scuba diver in a fish tank trying to communicate with aquarium visitors. (The comedian Norman Collier, for instance, used to perform a routine in which he played with the 'fourth wall' that was created by the raising and lowering of an imaginary car window.)

2. Stand-up techniques

This exercise has been taken from Oliver Double's book *Getting the Joke* (2005). The students of stand-up comedy use a microphone, but this is not needed for this improvisation exercise as its focus is on practising the building of empathy and interplay within a different context of live comic performance. You can perform this exercise 'in character' as part of the rehearsal process:

Here and now

The student behind the mike does all the talking, and may talk only about things that are happening in the here and now: the décor; the things people are wearing; somebody breathing heavily or sneezing; the thoughts and feelings passing through his or her head ... when the player strays from the here and now, the audience has to shout 'Here and now!' and the first person to do so takes up the position behind the mike, becoming the next player.

(2005: 265–6)

Audio visual

To see comedian Norman Collier playing with the concept of an imaginary barrier in his routine, type 'Norman Collier car window' into the search box.

Building a relationship with the audience

So, in as far as you require the formation of some form of interplay with your audience, you will also, in consequence, be building a relationship with them.

This relationship takes the form of establishing complicity with and, in turn, receiving some empathy from the audience. Building such an understanding with the audience (along with developing a comic transmission which becomes measurable through the quality of the spectators' laughter) takes a communication form that is 'phatic', that is, in which 'for communication to take place effectively some kind of psychological *rapport* must also be created' (Hartley, 1982: 71, italics in original). As the American stand-up comedian Milton Berle pronounced, 'the first thing is that an audience, I believe, have to like you' (in Double, 2005: 61), while the comedy actress Beryl Reid wrote:

> I have one or two theories about comedy, but it is impossible really to define. What I feel very strongly is that audiences must love the people before they can laugh at them ... the audience must feel affection for the person who is aiming to make them laugh. There has to be a great deal of affection going between the audience and the performers, whatever you're saying and however witty or clever you're being.
>
> (1985: 255)

For the comic performer this means that the character you portray can never be one-dimensional and wholly dislikeable, even if the role appears to be written that way. The performer has to radiate some humanity, often despite of and through the stereotype that is represented. The audience must like something about the way the comic actor presents the character that she or he plays, even when that character is inherently dislikeable or their character traits are essentially far from admirable – for example, Basil Fawlty's irascibility, David Brent's lack of self-awareness, Rigsby's cravenness, Edina's self-centredness. (Sitcom characters played, respectively, by John Cleese in *Fawlty Towers* (BBC, 1975, 1979); Ricky Gervais in *The Office* (BBC, 2001–2003); Leonard Rossiter in *Rising Damp* (ITV, 1974–1978); and Jennifer Saunders in *Absolutely Fabulous* (BBC, 1992–1996 and 2001–2005).)

This subversion of stereotype is created by humanising and rendering the qualities of the character as sympathetic rather than as merely one-dimensionally despicable or pitiable. The comic actor making the comedy character somehow likeable is one key component in achieving that false state which is understood as 'comic truth'. This might best be achieved through thinking about 'both-ness' in your character. So, as in life, we usually have more than one thing going on at a particular time. We are more likely to feel, say, simultaneously serious *and* naughty; or amused *and* disgusted or outraged *and* titillated or – indeed, happy *and* sad – than we are likely to be experiencing one pure, unadulterated emotion. The same holds true for the comic characters that you play. Finding the 'both-ness' in your character helps to humanise your role and diverts away from any stereotyping in playing, say the jealous villain, soppy lover, or bossy aunt.

One-dimensional characterisation can make comic performance seem stale. Somewhat surprisingly, perhaps, the audience is perfectly able to pick up on any 'both-ness' that is going on in the performance and more easily recognises implicit human-ness in the character. See, for instance, Ricky Gervais/ David Brent's uncertainties about whether his overbrash presentation of his idea of himself is actually working. This 'both-ness' makes his farcical egotism all the funnier and ultimately creates more empathy for the audience towards the character. We can similarly identify much more with, say, Kristen Wiig/Annie Walker's excessive and selfish behaviours in the film *Bridesmaids* (Feig, 2011) because we can clearly see the implicit fears (of loneliness and loss) that propel her outrageous playing out. The audience can identify – and identify with – Walker's very human drives and motivations. Rather than being presented with a purely comic stereotype (e.g. in this instance, an excessive female) we see the character's frailties as being the outward manifestations of the all-to-real characteristics of a rounded, human, everyman figure.

So, to put it another way, for the performer of comedy, it is a case of finding some chink in the character's armour and letting it shine through. You have to emanate some vulnerability in the person that you create for them to become as rounded and real as possible. You can always find a route into allowing the audience to relate to and empathise with your character, irrespective of how ridiculous or unappealing they might appear on the surface. As Peter Thomson describes this phenomenon, 'It is not simply that we like the actor in spite of the character, rather that, in defiance of our own moral judgment, we like the character because of the actor' (2000: 131).

GROUP AND INDIVIDUAL EXERCISES

I. Speech day

Try reading out various unlikely texts (e.g. excerpts from an instruction manual, a recipe for shepherd's pie, the rules of a board game) as if you are delivering it as an important public speech. For example, below are the instructions for changing a turbo on a Citroen Berlingo automobile. (These instructions have been translated from French into English by Google translate which gives the text an extra layer of absurdity):

Before mounting the turbocharger, made the engine run for a few seconds, oil supply hose disconnected from the turbocharger, in order to drain the oil into a container. The flow must be immediate and plentiful. The joint

(Continued)

(Continued)

compound job is to banish imperative. Remove all protective foams and caps turbocharger inputs and outputs. Present the turbocharger on the engine. Once the correct position found turbine housings and compressors, block with new screw. Empty any remaining oil reasoning. Flip the exchanger and wait 10 minutes. Check air filter elements, cleaning or replacing the appropriate box to air, the air-filter or oil in the case of oil bath filters. Fittings (hard or soft) should not undergo abnormal twists. Proceed fixing the turbocharger and its nozzles by using the original batch of seals. Check for the nut assembly of the inlet compressor wheel. It can be released because of a sudden stop of the whole roundabout. This is due to lack of lubrication or the passage of a foreign body in the turbocharger inlet. Clean your catalyst, certainly in charge of oil. Replace clamps.

Now try reading out your speech again, this time becoming gradually aware that the content of the speech is absurd, inappropriate or inaccurate. Try to mask the fact that you realise how ridiculous it is as you read out your speech. Carry on giving the speech as convincingly as you can.

As an added improvisation you can make an impassioned speech on the importance of retaining dignity at all times while gradually becoming aware that, say, your audience are all falling asleep, or that your trousers or tights are about to fall down. Does coping with this unseen dilemma make you, the speech-maker, come across as more vulnerable and human – and therefore make the scene funnier?

Similarly, you might try making a 'political' speech about something diametrically opposite to what you actually believe. You can explore with the group as audience afterwards whether the hidden vulnerability inherent in the situation (i.e. the lack of self-conviction or belief in what you are saying) was overt and whether, in turn, it made your performance seem truer and/or funnier.

2. Finding unconditional positive regard

The educational psychologist Carl Rogers talked about the need for teachers to have 'unconditional positive regard' (1956) for their learners and the same is true for comic performers and the characters that they inhabit. It is necessary to find something that you like about your character – even in the most seemingly stupid or repellent role – and to find their human core and what motivates them. For instance what 'both-ness' in terms of their feelings, hopes or fears might impel Pantalone's greed, Miles Gloriosus' swagger, Lady Wishfort's vanity, or Shirley Valentine's lack of self-fulfilment?

In finding the human core, vulnerability or inherent motivation of the characters you play, you will simultaneously develop your character's likeability and build some rapport with the audience. Humanising the character is fundamental for creating the conditions for deeper comic performance to occur.

Comedy and playfulness

Comic performance is very closely linked to playfulness. As a communicative activity that is firmly located in the 'here and now' (Hartley, 1982: 50) comic interplay is very similar to the characteristics employed by our early care-giving activities during the ubiquitous and universal engagement that is termed 'Child Directed Speech' (CDS). The CDS bonding interactions that we have all experienced as very young children subsequently affect our recognition and understanding of both what comedy and performance mean:

> The combination of cry and gurgle is identified as the ontogenesis of laughter. The expression occurs when bonding between the mother (or other caregivers) and child allows the child to identify the trusted protector.
>
> (Knight, 2011: 9)

CDS, quite simply, is the mode that adult carers use to communicate with babies. Carers' verbal and non-verbal communication employs many of the exact same tropes that feature in comic performance – for example, exaggerated expressions, repetitions, comforting articulations, vocalisations and physical engagements that contain humorous intent, and so on. As Wilkie and Saxton note, like CDS:

> Comic performance, in act and interpretation, is intrinsically located in early adult interaction ... [is] typified by a focus on the 'here-and-now' and the use of comic devices, which include surprise, familiarity, repetition, incongruity and nonsense ... [and] superiority ... early parent interaction constitutes the blueprint for comic performance itself and ... the quality of interaction between parent and child echoes the conditions for successful interplay between comedian and audience.
>
> (2010: 21)

Talking to babies is a highly incongruous activity in which the care-giver behaves just like a comic performer does in their attempts to amuse, distract and occupy the very young child. As in comic performance, the activities have to amuse and engage, and the child, like your audience, must be in a receptive frame of mind to allow amusement to occur. In this way, as John Morreall states:

> Incongruity ... must not only be different from what we are used to, but it must violate our conceptual patterns ... we have to be able to compare things and events, at least implicitly, with things and events of the relevant kind ... it also needs to be able to operate with its concepts in a non-practical, non theoretical, in short, in a *playful* way, so that the violation of its conceptual patterns won't evoke negative emotion or disorientation.
>
> (1987: 202)

The care-giver directly 'performs' to the young child to entertain and amuse her. In comic performance, characters such the comic interlocutor figure can clearly be seen to be soliciting the audience's collusion. Both types of performer must always take into account whether the baby (or audience) is favourably receiving the comic message by evaluating their response in laughter to the (inter)actions they are making.

Furthermore, CDS links to comic interplay in the use of repetitions. For example, in sitcom, the catchphrase – such as the 'I don't believe it' of Victor Meldrew (Richard Wilson) in *One Foot in the Grave* (BBC, 1990–2000) or the 'go on, go on, go on, go on' of Mrs Doyle (Pauline McGlynn) in *Father Ted* (Channel Four, 1995–1998) – is a device that builds familiarity through raising an expectation in the audience which is then satisfied. Repetitions are comforting and they remind us of how familiar and liked individuals communicated with us in our state of early childhood. As the Scottish comic actor and impressionist Janet Brown described this phenomenon:

> We had an Aunt Lizzie, a wonderful character with iron grey hair that stood up on end, just like Ken Dodd's, who whenever she came to see us used to call out from the kitchen, 'Toot toot, the light!' It's funny how these things stay with you.
>
> (1986: 11)

The conditions for comic performance to succeed require playfulness (and recognition and acceptance of that state of playfulness) communicating between the audience and the performer and vice versa. Both parties must become, to some extent, 'like a child' (Chekhov, 2002: 127) for any comic spark to be able to ignite. As the silent movie comedy director Hal Roach observed, 'one of the big secrets of successful comedy is relating it to childhood' (in Kerr, 1980: 111), and comic themes often mire the characters 'at sea', in situations of helplessness, further linking comedy to the child-like state. Take, for example, the comic films of the 'wacky ... never understated' (McCabe, 2005: 171) Mel Brooks, which 'trace the maturing of childish adults' (Yacowar, 1982: 196). Perhaps too, the connection between early cognitive and emotional responses made in babyhood to the stimuli of comic performance may partly explain why psychologists note that comedy can induce feelings of 'shame'. As Susanne Langer suggests, 'we often laugh at things in the theater that we might not find funny in actuality' (1953: 85). Freud described 'feeling ashamed over what one has been able to laugh at in a play' (1964: 219), and Charles Jennings, for instance, writes of his response to the Scottish stand-up comedian Billy Connolly as 'the way Connolly makes you laugh – exorbitantly, shamingly' (2001: 197). Comic performance's close links to early play may, in fact, create an unshakeable association of childishness to the laughter response within society and culture which has, in consequence, led to the perception of comic theatre being seen as a more puerile form, and therefore often treated as a less 'worthy', lower-status artistic phenomenon.

As an example of playfulness, violation of the fourth wall, building rapport and the manufacture of comic release, Leslie Halliwell writes of the northern comedian Frank Randle appearing as Buttons in the pantomime *Cinderella* at the Bolton Theatre Royal in the 1930s and gaining the quality of laughter that is the goal of many comic performers:

> He was being dressed for the ball and had trouble with the cut of his silken drawers. 'Come on, stand up straight', urged an Ugly Sister, 'I want to see your dignity come out'! Randle milked that one for five minutes, establishing instant rapport with his audience and in particular with a woman in the third row who did not so laugh much as cackle. Randle had only to bare his toothless gums at her for the cacophony to be resumed, leaving the rest of the audience – and the cast – in stitches.
> (Halliwell, 1987: 29–30)

In developing comic performance, play and games within the rehearsal room become particularly important in building the process. The teacher, facilitator or director should try to foster an ethos of exploration through playfulness, while the performers should be encouraged to play and explore together to create a true ensemble feel. The playful state bonds the group and enables connections to arise that translate into intuitive understanding of how others will respond within exchanges. The interconnections that are built through play in rehearsal, in turn, expand in live performance and then emanate further to allow the audience to join in the group and to participate in the game. The exercises described in this book should therefore all be approached in the spirit of play. They are intended to develop, equally, the individual's creativity and to sharpen up the ensemble's comic instincts. Just as in early learning,

> The spirit behind such games should be a spirit of joy, foolishness, exuberance, like the spirit behind all good games, including the game of trying to find out how the world works, which we call education.
> (Holt, 1976: 19)

GROUP AND INDIVIDUAL EXERCISES

Word games can develop vocal dexterity, encourage understanding of how rhythm works in comedy and bond the ensemble. They also provide a good vocal warm-up before students work with text. Here are, firstly, some examples of tongue twisters that can be used as vocal exercises:

1. Tongue twisters

How much wood would a woodchuck chuck if a woodchuck could chuck wood?
I want a proper cup of coffee from a copper coffee pot.
She stood upon the balcony, inimitably mimicking him hiccoughing and amicably welcoming him in.
We had a knocker up, and our knocker up had a knocker up, and our knocker up's knocker up didn't knock our knocker up. So our knocker up did knock us up, 'cos he's not up.
Rubber baby buggy bumpers.

To sit in solemn silence in a dull, dark dock,
In a pestilential prison, with a life-long lock,
Awaiting the sensation of a short, sharp shock,
From a cheap and chippy chopper on a big black block!
A dull, dark dock, a life-long lock,
A short, sharp shock, a big black block!
To sit in solemn silence in a pestilential prison,
And awaiting the sensation
From a cheap and chippy chopper on a big black block!

(From *The Mikado* by W. S. Gilbert)

2. Non-sense rhymes

A

'Twas brillig, and the slithy toves
Did gyre and gimble in the wabe:
All mimsy were the borogoves,
And the mome raths outgrabe.
'Beware the Jabberwock, my son!
The jaws that bite, the claws that catch!
Beware the Jubjub bird, and shun

The frumious Bandersnatch!'
He took his vorpal blade in hand;
Long time the manxome foe he sought-
So rested he by the Tumtum tree,
And stood a while in thought
And, as in uffish thought he stood,
The Jabberwock, with eyes of flame,
Came whiffling through the tulgey wood,
And burbled as it came!
One, two! One, two! And through and through
The vorpal blade went snicker-snack!
He left it dead, and with its head
He went galumphing back.
'And hast thou slain the Jabberwock?
Come to my arms, my beamish boy!
O frabjous day! Callooh, Callay!'
He chortled in his joy.

'Twas brillig, and the slithy toves
Did gyre and gimble in the wabe:
All mimsy were the borogroves,
And the mome raths outgrabe.

(*Jabberwocky* by Lewis Carroll)

B

On the Ning Nang Nong
Where the Cows go Bong!
And the monkeys all say 'BOO'!
There's a Nong Nang Ning
Where the trees go Ping!!
And the tea pots jibber jabber joo.
On the Nong Ning Nang
All the mice go Clang
And you just can't catch 'em, when they do!
So it's Ning Nang Nong
Cows go Bong
Nong Nang Ning

(Continued)

(Continued)

> Trees go ping
> Nong Ning Nang
> The mice go Clang
> What a noisy place to belong
> Is the Ning nang Ning Nang Nong!!!

(*On the Ning Nang Nong* by Spike Milligan)

3. Group word games

A. One smart fellow

> One smart fellow, he felt smart.
> Two smart fellows, they felt smart.
> Three smart fellows, they felt smart.
> Four smart fellows, they felt smart.
> Five smart fellows, they felt smart.
> Six smart fellows, they felt smart.

This can be played as a group chant or as a round. Any player who makes a verbal slip can be eliminated (not fatally, though)!

B. Random words

> Each player, in turn, says a word which begins with the last letter of the previous word spoken, for example, banana – apricot – tomato.
> The game can be played by using categories, for example, animals, transport, etc., or the words can just be randomised.

C. Word association

Each player, in turn, says a word which associates with the word before. Challenges can be introduced where a player has to explain or justify exactly how the word associates with, or links to, the previous one.

> These exercises all encourage playfulness and recreate the child-like state from which comic performance can emanate. They also allow the practice of being 'silly' and help build awareness – and enjoyment – of textual incongruities.

Comedy audiences

Comedy is a peculiarly performer-driven medium for conveyance of meaning, due to the fact that you must be attuned to, and to some extent control, the audience's responsiveness in laughter. The actor Donald Sinden described the process of such command of interplay as follows:

> It is the actors' job to treat the audience as a sheepdog does a flock of sheep. His ears are finely attuned: he must listen and isolate that portion of the audience that is quick off the mark and then, not as you might expect, play all the laugh lines to that portion – that would antagonise the remainder – but distribute his next laugh lines to the other parts of the house until the whole audience is acting as one.
>
> (1985: 213)

The experienced comic performer, it seems, learns to pitch the performance according to the response received, and each performance is subsequently shaped by the (different) audience's reactions on the night. Audiences, too, in some sense, need permission to laugh. An audience needs to 'know' that something is supposed to be funny before the full effect of a comedy can become possible. Laughter is a predominantly 'communal' activity (Cook, 1994: 248), and John Wright notes the importance of belonging and community membership that are created in response to comic performance, as 'a shared laugh is a shared feeling. Instantly we're all in each other's shoes; we've all gone to the same place and now we have a common understanding' (2007: 11). As Peter Bull recorded of the second night of Christopher Fry's verse drama *The Lady's Not for Burning* in 1950 (a play that was received in baffled silence by the first night audience):

> The net result of the notices was fascinating. The second performance was strangely enough a matinee and a riot at that. Old ladies fell tumbling into the aisles, and it was obvious that now they knew it was a comedy, they could be permitted to enjoy themselves.
>
> (1985: 99)

Bull's anecdote gives further credence to the idea that laughter is 'communal'. Scientific research at University College London supports the notion of the part that communality plays in effectively cueing laughter. Positive sounds, including laughter, were played to respondents and their brain activity was measured using an fMRI scanner. The test sounds triggered a response in the volunteers' brains and the study's findings indicated that laughter is partly 'infectious' and appears to be stimulated by activity in the premotor cortical region of the brain (Scott, 2006).

However, demonstrating audience awareness must also be treated with caution in performance. The actor Peter Bull ruefully confessed the dangerous and overaddictive nature of 'getting the laugh' at all costs in his early career, 'my whole existence in those days [1933] hinged on the public's reaction to the laugh line, which I tabulated in my diary every night, giving myself marks out of a hundred' (1985: 28). While the playwright

Simon Gray reported attending a performance of his own play *The Old Masters* (Gray, 2006) and noting how the audience's reaction directly and detrimentally affected the actors' playing:

> There were moments where they paused slightly too long to accommodate a response they'd become used to but last night didn't come, then suggested by other pauses or a break in a line that that they had become used to laughter there and there, but that didn't come either – so, assuming a slowness in the audience, they developed a thoughtful, expositional tone, to help it follow the line of the story.
>
> (2006: 236)

Repeatedly and consistently 'getting the laughs' for their own sake can become a dangerous aim if, of itself, it becomes the only desirable outcome for the comic performer. Audience laughter can indeed become intoxicating and it must be treated carefully, never becoming a *raison d'etre* or sole means to an end. Audience laughter must be gained *appropriately*, otherwise the overall effect becomes diluted and cheapened. As an example of this process, John Gielgud wrote, apropos of playing John Worthing in *The Importance of Being Earnest* (Wilde, 1885), of 'arousing a cumulative laughter from the audience ... the actor may easily ruin a passage by allowing the audience to laugh too soon' (1965: 81–82).

Predicting an audience's laughter can, too, be counterintuitive and become off-putting if it does not come as expected. Lack of expected laughter can have the consequence of throwing your performance out-of-kilter unless you remain careful. Keep in mind that each audience is different and is viewing the work afresh. Treat each new audience with the highest of expectations, assuming them to be an 'ideal' cooperative body. In so doing, only allow audience laughter to help shape your performance where the effect is to enhance, never to upstage, the intended comic message. Conversely, and concurrently, do not allow any lack of laughter or a muted response to change or force your performance for the worse. It is interesting how an audience that appeared seemingly 'quiet' or 'difficult' to the performers during the play will report to having found exactly the same elements of the piece as having been 'funny' (even 'hilarious') that a 'responsive' or 'great' audience clearly did. It is therefore a case of how you, the performer, once aware of how an audience's interplay can be used as a vital tool, choose to monitor and use their response. Simultaneously, treat any lack of response with suspicion and refuse to let it dupe you into radically altering or varying your performance. Keep a constant awareness that:

> Fluid concepts, such as an audience reaction or mood of the actor can both change the reception processes and alter the levels of signification, from performance to performance.
>
> (Aston and Savona, 1991: 108)

Drawing positively from the interplay between audience and performer is a subtle state that requires careful and ongoing nurturing. While the audience's reaction acts as a cue, or indication of the direction of the performance, it must never be allowed to overrule. In short, you, the performer, need to be the one in constant control. And, rather than allowing the audience to dictate the pace, direction or quality of the comic performance it is ultimately the performer's job to reflect whether the audience's response is providing a useful gauge or tool. Keep control of the process and never allow the audience's laughter to become the sole master of the process.

All this raises the question of how the comic performer can use interplay and retain any 'truthfulness' within a form of performance that relies on what Bernard Beckerman refers to as 'an acknowledged exchange between performer and spectator' (1990: 110). At the same time as unconsciously acknowledging that the audience are to some extent 'co-creating' your comic performance, you must not lose sight of the fundamental need of all performance – that is, that it must register as being 'truthful'. Stanislavskian and other methods to creating performance that you will encounter while studying drama hold equally true when creating and playing a comic role. Approaches to performance remain fundamentally the same – performers are expected to be responsible for internalising the creation of 'character from within', in which 'the actor ... [uses] imagination to believe in ourselves as the character in the imaginary circumstances in the play' (Gillett, 2007: 20). Comic performance, however, requires extra layers – namely, the interplay with the audience and the creation of a performative truth that is based on more complex conditions. To be an effective comic performer it is true that mastering non-comic acting skills is equally as important for performing comedy. For this reason, trying out acting exercises are useful to help you make the text come truly alive. As John Wright states in his excellent book on clowning and improvisation, *Why Is That So Funny?*, 'a writer can write a comic situation and carefully structure an incident and an action to wonderful climaxes but only you [the performer] can make it funny' (2007: 62).

It is your performance, just as much as the script, that will give rise to comic meaning, in so far as 'most deeply felt moments are not strongly textual, they rely on subtextual exposure or intensity, on changes of tempo, rhythm, texture or weight' (Russell Brown, 1993: 194). It is in working through ways to bring out the 'subtextual' – perhaps by adding a layer of comic sparkle, 'brio' (Callow, 1991: 35) or 'irrepressibility' (Goldman in Gruber, 1986: 189) that comic performance becomes alive and, in its unique way, ineffably 'true' and real.

Ultimately, experimenting with the acting exercises that you encounter in the studio, attempting variations in rehearsal and finally, through really hearing, reflecting upon and responding to your audience's reception of your performance is the best way to create truly effective comic performance.

GROUP EXERCISES

Hammy contrasts

Firstly, try acting out these 'demonstrations of the passions, feelings etc.' as recommended by the Victorian elocution guide *The Academic Speaker* dated 1861 in as truthful a way as possible.

Then try them out following the descriptions given. The demonstrations themselves should prove enjoyable to perform!

Thirdly, try performing the hammy responses in response to a narrated story or poem using the different 'passions' to illustrate the various mood changes as the text unfolds.

See which of the demonstrations proves funniest and why. The incongruity of the over-the-top actions in conjunction with the 'dry' text should stimulate laughter from your fellow students acting as the audience. Note where and when each effect proved funniest.

Below are the description of the attitudes as taken verbatim from *The Academic Speaker* – try performing the actions exactly as suggested:

Abhorrence: *draws back the body, averts the head, hold up the hands, with the palms turned outwards in a repelling manner; an expression of loathing on the countenance.*

Adoration: *bends the knees, the body forward, spreads the arms, hands open, tone of voice trembling, words slowly delivered.*

Anger: *stretches the neck, shakes the head, inflames the eyes, knits the brows, opens the mouth wide, wrinkles and blunts the face, gnashes the teeth, convulses the chest, clenches the fists, stamps with the feet, interrupts the breath, agitates the whole body, utters the words with harshness, rapidity, noise, and violence.*

Apprehension: *with apparent unconsciousness agitates the hands, raises them sometimes to the bosom, sometimes to the head, produces sudden intervals of rest and motion, and gives the body an appearance of watching for something.*

Cunning: *throws up the hands, gives the eyes a vacant stare, puts the legs close, bends the knees, gives the whole figure an air of simplicity; an occasional meaning glance from eyes takes away the appearance of stupidity.*

Despair: *bends the eyebrows, clouds the forehead, rolls the eyes frightfully, opens the mouth, bites the lips, widens the nostrils, gnashes the teeth; the head hung down upon the breast; the arms bent at the elbows; the fists clenched hard; veins and muscles swelled; the whole body strained and violently agitated; groans expressive of outward torture, words sullen, with eager bitterness; tone loud and furious.*

Fear: *opens the mouth and eyes wide, shortens the nose, eyebrows downcast, gives the face a deadly paleness, and gives it an air of wildness; draws back the elbows close to the sides, lifts up the open hands, the fingers together, to the height of the breast, so that the palms face the dreadful object as shields opposed to it; the body shrinking and seemingly in a posture of defence; breath quick and short; the body thrown into general tremor, voice weak and trembling; sentences short, confused and incoherent.*

Joy: *clapping the hands; exulting and weeping; the eyes opened wide, sometimes filled with tears, often raised to heaven; the countenance smiling, the voice rising at times to very high notes.*

Which of the over-the-top effects provoked most laughter – and why?

These exercises allow you to experiment with truthful and real responses as compared to surface and superficial presentations.

Conclusion

Interplay is in some ways a hidden phenomenon in comic performing. Performers are often reluctant to admit that they use the audience's response (or lack of it) as a guide to their live practice. Such reflection-on-action may indeed be viewed as 'bad' acting by some practitioners in the sense that the

performer feels that they have not, in a fully Stanislavskian way, immersed themselves sufficiently in their character. But live performance in which the audience is totally excluded and ignored often remains sterile, dry and purely functional. In comic performance, laughter (or the provocation of amusement) and complicity with an audience actually defines the art. And, as the playwright David Mamet notes, 'the audience will teach you how to act' (1998: 19).

More on the subject of truth in comic performance follows in the next chapter.

Suggested further study

Reading

The texts below describe the processes that the stand-up comedian uses. These can be used to influence your approach to the performance of scripted comedy.

Double, Oliver (1997) *Stand-up: On Being a Comedian*, London: Methuen
Double, Oliver (2005) *Getting the Joke*, London: Methuen
Ritchie, Chris (2012) *Performing Live Comedy*, London: Methuen

Examples

Comedy's links to CDS and to early childhood interactions

It is worth looking at what amuses babies and small children. This is often the case of a recognised and familiar carer 'performing' (pleasant) surprises, uttering repetitions, indulging in playfulness and communicating oddities, incongruities and violations of the norm, both vocally and physically. These are, fundamentally, many of the same elements that occur in comic performance.

The YouTube video entitled *Ha ha ha small daring boy* (sic) neatly illustrates the situation of many of the basics of comic performance in action. With numerous versions and many tens of thousands of 'hits' (and growing), the video provides a global illustration of the CDS process. In the short (European) video an unseen (male) carer amuses a baby through an interplay interaction involving the use of sudden, alternating high-pitched and staccato nonsense sounds to cue laughter. The baby interacts with the carer, stimulating, in turn, the comic provocations through the reward of (highly infectious and endearing) laughter. The interplay is essentially comic in the manifestation of the 'peep-bo (sic) situation [that] is for ever recurring in the early years of a child' (Greig, 1969: 55). The 'performer', the carer, demonstrates comic 'expertise' – he times the interjections using pauses, playful anticipations and hesitations to cue the baby's responses (indeed the baby laughs once in sheer expectation, even though the carer has produced no noise at all)! The sounds that the carer makes are incongruous and the suddenness of their articulation stimulates surprise. The baby's laughter is, literally, the laughter of release. The baby is also being conditioned to recognise and respond to comic signals. This is a demonstration of the process of the situating of comic performance in our psyches, in which, as Meltzoff states, 'for human beings, nurture is our nature' (in Bock, 2005) and substantiating Hobbes' claim that 'the comic is largely behavioural' (in McKellar, 1968: 219). The baby, as 'audience', reciprocates by rewarding the performer with laughter, egging the carer on to provide further stimuli. Here, CDS is, like comic performance, a specialised system of reciprocated signs that are transmitted by the performer and received by the spectator that, in turn, cues laughter.

Audio visual

There are literally hundreds of videos available on YouTube of babies being amused by care-givers. You will see many of the features of comic performance being used here – surprise, repetition, empathy, interplay, incongruous movement, vocal play, etc.

The video example is viewable by entering the terms 'Hahaha small daring (sic) boy' into the search box.

Tommy Cooper's 'Hats'

An example of a comic performer using interplay can be seen in the 'Hats' routine by the British comedian Tommy Cooper (1921–1984). Cooper's familiarity to the British television audience of the period provided one element of the successful meaning-making in the comic performance, in so far as 'actors who develop personae can become familiars, commonplaces, semiotic markers' (Sante and Holbrook Pierson, 1999: xiii). Audiences expected Cooper to be 'naturally' funny. As Terence Hawkes states, signification at this level is:

> A covert producer of meaning at a level where an impression of 'god given' or 'natural' reality prevails, largely because we are not normally able to perceive the processes by which it has been manufactured.
>
> (1997: 133)

Below is an attempt to break down the 'processes' by which Cooper's comic performance is achieved.

This is a clear example of a comedian using interplay and deliberately breaking the fourth wall. Referring to Cooper, the comedian Ade Edmondson asserted, 'he could make funny things out of absolutely nothing at all' (Edmondson, 1989). In a one-man sketch broadcast in 1974, Cooper performed the 'hats' routine during his Thames Television show entitled *The Tommy Cooper Hour* (ITV, Thames, 1973–1975). The premise of the sketch is Cooper's recounting of a shaggy dog story ('T'was New Year's Eve in Joe's Pub') – a rhyming tale that ostensibly recounts a fracas that arises between a tramp, his wife and various other drinkers in a bar. Cooper uses a box of hats to delineate the cast of various characters that make up the clientele of Joe's pub. A reading of the comic performance elements that are at play helps to explain why the humour works so effectively and specifically when performed live.

Cooper was an enormously popular star comedian in the UK by the time the sketch was broadcast. Famous for his bumbling, apparently shambling persona – particularly in the performance of his magic tricks – Cooper draws on some ambiguity regarding his competence in completing the monologue – he may or may not, for example, be slightly drunk – and he may or may not accidentally or deliberately forget his lines. Nevertheless, Cooper's sheer comic expertise is evident in this sketch. He had, in fact, been regularly performing a version of the same routine since 1955, and as Cooper's biographer John Fisher notes, 'such lapses proved the making of the routine' (2007: 218). Nevertheless, Cooper's exhibition of 'forgetfulness' after donning the cowboy hat allows him explicitly to use interplay and complicity with the audience. He addresses them directly ('I won't be a second ... oh, yes') while pointing up the difficulty of the task (i.e. the expertise required in the switching between eleven different characters while remembering the poem) by pausing to mutter his way through the poem from the beginning again in order to find his place. This apparently guileless mode of aide-de-memoir evokes audience laughter in the incongruity of its inappropriateness. As Fisher notes of Cooper in general, his comic expertise was – like his abilities as a magician – deceptively reliant on distraction and concealment: 'analyse his performance and he is seen to represent a far more complex range of expression and body language than the immediate impact of his branding suggests' (ibid.: 4).

Cooper resorts to further interplay and complicity with the audience as the sketch unfolds, donning the 'wrong' hat and laughing at his own 'confusion'. He throws one hat away, admitting 'I don't know what that is'. John Fisher also refers to Cooper's employment of a direct interplay technique, alluding to his trademark 'guilty look of complicity' (ibid.: 4).

Cooper's performance includes the introduction of childhood playfulness in the use of the 'dressing up box'. The creation of sudden incongruities afforded through the deployment of the different hats invokes the 'peek-a-boo' articulations of CDS. As Ruqaiya Hasan notes, 'everywhere in the world children play a variety of pretend games' (1989: 2) and these usually involve repetition, 'itself a meaning-making device' (ibid.: 4). Here, Cooper's activities in the playful activity of donning and rejecting various hats recreate early CDS interactions (and concurrently induce feelings of warmth towards the initiator), subconsciously reminding the audience of a state when, 'for the young child, appreciation is confined to 'receiving with pleasure' (ibid.: 26).

There are, furthermore, many incongruities contributing to the comic effect. The hats are, in themselves, 'visual signifiers' (Marshall and Werndly, 2002: 26). On the surface, they serve simply to signify character 'types' (a policeman, a soldier, an older woman), allowing what Metz terms 'the language of objects' (1974: 142) to ensue. But by adding a layer of incongruity, they also serve to make Cooper look instantly absurd as he perches them on top of his large head – from the woman's small, feathered headgear to the cowboy's over-large and floppy hat. The further absurdity of a cowboy drinking in what is clearly depicted as the setting of a British working man's pub is another incongruous addition within Cooper's manipulations. The hats are intended to be read comically within Cooper's overall playing of the comedy (a sham serious delivery of a dramatic monologue). The activity is performed in a way that the audience is expected to perceive as being funny, even if the intention is portrayed otherwise within the manner of performance – Cooper's apparent seriousness and desperation to get it 'right' counterpoints the absurdities within the presentation.

Cooper also demonstrates some slapstick expertise – suddenly and violently hitting his own head with the hard fireman's hat as he pulls it out of the box. This device further allows him to play with the narrative frame by introducing an unseen, offstage character – an imaginary stagehand assistant whom Cooper berates for not having padded the helmet in advance. Cooper once more directly addresses the audience 'you could be cutting your head wide open with that!' Later the offstage assistant device is used to gain further interplay with the audience as Cooper once more breaks the frame to demand an offstage policeman's whistle sound effect from his 'assistant'. In so doing, Cooper deliberately sets up a complicit joke at the incompetent 'stage hand's' expense with the audience. Referring to the missed whistle effect Cooper addresses the audience with 'in'it marvelous? That's all he had to do ... *and* he's wearing make-up!' The incongruity of this image gains studio audience laughter and extended applause which compensates for (and lasts through) the rather weak tag to the sketch (i.e. as Cooper dons a policeman's helmet and states 'and a policeman came and pinched the whole damn lot of them' followed by a quick statement of 'thank you. Goodbye').

Audio visual

The Hats clip is available by typing in 'Tommy Cooper Hats Routine' into the search box.

Let's turn now to developing your (truthful) comic performance expertise and crafting your ensemble skills.

Chapter 3

Expertise, truth and ensemble interplay

> Ah, dear reader, if only I could now rise from the page and demonstrate just for you how these lines when spoken and given with a special delivery of vocal intonation, and timing, plus facial contortion, can become formidable lines of dialogue in a surrealist manner.
>
> (Max Wall, 1975: 187)

Comic performance expertise: the 'craft' skills

The above statement made by the comic Max Wall shows the difficulty in describing masterful comic performance without actually being able to see it. Effective comic performance is certainly something that is recognised by the audience, albeit mainly on a subconscious level. Equally, inexpert comic performance is registered negatively and is subliminally rejected. For the performer, comic expertise, like developing interplay, is something best discovered through experience, by exposure to live audiences. Once seen and experienced, demonstrably masterful comic performance means that the audience is aware that they are in the 'safe' hands of someone who is good at their craft. This is reassuring to an audience. They relax accordingly and are able to enjoy and access the comedy without any hindrance. True comedy – and deep laughter – simply cannot be achieved by any performer who is not adept at the craft skills required for acting comically. Brett Mills notes the importance that the performer's expertise plays in successfully delivering the overall message – 'for comic performance to offer pleasure it must demonstrate the abilities of the person performing it far more obviously than non-comic forms do' (2005: 70).

Comic expertise can thus be best gained through practice – through exposure to audiences and through repeated experience. It is also something that can be developed in the studio and by using some of the exercises in this book. Practice will help you to develop and hone your comic performance skills. And, just as interplay with the audience is one key feature of effective comic performance, so too is interplay with your co-performers. As you will have noticed, many of the exercises in this book require group work, in which the rest of the students act as the *de facto* audience. This is necessary for allowing the interplay and cause-and-effect responsiveness which is a crucial part of comedy performance. Comic theatre cannot, in fact, exist without the vital presence and participation of an audience. This is evident even in the telling of a simple joke. Making a joke is itself a mini-performance which requires a teller and a hearer – and in the case of a 'knock, knock' joke – a responder:

Questioner:	Knock, knock.
Answerer:	Who's there?
Q.	Boo.
A.	Boo who?
Q.	There's no need to cry about it.

The group exercises herein, in which you are expected to interact with your co-actors in performing them, will also allow you to hone your ensemble skills – developing interplay between you and your fellow performers.

GROUP EXERCISES

Joking

Take turns to tell simple, old jokes. Experiment with different ways of delivering your joke. Try impersonating the different characters; add touches of detail and colour; emphasise certain lines while glossing over others; and use different inflections to see what ways of telling the joke evoke the most laughter.

Here are some examples of the kind of jokes you might try telling:

1

My auntie Agnes had kept this parrot for three years and in all that time it had never said a word. Despite auntie trying to coax the bird to speak, it never ever did. Then one day, as she was feeding it a little bit of lettuce, the parrot suddenly pipes up, 'Yuk! There's a caterpillar on it! There's a caterpillar on it!'

Auntie Agnes was amazed. 'You can talk! But why on earth, in all these years, haven't you said a word before?'

'Oh', says the parrot, 'Well, up till now the food has always been excellent'.

2

A woman called over the usher at a cinema.

'Excuse me but there's a man sprawled out in the row behind me making loud groaning noises. You're the usher, can you 'ush him up?'

So the usher whispers to the man, 'are you alright, sir?'

'Ooooo-aaargh!' replies the man.

'Shhhhhhh!' ushes the usher.

'Ooooo-arrrrgggh!' comes the reply.

'Where are you from, sir?'

The man gasps out. 'From ... the ... balcony!'

3

This poor chap was in a hospital bed having been given medicine for his severe stomach cramps. He suddenly and urgently needed to use the toilet. Too late! In a state of embarrassment, he leapt out of bed, gathered up the soiled bed sheets and chucked them out of the window.

On the street below, a drunk was walking past the hospital when the sheets landed on him. The drunk starts shouting and swearing and swinging his arms about, trying to get them off, and the sheets eventually end up in a tangled pile at his feet.

A passer-by asks him, 'what on earth is going on here?'

The drunk, still staring down, replied, 'I don't know. But I think I just beat the **** out of a ghost'.

Which ways of telling the jokes and which additions made by the performer provoked the most laughter? Why might this be?

To practise ensemble interplay skills, retell the jokes as narrator, with your co-performers enacting the characters and dialogue. Try inserting reactions between the narrator and the player(s) to see what makes the joke/scene funniest.

Comic performance, in its pursuit of laughter, constitutes a specialised category, that of 'humour ... dependent on performance skills' (Palmer, 1994: 165). The fully equipped comic performer therefore needs to become an expert in delivering both verbal and physical comedy.

Verbal (or spoken) comedy requires expertise in the development of comic timing, plus having awareness of how rhythm works (and for more on this, see the next chapter). In a play, the language you use is normally not your own, in that the text has been written by another person to be articulated by the writer's imagined character. However, in further co-creating your own version of that character for performance purposes, you have to be aware of how that individual might use verbal rhythms and/or have any spoken peculiarities or other special vocal characteristics. Mastering verbal expertise might become essential in order for you to create a properly rounded, fully effective comic character.

Performing physical comedy expertly, meanwhile, relies on the actor being in control of, and expertly expressing, bodily utterances that impel the comic artic- ulation of the character within the play. You might find it counterintuitive that the most fundamental physical skill that the comic performer can acquire is the practice and mastery of doing any action reasonably well that may be required by the script to be done by the character badly or 'off-kilter'! For example, to sing consistently comically badly in performance, you really have to understand how to sing well (take the example of the singer Jo Stafford performing as 'Darlene Edwards'). Or, to play the piano consistently comically badly, you have to know how to play the piano properly (c.f. the comedian Les Dawson in musical mode). You must be able to, firstly, do something (or at least under- stand the mechanics of doing something) sufficiently adeptly that you may then have to perform 'inexpertly'. As W. H. Auden notes in the case of the clown,

> In appearance, he is the clumsy man whom inanimate objects conspire against to torment; this is in itself funny to watch, but our profounder amusement is derived from our knowledge that this is only an appear- ance, that, in reality, the accuracy with which the objects trip him up or hit him on the head is caused by the clown's own skill.
>
> (1963: 373)

So, to take Buster Keaton's pratfalls, Charlie Chaplin's boxing, Jacques Tati's ungainliness, Lucille Ball's ineptness – all these are made more comi- cally sublime by the fact that the comic performers' incongruous bodily characteristics actually mask their expert physical abilities. In comic thea- tre, a series of incongruities prevail within the narratives of plays. Within these odd premises, nevertheless, the comic performer must appear just like an 'ordinary man', except (to borrow the American comedian Ed Wynn's terms) he might either present himself as a man who 'does funny things' or a man who 'does things funny' (in Marowitz, 1996: 117).

In order to 'do funny things' or to 'do things funny', it is your comic per- formance that will elevate the written text and, ultimately, will be what makes the comedy work. As the theatre director Peter Brook states, 'all the printed word can tell us is what was written on paper, not how it was … brought to life' (1968: 14). Your expertise in comic performance is, there- fore, a major constituent factor in ensuring the success of a play. Expertise in performance (what Andy Medhurst terms the 'craft skills'; 2003: 67) need you, the performer, to bring both your own physicality and mental agility to enliven the roles you play. In exercising your 'instrument' you have the potential not merely to support but to enhance the comic text. As Michael Chekhov mused, 'every role offers an actor the opportunity to improvise, to collaborate and truly co-create with the author and director' (2002: 36).

In comic performance, as in life, much of the communication made is non-verbal (indeed, different studies claim that somewhere between 65% and 95% of all human communication is non-verbal). Ray Birdwhistell, for example, estimates there are 250,000 different facial expressions alone (in Pease, 2004: 9–10). Below are some exercises and games which employ non-verbal, purely physical activity. Practising these skills – and experimenting and evaluating what works and what does not – will help you develop your craft skills and expertise in performing physical comedy.

GROUP EXERCISES

1. Spaghetti limbs (with thanks to Britt Forsberg who taught me this one)

A good warm-up exercise – and one which breaks down any barriers about appearing 'silly' (a necessary condition for allowing free comic expression in performance to occur) is this 'spaghetti limbs' exercise. Students move around the space while the facilitator instructs different limbs, hands and feet, in turn, to morph into 'spaghetti' or 'jelly'. Gibberish or inchoate noises can be added by the students to 'converse' with each other as they move around the studio.

For building the ensemble, following or copying the 'leader' can be built in to the exercise.

2. Pass the laugh

Another exercise from Dymphna Callery's book:

> Someone enters with the laugh merely a glint in their eye. As they make eye contact with the next person they 'pass the laugh' and it becomes a slight twitch of the mouth. As it is passed along the line of players, each raises the level of 'laugh-energy' so that they move from smile to giggle to belly-laugh – and to tears eventually.
>
> (2001: 31)

3. Boal's back dancing

This is taken from Augusto Boal's *Games for Actors and Non-Actors*.

> Two actors set themselves back to back and dance, without music. Each must try to intuit what the other wants to do, and where he wants to go. Back to back contact must never be broken.
>
> (2002: 60)
>
> (Continued)

(Continued)

4. Hats

Picking up on the Tommy Cooper 'Hats' sketch from the previous chapter, below are stage directions from Samuel Beckett's *Waiting for Godot*. The scene recreates an old vaudeville routine in which the 'business' of swapping hats is played out. It is a good, physical routine for a group of three to practise and then perform.

> Estragon takes Vladimir's hat. Vladimir adjusts Lucky's hat on his head. Estragon puts on Vladimir's hat in place of his own which he hands to Vladimir. Vladimir takes Estragon's hat. Estragon adjusts Vladimir's hat on his head. Vladimir puts on Estragon's hat in place of Lucky's which he hands to Estragon. Estragon takes Lucky's hat. Vladimir adjusts Estragon's hat on his head. Estragon puts on Lucky's hat in place of Vladimir's which he hands to Vladimir. Vladimir takes his hat. Estragon adjusts Lucky's hat on his head. Vladimir puts on his hat in place of Estragon's which he hands to Estragon. Estragon takes his hat. Vladimir adjusts his hat on his head. Estragon puts on his hat in place of Lucky's which he hands to Vladimir. Vladimir takes Lucky's

> hat. Estragon adjusts his hat on his head. Vladimir puts on Lucky's hat in place of his own which he hands to Estragon. Estragon takes Vladimir's hat. Vladimir adjusts Lucky's hat on his head. Estragon hands Vladimir's hat back to Vladimir who takes it and hands it back to Estragon who takes it and hands it back to Vladimir who takes it and throws it down.
>
> (Act II: 71–72)
>
> These exercises are useful for developing physical comedy and for play, collaboration and building and fostering the ensemble.

The theorist Henri Bergson viewed the release afforded through laughter as having a primarily 'social function' (1900, 1994: 117). In his 'automaton' or 'mechanical inelasticity' theory (ibid.: 108, 117), he posited that it is whenever a man acts most like a machine that the laughter of relief is provoked. He stated that 'the attitudes, gestures and movements of the human body are laughable in exact proportion as that body reminds us of a mere machine' (1900, 1960: 49). His theory of 'something mechanical encrusted on the living' includes 'rigidity', 'loss of elasticity' or 'a person [giving] the impression of being a thing' (ibid.: 49–52). This 'mechanical inelasticity' theory also indicates, of course, an essential form of incongruity in action – as seen, for example, in Buster Keaton's seemingly improbable, acrobatic self-propulsion in his movies, or in Charlie Chaplin, in *Modern Times* (1936), literally acting as part of a machine, with 'his losing battle with a moving conveyor-belt, his entrapment in and regurgitation by the giant cogs of machinery, his insane dance with the oilcan' (Kerr, 1980: 38). The key thing is that the actions are performed with seriousness; they are done purposefully and, in their own comic way, expertly. This is what makes them funny – and, arguably, in their symptomatic illustration of the struggle against some form of normality – vulnerably human.

Meanwhile, John Wright states that in clowning and physical theatre 'the strongest comedy comes from the greatest seriousness' (2007: 326), while Halpern and Close note too that, in comic improvisation events, 'the more ridiculous the situation, the more seriously it must be played ... the actors must be totally committed to their characters and play them with complete integrity to achieve maximum laughs' (2001: 25). Maintaining seriousness and integrity holds equally true within comic performance generally.

Mastery of comic performance elevates the actor to being a true 'comedian', which, according to the American comic Joe Franklin's definition, is any performer who brings to life 'a definitive comic creation ... above and beyond an actor reading someone else's funny lines' (1979: 10). In the next chapter we will look at ways of employing comic expertise within scripted text.

Audio visual

For Chaplin in his final silent film *Modern Times* (Chaplin, 1936), type in 'Chaplin Modern Times'. This is a literal evocation of Bergson's notion of 'automaton' or 'man acting as a machine'!

Working in the ensemble: building interplay with your co-performers

As a comic performer, you will be working with others to (re)create the comic narrative. In effect, you will be telling a story as a group. You will tell your own bits of the story with comic expertise when you are the sole focus of the audience's attention and, equally, you should be aware of how to support and continue to augment the comic narrative when you are playing a more secondary function within the piece. In other words, having an awareness of 'action and reaction' – and when each is the appropriate performance mode – is vital. It is, for example, all too easy to kill a true laugh by upstaging, pulling focus or otherwise drawing the audience's attention inappropriately in a comedy. It is as possible to physically misemphasise as it is to verbally misemphasise something and this means that the comic timing is 'fluffed'. Working in the ensemble means that you, the comic performer, are adopting yet another layer of interplay into your skills bank. In addition to your measured awareness of the audience and their reactions, you must also become fully attuned to what your co-players are doing. You have to collaborate in ensuring the holistic gaining of the laughter. This might mean adjusting your own performance in the live situation (perhaps in setting up a gag line or allowing someone's reaction to read) according to what actually needs to be happening. It is important to keep the overall intention of a scene or moment at the forefront of your mind. What is the response (if applicable) that should be elicited at each stage? How can this best be achieved by the group through their mutual performance contributions to that scene or moment? What is your function within achieving that whole?

To use a musical analogy, playing in a comedy, in performance, can be likened to a musical concert – in which there exists a concert hall, an audience, a conductor, a stage and effects crew, plus a complete musical score to be conveyed. Within these parameters, the comic performer must operate, sometimes as a solo instrument, sometimes as a collaborative player. The performer collaborates as a musical stylist to be a fully rounded and effective member of that ensemble.

To some extent, the comic performer is also akin to Roland Barthes' wrestler figure in his essay 'The World of Wrestling' in *Mythologies* (1957, 2009). (Please do bear with me on this analogy!) Like the wrestler, the comic performer must always remain fully aware of what their role in the performance signifies. He (to use Barthes' choice of pronoun) understands the cause and effects of what he performs and what this is supposed to evoke in the audience. He knows when it is appropriate for him to drive and impel the action and when to accede to his fellow performer(s). Both the comic performer and the wrestler's use of interplay also has resonance in the very imagery that Barthes uses; he wrote that 'we are ... dealing with a real Human Comedy ... an immediate pantomime', noting that 'some wrestlers ... are great comedians ... because they succeed in imposing an immediate reading of their inner nature' (ibid.: 7). Like comedy too, wrestling 'demands an immediate reading of juxtaposed meanings' (ibid.: 4) and 'wrestlers ... have a physique as peremptory as those of the characters of the Commedia dell'arte who display in advance, in their costumes and attitudes, the future contents of their parts' (ibid.: 6).

The comic performer, moreover, like the wrestler, must conform to, and operate within, a highly prescribed world. In wrestling, 'the function of the wrestler ... is to go exactly through the motions expected of him' (ibid.: 4). The same thing can be said to apply in comic performance – this may be seen most obviously in the portrayal of the comic stereotype (e.g. the domineering mother-in-law, trickster figure, braggart, pompous authoritarian) in which, correspondingly, 'the public is overwhelmed with the obviousness of the roles' (ibid.: 5). As is often the case in comic performance too, 'wrestling ... offers excessive gestures, exploited to the limit of their meaning' (ibid.: 4) seen most obviously in the comic performer's execution of a larger-than-life reaction guaranteed to cue the laugh (as, say, for example early film comic actor James Finlayson's 'double take and fade away') (Halliwell, 1987: 309).

GROUP EXERCISES FOR BUILDING ENSEMBLE INTERPLAY

1. Wrestling boasts

Take turns to present your imaginary wrestling persona to the 'camera'. Invent a name and a characteristic for your creation – 'The Carshalton Crusher', 'the Martian Marauder', 'the Ballerina Bruiser', or whatever.

Describe the elaborate pummelling that you are going to mete out to your opponents. The more outrageous and over-the-top the claims, the better.

To develop ensemble working skills, incorporate and mock the characteristics that your opponents have described in their boasts in a second, follow up series of boasting monologues (e.g. 'I'm going to take a chunk out of that phoney Russian Rottweiler and send him back to Moscow with a red face', etc.).

Alternatively, stage the monologues jointly in a 'boast battle' dialogue.

(Continued)

(Continued)

2. Improbable pitches

Imagine you are trying to sell unlikely items (e.g. roller skates for squirrels, houses made of bread, a new religion based on the worship of lawnmowers) at a fair, market or exhibition. The object is to try hard to persuade the rest of the group to take an interest in your wares.

This can be extended into:

3. Flyting

Flyting was an ancient form, an Anglo-Saxon literary exchange of insults. In Scotland, in the fifteenth century, it became a performed verse battle between poets. (I like to believe it was the originator of rap battles!)

Students split into teams and they invent improbable insults to berate the other side. The more extreme and bizarre, the better. (The French soldier played by John Cleese in the film *Mothy Python and the Holy Grail* (Gilliam and Jones, 1975) is a good reference – 'you empty headed animal food trough wiper! I fart in your general direction, your mother was a hamster and your father smelt of elderberries'.) Sell these absurd insults (they should never descend into anything real, personal or genuinely hurtful) with as much gusto as you can.

You can experiment with form, using rhymes, rhythms and movements to get your comic insults across.

Again, incorporate and use your opponents' outlandish insults against them in a second series of flyting.

4. 'Walk this way ... '

This exercise replicates an old vaudeville gag where one character walks off and the others follow behind, copying the walk. It is usually a snooty butler-type who gets copied (see, for example, the Mel Brook's film *The Producers* (1967)). Everyone should follow the leader copying the person in front, impersonating the original eccentric gait.

The trick is to start off and mimic the walk as seriously as possible – and the more people that are involved in the chain, the funnier it should prove.

The exercise also tells us something, through the use of non-verbal body language, about the status of the characters at play. Mockery, or the 'sending up' of perceived pretension, is a subversive working of the mechanism of the superiority principle in comedy.

(Continued)

(Continued)

This exercise also encourages ensemble work as the group has to follow and closely mimic the originator of the walk.

Finally, a few simple warm-up exercises that also build ensemble:

5. Wink murder

Students stand in a circle. A 'detective' is chosen who steps outside the room while a 'murderer' is selected. Whenever the murderer winks at you, you must play dead. (Try not to die immediately as this can give the game away to the detective whose job it is to identify and catch the murderer.)

Again, performing a hammy death is permissible!

6. Radiation

This exercise simply requires students to count up to 20 without overlapping each other. The group stands in a circle and must (randomly) count up from 1 to 20 without anyone speaking over anyone else. No cueing is allowed and everyone in the group should contribute the articulation of at least one number.

To manage this counting as a group, each individual must listen to the silences and develop an awareness of when it is appropriate to add a number without destroying the uninterrupted sequence. It is surprisingly difficult and requires a lot of group concentration.

7. Slow-motion race

This is an adaptation of a Boal exercise from Dymphna Callery's book *Through the Body*:

> Actors line up as runners for a 100m sprint ... Spare actors become specta-tors at the race, reacting and responding to what occurs on the track. All this happens in real time' with vocalisation. As the referee calls the start of the race, everything goes into 'slow-motion' (like a TV action replay) and silence. The aim of each runner is to lose the race by being the slowest.
>
> (2001: 26)

8. Lifting the glass

Another exercise from Dymphna Callery's book:

> Players stand in a circle with equal spaces between them. They imagine a large circular plate of glass on the floor. They work together to lift the glass off the

(Continued)

(Continued)

> ground. Then they are asked to move it to a new position and replace it gently on the ground, without any potential breakage! The exercise takes place in silence. Only eye contact between players operates as communication.
>
> (2001:89)

These exercises also encourage collaboration and develop awareness of what the group, as a whole, is doing. Physical interplay and expertise are also built. The physical effects only work if everyone pulls together. One lapse in concentration can mean that the group cohesion is compromised and the illusion of unity of the ensemble all working together is destroyed.

The point of all these exercises is to help create the ensemble mode and to develop the group's skills in both reading the audience and in reading each other. Repeating these and similar exercises can continue to bond the ensemble and develop the picking up of cues, both verbal and non-verbal. Note, too, how this ensemble interplay is achieved through playfulness and playing together. This, in turn, is highly reminiscent of CDS interactions and imitates the basic process of how we learn.

Causes, effects and finding the vulnerability in your character

One tricky thing is that expertise in comic performance must contain the weaving and sustaining of a sense of comic 'truth', whether working as an individual or as part of an ensemble. This proves a real test of the skills of the comic performer. The actress Athene Seyle termed the maintaining of believability within a comic framing to be a form of 'tightrope walking' which is 'the craft of appearing to believe in the balance of a thing one knows is out of balance' (1943, 1990: 12). It is undeniable that comic 'truth' is harder to find within comic text which often relies on the use of expected tropes such as absurdities, incongruities, larger-than-life characterisations, happy endings, etc. Prescribed stock characters, moreover, abound in comic drama. Your performance will often take place in a world of heightened or distorted reality in which comic 'types' prevail – 'the wise fools ... "little men" ... con men and tricksters' (Mintz in Raskin, 2008: 295). It becomes your difficult job to imbue the roles that you play with reality despite all the unreality of the situation. You will recreate a form of recognisable truthfulness within the fiction. The theorist Henri Bergson defines the operation of truth in comedy thus – 'when a certain comic effect has its origin in a certain cause, the more natural we regard the cause to be, the more comic shall we find the effect' (1900, 1994: 122). It is the job of the writer to supply some material bases to alert the performer to the cause and effects of the play, but on occasions where these 'clues' are unclear, or simply do not exist, it becomes the performers' duty to find and implicitly portray these fundamental sources of cause and effect. To do this, as David Mamet suggests, 'learn to ask: What does the character in the script want? What does he or she do to get it? What is that like in my experience?' (1998: 99).

Take, for example, the character of 'Joxer' Daly in Sean O'Casey's play of 1924, *Juno and the Paycock*. O'Casey described the play as 'a tragedy in three acts' but the 'Paycock' – Joxer Daly – is the drinking crony of 'Captain' Jack Boyle in 1920s' Dublin, and he provides some comic relief within the play. O'Casey gives an unusually full and detailed description of Joxer's character:

> He may be younger than the Captain but he looks a lot older. His face is like a bundle of crinkled paper; his eyes have a cunning twinkle; he is spare and loosely built; he has a habit of constantly shrugging his shoulders with a peculiar twitching movement, meant to be ingratiating. His face is invariably ornamented with a grin.

Below is an extract from the play, in which Joxer sings (badly) to the amusement of the other characters in the scene (and to the audience):

Boyle:	Joxer's song, Joxer's song – give us wan of your shut-eyed ones,
	(Joxer settles himself in his chair; takes a drink; clears his throat; solemnly closes his eyes, and begins to sing in a very querulous voice:
	She is far from the 'lan; where her young hero sleeps,
	An' lovers around her are sighing (He hesitates).
	An' lovers around her are sighin' ... sighin' ... sighin' (A pause).)
	Boyle (imitating Joxer): And lovers around her are sighing!
	What's the use of you thryin' to sing the song if you don't know it?
Mary:	Thry another one, Mr. Daly – maybe you'd be more fortunate.
Mrs Madigan:	Gawn, Joxer; thry another wan.
Joxer (starting again):	
	I have heard the mavis singin' his love song to the morn; I have seen the dew-dhrop clingin' to the rose jus' newly born; but ... but ... (frantically) to the rose jus' newly born ... newly born ... born.

Johnny:	Mother, put on the gramophone, for God's sake, an' stop Joxer's bawlin'.
Boyle *(commandingly):*	Gramophone! ... I hate to see fellas thryin' to do what they're not able to do. (O'Casey, 1924, 1963)

Joxer's role in the play is to supply some light relief from the bleak overall situation that is depicted. He represents the cosy, parochial, domestic buffoon – someone who is oblivious to the political situation in a time of great national upheaval. He may, indeed, be intended to epitomise the old order of Ireland at the time. At any rate, there a few further clues given by O'Casey to suggest Joxer's causes and effects – what the reasons are for him being the way that he is. It is down to the performer to choose how to supply the cause and effect of Joxer's character and actions in the play, in order to portray him as a real human being, albeit someone whose odd, strutting insouciance and sly manipulations are still the stuff of comedy. At the very least, the performer must uncover some hidden charm or sparkle in Joxer that sufficiently amuses the Captain to consider him as an albeit unlikely companion.

INDIVIDUAL AND GROUP EXERCISE

Finding the causes and effects

In this exercise you will research, evaluate and discuss the causes and effects that comic characters have on the other characters in the play and on the audience. This is the first stage of being a reflective practitioner.

Plot the causes and effects of a character you are performing in a comic text. Compare, discuss and, perhaps, resolve whether and to what extent your co-actors' characters' causes and effects map – or conflict – with yours.

Describe what effects your character causes on the rest of the characters at key points in the play. Discuss what effects the character should cause on the audience at key points in the play. Describe what has caused or causes the character to react in the way he/she does at key moments in the play. Discuss what other characters' causes and effects mean for your conception of what your selected character does.

Or, as a group, select different characters from a comic play, for example, *The Comedy of Errors*, or from a farce such as *A Flea in Her Ear* or *A Servant of Two Masters* and apply the above questions.

As an example, try finding what causes and effects the character of the arch-gossip, the Duchess of Berwick, in Oscar Wilde's *Lady Windermere's Fan* (1893) has on the other character(s) and on the audience. What might have caused the Duchess to become such a society gossip? Do these causes make her more human, vulnerable and (genuinely) funny?

DUCHESS OF BERWICK: Ah, what indeed, dear? That is the point. He goes to see her continually, and stops for hours at a time, and while he is there she is not at home to anyone. Not that many ladies call on her, dear, but she has a great many disreputable men friends – my own brother particularly, as I told you – and that is what makes it so dreadful about Windermere. We looked upon him as being such a model husband, but I am afraid there is no doubt about it. My dear nieces – you know the Saville girls, don't you? – such nice domestic creatures – plain, dreadfully plain, – but so good – well, they're always at the window doing fancy work, and making ugly things for the poor, which I think so useful of them in these dreadful socialistic days, and this terrible woman has taken a house in Curzon Street, right opposite them – such a respectable street, too! I don't know what we're coming to! And they tell me that Windermere goes there four and five times a week – they see him. They can't help it – and although they never talk scandal, they – well, of course – they remark on it to everyone. And the worst of it all is that I have been told that this woman has got a great deal of money out of somebody, for it seems that she came to London six months ago without anything at all to speak of, and now she has this charming house in Mayfair, drives her ponies in the Park every afternoon and all – well, all – since she has known poor dear Windermere. It's quite true, my dear. The whole of London knows about it. That is why I felt it was better to come and talk to you, and advise you to take Windermere away at once to Homburg or to Aix, where he'll have something to amuse him, and where you can watch him all day long. I assure you, my dear, that on several occasions after I was first married, I had to pretend to be very ill, and was obliged to drink the most unpleasant mineral waters, merely to get Berwick out of town. He was so extremely susceptible. Though I am bound to say he never gave away any large sums of money to anybody. He is far too high-principled for that!

(Wilde, 1893)

Maintaining comic seriousness and depicting the integrity of the character are important factors in developing expertise in comic performance. These contribute to the sense of overall comic truth. In the 'tightrope walk' of conjuring up a sense of reality within the unreal – 'the essential element of truth in a ... comedy situation has to exist, or the audience will stop laughing'

(Parsons, 1994: 146). Ultimately, any sense of 'comic truth' is valid only if it also registers as 'true' by the audience. An audience is quickly able to detect and reject as 'phoney' or 'untrue' any interaction or piece of 'business' that seems fake, and comic performance is, unfortunately, frequently full of such false signals which disestablish any sense of comic truth. Examples of what the American comic performer Phil Silvers described as 'hokum' (1973: 27) and that exist only in the realm of hackneyed comic performance include a performer spitting out water on hearing 'shock' news or allowing their character to continue to chatter on before suddenly stopping to register a surprising piece of information. Eric Weitz refers to 'one of the oldest farcical punchlines in the book' (2009: 167) in Trofimov's charge offstage followed by a crash, as if he has fallen downstairs in Anton Chekhov's *Uncle Vanya* (1897). When any of these bits of 'business' are poorly performed, the audience registers the falseness and lack of truth contained in the action above anything else. The actress Molly Weir also refers to the ubiquitous 'cod dry up' – a device sometimes utilised by comic performers to ensure audience laughter as 'a desperate ruse where the performer pretends he's convulsed with laughter and can't go on with his dialogue, just to get the audience laughing at him' (1979: 94). As Northrop Frye states, 'laughter is partly a reflex ... and [it] can be conditioned' (in Enck, 1960: 88). This therefore means that a laugh can also be lazily gained through 'easy' tricks – for example, as from the stand-up comedian who swears just for the sake of it; by a character dressing up in 'inappropriate' clothing; or, simply, through a custard pie to the face. The last being something that very rarely happens in real life. In short, falling into the trap of reproducing tricks, what W. S. Gilbert remarked in the quote in Chapter 1, as the 'sitting on a pork pie', provokes a laugh but one that is cheap, superficial and actually proves counterproductive. Such 'extorted' (Mamet, 1998: 126) effects are, moreover, what Brett Mills refers to as the 'excess' which have become the pejorative 'traditions of comic acting' (2010: 131, 137). These are what the comic actor Kenneth Williams despairingly referred to as 'lines, business and cracks – corn – the lot – false noses if necessary – just get your laughs any way you can and devil take the hindmost' (1993: 124).

Such cod playing to bank a guaranteed, easy laugh is to be scrupulously avoided, however tempting it may be! Playing real comedy, while managing to remain 'truthful', presents you with the challenge of mastering a highly sophisticated and intricate form of acting. Craft and expertise requirements involve the mobilising of skilled physical and verbal expression. Both require the enhanced use of rhythms and the ability to employ timing to make your effects work (as we will see in more detail in the next chapter). Sustaining the impression of comic truth and balancing portrayals of realism within the heightened, quasi-realistic, skewed world of comic text can require the performer to project some form of vulnerability or essential humanity or likeability within the character. For the comic actor this often means finding ways to humanise a stereotype. Note how a skilled comic performer can take what is, on the surface, a comic stereotype and make that character real – for example, see the domineering mother-in-law as played by Doris Roberts in *Everybody Loves Raymond* (CBS, 1996–2005); the braggart soldier as portrayed by Arthur Lowe in *Dad's Army* (BBC, 1968–1976); or the hapless, would-be lover as depicted by Tamsin Greig in *Green Wing* (Channel 4, 2004–2007). These highly skilled performers elevate the superficial through their ability to make their characters real, living beings, whose human frailty and faults are rendered wholly recognisable to the audience. These actors subvert any caricature that their roles contain and imbue their, apparently, on-the-surface stereotypes with understandable human traits. The characters clearly have beating hearts that make the comedy all the funnier. As the comic actor Kenneth Williams recorded in his diaries, this is a case of 'proper acting – i.e. vulnerable acting' (ibid.: 203). Finding this vulnerability may involve some element of being prepared to make yourself (as your character) look absurd or foolish. For this reason, some 'star' performers in the world of film, who already have a strongly defined image and guarding the dignity that their success and power have imbued them with, have not fared so well in the playing of comedy!

Ultimately, finding some human vulnerability in your character can simply take the form of identifying the source of the underlying seriousness which underpins everything that they do. We all have some characteristic of underlying seriousness about our motivations and what impels us, and, often, when you think about it, this basic impetus is often actually rather ridiculous!

As humans, moreover, we have the ability to pick up on all sorts of subliminal clues from each other. We tend to be able to 'read' people less from what they say and do on the surface but are able to deduce what really impels them from their actions, behaviours or 'give-aways'. We are, generally speaking, extremely gifted in being able to see through the 'front' which someone presents to the real person underneath. We can, essentially, 'intuit' what it is that motivates people – sometimes even better than they know it themselves. And, just as it happens in life, the same thing applies in performing comedy. Audiences will easily read the underlying seriousness that impels a comic character if you, the performer, are aware of it and have absorbed this into your construct of the character. For the purposes of the comic performer, this means, in effect, that finding the seriousness is the same as revealing the vulnerability that underlies the – often rather unappealing – strictures of characterisation and action as depicted by the author. George Santayana noted that 'the essence of what we call humour is that amusing weakness should be combined with an amicable humanity' (1896: 96). John Russell Brown, speaking of the great Shakespearean clowns, opined further that 'one of the greatest strengths of the clowns was their ability to call forth abnormal responses, to make pathos, villainy, wisdom, or cowardice both funny and acceptable' (1993: 89).

For instance, an interesting example of how human frailty is presented with both reality and a sense of humanity is suggested by the playing of the cast of the American sitcom *Seinfeld* (NBC, 1989–1998), where, as the British sitcom writer Alan Simpson notes, despite the fact that 'the characters are quite nasty underneath' (in Hall, 2006: 208) they remain endearing and likeable. Similarly, take the case of the protagonists of the film *This Is Spinal Tap* (Reiner, 1984), where 'even while Spinal Tap are egotistical idiots who make terrible music, you can't help but like them. Hilarious' (Gilbert, 2009: 47). Or, as Bob Monkhouse observed about John Cleese's characterisation of Basil Fawlty in *Fawlty Towers* (BBC, 1975, 1979):

> For all his comic ghastliness, the frustrated hotelier evoked a response of warmth in us, recognition and pity for his reality, that only the defenceless honesty of the actor could achieve.
>
> (1998: 47)

Some tantalising detail about humanising the stereotype or fleshing out the caricature propounded in a literary form of comic characterisation is to be found in T. C. Worsley's description of Donald Wolfit, as Lord Ogleby in *The Clandestine Marriage* (Colman and Garrick, 1766) in the 1951 Old Vic production:

> There are conventions and clichés for representing ... all characters ... The good craftsman-actor doesn't get beyond putting over a more or less sensitive selection of these clichés: and usually we accept them. But how dull and insufficient that seems when alongside it we suddenly find an artist-actor really creating, not merely imitating, and so, apparently, not acting but being. Every little gesture, grunt, wheeze, inflection, tic, in Mr. Wolfit's Lord Ogleby seems to grow organically out from the centre of an actual living man. A foolish old man it is true, but the man is presented to us mixed up with his folly; and so behaviour which might in other hands be odious or simply ridiculous touches a layer of affection under our laughter.
>
> (1952: 255–256)

To present 'being', it is, therefore, the job of the comic performer to find what has caused their character to become – or what, in the play, motivates them to be – the way they are. Does the domineering mother-in-law's behaviour stem from an inherently noble, if overdeveloped, sense of protection for her children? Did she, perhaps, have an overbearing – or absent – mother herself? Does she fear being no longer required or being left alone? Does the absent-minded professor actually fear his memory lapses? Or does he deliberately forget some things? Is he really as absent-minded as he appears – or is it a protective shell? Is the lovesick young man really so deluded and pathetic?

What if he knows – and is correct in his assumption – that he will never again meet anyone whom he will feel so passionately about as that scheming strumpet who is out to con him? What if he is also rather scared of this glorious passion that consumes all his thoughts and overwhelms his very sense of self?

Even the most apparently superficial or buffoonish character has many potential underlying dimensions, which, although never necessarily made overt or brought explicitly to the surface of your performance, will help you to find the seriousness and vulnerability that underlies the character. Finding the human core will help you to subvert the stereotype and provide a more realistic and 'true' comic characterisation.

Becoming reflective on your craft skills

Building the craft or expertise skills cannot be overlooked in the achievement of successful comic performance:

> Performative skill can weave spells from even smaller units of 'text', mining comic gold from the tiniest of territories, so that an unexceptional single word, or even part of a word, can become a memorable comic moment if the performance is bold, crafty and precise enough.
>
> (Medhurst, 2003: 3)

Building up a craft skills bank involves being aware of what works and what does not in performance – and continuing to learn from this. It also means constantly refining what works and rejecting anything that does not. In becoming reflective, you will underpin your practice with theory – and vice versa – in a process which enriches your expertise in producing true comic performance. Becoming a reflective practitioner in the way that this book encourages means that you will think about, articulate, experiment with and try out your craft using 'reflection-in-action' and 'reflection-on-action' (Schön, 1987: 14). This will make it easier for you to discuss, evaluate and expand your practice in collaboration with others who are involved. However, you may find that there may be some initial scepticism about embarking on this process from some quarters. This may partly be because there is some 'distrust of method and analysis in acting' (Redgrave, 1995: 10) from certain practitioners. As William Cook notes, 'most of the actors I've met have displayed a marked disinclination to discuss their craft' (1994: 4), while Morris Carnovsky observed that,

> My colleagues were some of the finest actors of the day – Dudley Digges, Henry Travers, the Lunts, Edward G. Robinson, many others ... it was curious, but none of these good craftsmen seemed able or willing to talk about their craft.
>
> (Corrigan, 1964: 304)

Comedy, moreover, is often (erroneously) thought to be something that is antithetical to analysis. As early as 1751, Samuel Johnson noted in *The Rambler* that 'comedy has been particularly unpropitious in definers' (370), while Michael Mulkay pointed out that 'analysts of humour operate within a different discursive mode from participants in humour' (1988: 28). What is certainly true, as Brett Mills notes, is that 'the analysis of performance is one informed by the lack of critical thought and vocabulary available' (2005: 68). This should not deter you from attempting to evaluate the processes, causes and effects that you will encounter when making comic performance. Unhelpfully, both comedy and performing are sometimes presumed to operate through entirely subconscious or intuitive processes and there exists a belief among some actors that conscious analysis of the execution of practice is somehow dangerous. As Geoff King notes, for some performers, evaluation of practice methods might actually appear to be a threatening or destabilising activity, referring to 'practitioners for whom excessive analytical probing might threaten a form of creativity that draws on a range of unstated and unselfconscious assumptions' (2006: 4).

Alongside some second-hand reluctance towards analysis, you may also find that it is difficult to find the right words or terminology to capture abstract concepts or ideas whenever you attempt to describe your practice and processes. Available language is often inadequate when attempting to describe what it is that you are trying to do (or uncover) in a creative art discipline. Words are slippery things and you will find that descriptors of craft/expertise skills often tend to be reductive or somewhat simplistic. Such descriptions often do not get beyond the physical dwelling on Bergsonian, bodily misalliances, relegating the performative technical abilities, practice or process elements to the outer fringes of the farcical, pantomimic or broadly comic. Commentators' attempts to capture comic performers' input often emphasise the act of 'telegraphing', or merely describe the more obvious physical incongruities. Miranda Hart, eponymous star of the sitcom *Miranda* (BBC, 2010–2014), has been described by one reviewer as 'a skilful comedian making silly faces at the camera and falling over ... [there is] her size (6ft 1) and physical awkwardness' (Hanks, 2011: 31). This difficulty in capturing what it is that comic performers do (rather than just explaining what they 'are') in their endeavours to cue laughter is undoubtedly due to the paucity of critical 'vocabulary' that exists to enable deeper description. For example, even the silent movie expert John McCabe struggles with describing the craft/expertise skills, hinting merely at some mastery of incongruity or absurdity, when he writes, apropos of the early movie comedians and their use of traditional Commedia dell'arte tropes, of:

Lazzi – or comic tricks. These perhaps look simple to people – like bumping into someone you don't see at first and then backing off in surprise and fear – but these thing are not easy to do gracefully and do funnily ... it is only a master like Stan [Laurel] or Charlie [Chaplin] who can do these things in a very, very funny way to make us laugh out loud, heartily.

(1966: 137, italics in original)

Nevertheless, it is worth persisting with reflection to uncover your character's hidden motivations and their essential human-ness. Evaluate your effects during the rehearsal and performance stages. Further, when analysing your craft jointly, evaluate your various characters' drives as a group. Thus you can play within the text and in so doing, will make discoveries about the layers and textures of the work. This kind of reflection – exploring what impels the underlying seriousness of your different comic characters and the various causes and effects they contain – is all to the betterment of the play. Reflection becomes a skill which can only help you to imbue your performance with the necessary truth and vulnerability which will humanise your role. All this, ultimately, will make the comedy even funnier.

An audience can recognise great comedy acting when witnessed, but without necessarily being fully able to describe what has been seen. Take, for instance, a contemporary account in which Georg Christoph Lichtenberg describes the craft/expertise skills evident in Thomas Weston's playing of comic 'business' as Scrub in a 1770s' production of *The Beaux Stratagem*:

> While Garrick sits there at ease with an agreeable carelessness of demeanour, Weston attempts, with back stiff as a poker, to draw himself up to the other's height, partly for the sake of decorum, and partly to steal a glance now and then, when Garrick is looking the other way, so as to improve on his imitation of the latter's manner. When Archer at last with an easy gesture crosses his legs, Scrub tries to do the same, in which he eventually succeeds, though not without some help from his hands, and with eyes all the time either gaping or making furtive comparisons. And when Archer begins to stroke his magnificent silken calves, Weston tries to do the same with his miserable red woollen ones, but, thinking better of it, slowly pulls his green apron over them with an abjectness of demeanour, arousing pity in every breast. In this scene Weston almost excels Garrick by means of the foolish expression natural to him.
>
> (in Thomson, 2000: 105)

Through reflection, the performer gains the ability to provide first-hand insight into the process and practice of creating a character.

A rare example of such (self) reflection-on-action comes from the actor Donald Sinden (1923–2014). By the late 1980s, Sinden was a highly familiar performer to audiences of the time, having become well known from cinema appearances (as an alumnus of the Rank film school from the 1950s) and his subsequent work in a number of TV sitcoms, including *Two's Company* (ITV,

1975–1976) and *Never the Twain* (ITV, 1981–1991). In 1988, Sinden was invited, along with a number of other 'players of Shakespeare', to discuss his own portrayal of a famous character from the canon. In his own text, Sinden discussed his playing of Malvolio in the RSC production of Shakespeare's *Twelfth Night* in 1969/1970. In his reflection on the craft skills, the presence of the comic principles of superiority, relief and incongruity appears in Sinden's account. He notes that 'laughs are not normally recorded, but the comic actor is always striving for them' (Sinden in Brockbank, 1988: 45–46) and he proceeds to enumerate and 'rate' the audience laughter, prompted by his own vocal, physical and 'business' interventions. He grades the responses 'from 1–9, between the largest that can be expected (ibid.: 9) and the smallest (ibid.: 1) still worth trying for' (ibid.: 46). Describing how the comic performer can facilitate the effect of audience laughter, Sinden also includes a reflection on the craft/expertise skills necessary for this, characterised by the use of vocal, facial and bodily inflections; the employment of particular, pre-selected interactions with other actors; and the invention of comic 'business' with costume and props (e.g. the later interpolation of a piece of business with an onstage sundial (ibid.: 61–62; and also in Sinden, 1985: 282–283)). Thus, in the scene where Malvolio has been tricked into thinking that his mistress Olivia is in love with him, Sinden elaborates on his own performative input as follows:

> A discreet cough. She turns! 'How now, Malvolio?'; not quite the reaction I expected; but of course! I have forgotten the smile! Here goes (laugh 4). Very musically, almost sung, 'Sweet Lady', and then – as written – flatly, with no humour at all, 'Ho Ho' (laugh 4). The parallel fingers of my R hand punctuate both 'Ho's' like castanets ...
> (Sinden, 1985: 60 [note that Sinden is using 'L' for moving left, 'R' for right, 'U' for upstage])

Crucially, it is noteworthy that the choices as described by the performer are affected through a form of interplay with the audience – a process described by Sinden as:

> I am now one-hundred-per-cent Malvolio, but in a comedy I, the actor, must remain one-hundred-per-cent myself, standing outside my character, my ears out on stalks, listening for the very slightest sound from the audience, controlling them, so that I am able to steer a 'cue', 'punch' or 'tag' line clear of any interruption. If on any night Malvolio takes over, the precision, the immaculate timing, the control, suffer. If the actor takes over, the performance becomes 'technical' and the audience is always aware of it.
> (Ibid.: 46–47)

Building complicity through interplay with the audience also takes the form of unscripted, performer-driven signalling to comic effect, 'and puzzled,

I ask if the audience know the word' (ibid.: 57); 'He [Malvolio] flashes a plea to the audience' (ibid.: 58); 'I address the audience again – orchestra stalls now' (ibid.: 61). Moreover,

> I must forestall the audience's reaction. Malvolio doesn't intend the bawdry, but Shakespeare does ... He throws the letter aside and starts to move U. his eyes roam the audience (I would not dream of reading anyone else's letter). His fingers run along the back of the chair R to L. As it reaches the end ... did his foot slip? Or how is it that he has now lost 18 inches in height and has the back of the chair under his R armpit (laugh 4).
>
> (Ibid.: 55)

Sinden advances interplay and timing, while describing expertise skills and the finding of the underlying seriousness and vulnerability that impel the character's motivations:

> I am deeply hurt that she [Olivia] should speak thus to me – but what am I to do? Pained and distressed I reply: 'Madam' (I'm sorry you should behave like this) 'I will'. I turn L, the staff is held by its centre, horizontally, in the right hand and I execute what must be the slowest run ever ... as if crossing a series of puddles just wider than an extended pace. I exit L (laugh 8, and a round of applause).
>
> (Ibid.: 48)

This example of reflection also reveals the actor drawing on the repertoire of techniques used by the stand-up comedian, elsewhere described by the British comedian Bob Monkhouse as basic interplay skills which manufacture an impression of intimacy and attempt to create a form of complicity between comedian and spectator, through the use of:

> The perfect pause, the subtlest shading of a word, the sidelong glance, the sudden switch of expression, mock shock, simulated sanctimony, shared secrecy, faked frankness, genuine on-the-spot invention.
>
> (1993: 319)

GROUP EXERCISES

Reflection-on-action

Record yourself performing a comic monologue or improvisation in front of the group. When playing back the recording, listen for audience's reactions.

(Continued)

(Continued)

Note what you did that especially got laughs? Analyse and evaluate which elements raised the most laughter. Was this gained through any direct communication with the audience? From pausing to allow a laugh to ignite and then grow? Or by bringing certain moments to life through particular vocal or physical characterisation?

Now evaluate whether the laughs gained were from truthful causes and effects on your part. Was the quality of the laughter 'deep' or 'surface'? If the laughter is the product of a truthful, genuine and recognisably human provocation through your performance then it will sound suitably deep and (lastingly) real.

If, however, the quality of the laughter sounds shallow, obvious or easily gained, the chances are that it was triggered by tricks or 'hokum'. This is a case of the superficial laughter of (instant and fleeting) release.

From what you have learned through this reflective exercise, what might you do differently next time?

It is also worth keeping a reflective note book, log or journal – it is valuable to record the process you arrive at as you go through the process and to evaluate the effects of your practice in an ongoing way (reflecting both 'in-action' and 'on-action'). Reflection-in-action is much easier in comedy where the audience's reaction needs to be taken into account as an important aspect of evaluating the effectiveness of your performance.

Suggested further study

Reading

Barthes, Roland (1957, 2009) *Mythologies*, London: Vintage Books. Useful, if you want to know more about drawing comparisons between how the comic performer and the wrestler produce meaning-making 'significations' in performance.

Bergson, Henri (1900) 'Laughter'. In Sypher, Wylie (1994) *Comedy*, London: John Hopkins University Press. Also in Morreall, John (ed.) (1987) *The Philosophy of Laughter and Humor*, New York: Albany. Also in Enck, John J., Forter, Elizabeth T. and Whitley, Alvin (eds) (1960) *The Comic in Theory and Practice*, New York: Appleton-Century Crofts. A theorist offers an influential interpretation of how comedy works.

Brockbank, Philip (ed.) (1988) *Players of Shakespeare 1*, Cambridge: Cambridge University Press. Actors talk about performing Shakespeare in both comic and non-comic roles.

Olsen, Christopher (ed.) (2015) *Acting Comedy*, London: Routledge. Different practitioners offer perspectives on the craft of acting in comedy.

Schön, Donald (1987) *Educating the Reflective Practitioner: Towards a New Design for Teaching and Learning in the Professions*, San Francisco: Jossey-Bass. An account of what becoming a reflective practitioner involves.

Example

In an example of what might be considered a 'classic' film performance, the comic performer's input and craft skills can be seen as more than just a simple case of physical or performative dexterity. In the film *Laughter in Paradise* (Zampi, 1951), Alastair Sim plays Captain Deniston Russell, the otherwise genteel author of hard-boiled thrillers, who is forced to commit a crime in order to inherit a bequest. Steven H. Scheuer refers to this film as 'an amusing British comedy … [comprising a] first rate cast with great depth' (1992: 593). Michael Brooke's description of Sim's performance in the film captures the essence of the performer's input as:

> His single-take essay in self-conscious surreptitiousness … his body language betraying both his inexperience and his disgust at the depths to which he has sunk in order to inherit a fortune.
>
> (2005: n.p.)

Clearly, Sims' acting – his 'playing' of the comic situation – in both his expressive expertise and in his transmission of the character's 'feelings' is fundamental to the overall comic message that is being depicted. The performer is clearly functioning as what Andy Medhurst terms the 'crucial conduit' (2003: 67). However, while accepting that the success of any performed comedy is, of course, reliant on the collaborative skills of a team of people, including the writer, director, camera and music supervisors, editor, etc., it is illuminating that the co-writer of the screenplay of *Laughter in Paradise*, Michael Pertwee, later felt obliged to defend the supremacy of his written text as the primary agent in creating the comedy. He argued against any charge that Sim's performative input should be viewed as the preeminent factor in dictating the effectiveness of the comedy, writing in his (highly entertaining) biography *Name Dropping*, that:

> True, there were two sequences without dialogue, but carefully written and worked out, in which Alastair Sim performed brilliantly … but he was not abandoning the script. He was following it and interpreting it in his own inimitable way.
>
> (1974: 113)

However, a review of the original shooting script of *Laughter in Paradise* in the British Film Institute Library would suggest otherwise. Rather than the wordless sections being 'carefully written and worked out', the 'acting' directions in the shooting script are terse, factual and mechanistic:

Scene 269 CS Jeweller's Shop

DENISTON pauses in front of a window and looks at the brick in his hand. Everything about him is indicative of desperate resolve. He braces himself to throw the brick and is about to do so when an ASSISTANT inside the shop suddenly appears in the window at the exact spot where the brick would have landed.

DENISTON lowers his arms and mops his brow ...

Scene 270 CAMERA DRAWS BACK as DENISTON gives a start, drops the brick and swings round, and SHEILA comes into the picture.

(Pertwee and Davies, 1950: n.p. [original shooting script])

Later in the script, acting directions include such bald instructions as 'Deniston is moved by her loyalty and enthusiasm' or 'he reacts with horror' and, later, 'increasing horror'. Such directions can, in no way, serve to capture or, indeed, describe the pre-eminence that the performer's skills of interpretation – the craft element – actually play in the creation of the comic possibility and in enabling the successful reading of the overall text as humorous. Far from simply 'following' the script and 'interpreting' it, Sim's comic reinterpretation and transmission were, arguably, utterly crucial to the process of successful comic communication and, doubtlessly, in creating the enduring appeal that has subsequently afforded these scenes a 'classic' status. Sim, the comic performer, is in short the producer or 'transmitter-in-chief' (Elam, 1994: 85) of what makes this scene funny. Sim's craft skills – his comic performance skills – are the main driver in what make these scenes funny. There is a believability depicted in his out-of-character behaviour. It is easy for the viewer to read the discomfort and determination in Deniston's actions – but this is achieved through Sim's playing of the text. The comic performer is, here, a creative, active, central agent of the making of the overall comic text. Far from being some kind of passive interpreter, the comic performer clearly controls and manipulates the comic discourse.

Audio visual

The Sim scene is available on YouTube. Type in 'Laughter in Paradise'/'Captain Russell commits a crime'. The film is also available on DVD – *Alistair Sim Collection*, Studio Canal DVD.

Chapter 4

Rhythm and timing

> There are a few basic rules of timing which any competent actor ought to be able to follow, like facing out front to deliver a punch line and giving a little cough at the end of it, or doing a false trip and blowing a raspberry as you exit, but these are just the tip of the timing iceberg.
>
> (Planer as 'Craig', 1989: 84)

The above cliché comes from the caricatured thespian 'Nicholas Craig' in Nigel Planer's spoof biography *I, An Actor*. But 'Craig' is correct in his basic assertion that timing in playing comedy is important! The issue of comic 'timing' is indeed something that comes up a lot in analyses of performance of comedy. The British comic actor Steve Coogan stated that 'comedy is somewhere between mathematics and music – there's a rhythm to it' (Burrell, 2007: 5), while the American film actor Willem Dafoe said, 'I think comic acting is more difficult because of the timing factor' (Luckhurst and Veltman, 2001:32). Meanwhile, the British comic actor and writer Eric Sykes averred that 'the most important element of comedy is timing' (2005: 380). While discussing the legendary clown, Grock, Max Wall referred to his 'timing' as 'the focal point of all comedy' (1975: 70).

Comedy most definitely relies on rhythm and timing. Comic cause and effect depends on a whole series of accurately timed elements coming together irresistibly and 'rightly'. All the rhythms – the 'flow' of the scene – have to be correct for optimum amusement to occur. A mistimed entrance, fluffed cue or wrongly emphasised line can mean the difference between the effective stimulation of laughter and the failure to trigger the desired response. But what does the notion of comic timing actually mean? On one hand, it can be seen merely as a set of technical tricks that can be learned and passed on from one actor to another. Athene Seyler, for example, notes the technical use of 'slowing up the pace', 'throwing away a line' or the 'topping of one another's tone' (1943, 1990: 41–42). Comic timing, however, cannot simply be stated as something that is mechanical and rote-like in execution. Accurate use of rhythm in performance is something more complex and profound. In performance, achieving rhythmic accuracy is something akin to Csikszentmihalyi's notion of 'flow' (1990) in which the performer achieves their effects while in a state of creative absorption. Comic rhythm requires immersion and a state of being 'in the zone'. It is a form of 'flow within flow'. This rhythmic flow can be learned and tested through practice in front of a live and responsive audience. It can also be achieved through continuing cooperative work with your fellow actors within a give and take, reactive and responsive, ethos – one in which you can spark off each other.

Furthermore, if, as Brett Mills claims,

> Comedy acting ... is marked by its distinctiveness from ... naturalistic or realist performance, often employing ... a wider vocal range, and more common stresses on the rhythms of language than would be the case for the majority of 'straight' drama.
>
> (2010: 131)

Then, the question is, can this 'wider vocal range' and use of 'stresses on the rhythm of language' become embedded in your practice of comedy performance? Certainly, reflecting on what works vocally can easily be achieved through the experience of working in front of a live audience and it can also be practised in studio situations. Be aware that the latter state only works if your fellow ensemble members act (genuinely and positively) as a *de facto* audience would. Rather than offering sycophantic responses (because they know and like you and want to be uncritically supportive), the ideal conditions for mutual reflection-in and on-action can only be created in rehearsal if your colleagues operate as 'critical friends'. Then it becomes possible to practise and develop your comic timing with some degree of reassurance. It is true that, even when any theatrical context is taken away, the development of comic timing is a highly satisfying discovery for anyone who practises it. From the child who gets a laugh from a parent, to friends who tell each other jokes and funny stories, it proves very gratifying to be the one who prompts an amused response. The child who tries to provoke a smile is simply finding out what works and what does not when attempting to behave comically. As Freud had it, 'play with words and thoughts, motivated by certain pleasurable effects of economy, would be the first stage of jokes' (1905, 1964: 128). A child soon learns that gaining a laugh is also dependent on the way she tells her story and it is the manner in which the utterances are made (both verbally and non-verbally) that will gain the most laughter. Successful reception of any comic 'telling' – from a joke to an entire scenario or play – is predicated on the timing of all the elements involved being complete. The rhythmic flow is what drives the comic story being told.

To break it down, comic timing is predicated on an awareness of rhythm and how beats (/) and pauses (-) work in communication. It is an understanding of how to employ emphases and/or pauses (both vocally and physically) in the articulation of a performance. So, while the telling of the simplest joke requires awareness of how rhythm works in the expression of the wordplay, as in, for example, the gag:

> I went to an animal enclosure the other day -
> It was rubbish. They only had one dog /
> It was a shitzu.

It is clear that without leaving a pause between the words 'day' and 'It was rubbish' and giving a beat after 'dog' and 'It was a shitzu', the clarity of the communication of the joke is less effective.

Similarly, to take another dog-themed joke:

> A postman complained to the owner of a house:
> Your dog just chased me down the path and ate my cap. Look it's left these teeth marks.
> 'Oh, big deal', replied the dog owner.
> 'Big deal? Listen mate', replied the postie, I don't like your attitude.
> The man says, 'it's not my attitude, it's your 'at it chewed ... '

The timing of the (admittedly weak) punchline requires explicit 'play' on words and needs the emphasis to fall on the final word. Otherwise, again, the effect of the joke is blurred.

Meanwhile, all 'knock-knock' jokes require mutual knowledge of a well-established rhythm to work:

> Knock knock/
> Who's there?
> Little old lady
> Little old lady who?
> I didn't know you could yodel.

A prodigiously talented comedian can actually subvert the expected rhythms or emphases and still get the laugh. In articulating scripted text, however, the comic performer needs to be aware of, and be able to exploit, the rhythmic clues that the writer has supplied and which will impel the full comic meaning. In delivering the verbal timing of a comic script the performer operates like a musician, whether playing at times as an individual (solo instrumentalist) or, at others, as a member of the ensemble (orchestral player). The actor Bill Paterson, apropos of playing Estragon in *Waiting for Godot*, refers to the play being like 'a piece for a string quartet, where everyone must know the players alongside them as well as themselves' (Pollock, 2015: 8). Writing about stand-up performers, Oliver Double notes that timing is reliant upon 'an understanding of rhythm' (2005: 202) and the very same thing holds true for comic performers working in plays. The actress Margaret Rutherford wrote about playing Mrs Malaprop in *The Rivals* (Sheridan, 1775), 'as in all comedy the timing had to be precise. Catch the split second and the laughs come. Miss two beats and they are gone' (1972: 201).

It is therefore important to work on keeping your comic timing sharp. I remember once being involved in a comic play and agonising as to why a certain line I delivered – which I knew *should* be funny – was not getting a laugh in performance. I asked a fellow actor who was also in the scene why he thought this was the case. He (the wonderfully talented and late-lamented Jeffrey Perry) reflected for a moment and said 'try saying it louder'. Incredulous, I put this (seemingly trite) advice into practice at the next performance and to my amazement it worked and continued to do so! Where I had thought that, timing-wise, a downward inflection and a 'throwaway' approach to the line in question was what was required, it actually transpired that the impetus built by previous lines needed a louder emphasis and a bit of a crescendo to work properly.

As performers very often identify timing and rhythm as key to performing comedy (see Chapter 7), there may be some credence in the theory that comedy and musicality are closely allied. Many well-known comic performers, in fact, also demonstrate a surprisingly high level of musical ability, for example, apart from such excellent comedy musicians as Bill Bailey, Mitch Benn, Tim Minchin, Tom Lehrer, Dillie Keane, Victor Borge and Anna Russell, comedians who also happened to be talented piano players have included Les Dawson, Eric Morecambe, Max Wall, Bruce Forsyth, Norman Wisdom and Rikki Fulton, while Phyllis Diller, Steve Allen and Dudley Moore all played the keyboard to concert standard. Comic performers too often resort to musical or horological imagery to try to explain their timing (e.g. Ken Dodd described his timing as 'a watch mechanism ... it's all rhythm'; Griffin, 2005: 89). Similar metaphors were used by Eric Morecambe – 'if you try to take us apart to find out what makes us tick ... the watch stops' (ibid.: 235). The farceur Marcel Achard wrote in his introduction to Feydeau's *Theatre Couplet* (1958) that attempting to write about farce was 'somewhat like being in the position of a clockmaker who has to dismantle the carillon on the Strasbourg Cathedral' (Bentley, 1958: 77).

GROUP EXERCISES

Fizz buzz boing

This is a game where students cue each other and must stay alert to rhythmic cues and responses. Students stand in a circle. In rotation, students pass and repeat the cue 'fizz', to the person to their left. The response 'buzz' changes the direction of the 'fizz' cue, while 'boing' means that the recipient of the 'fizz' can 'throw' the next 'fizz' response onto anyone else in the circle. Whoever starts

the game can say either 'fizz', 'buzz' or 'boing'. 'Fizz' is the key directive of the action. Students can also experiment with *how* they say 'fizz' or 'buzz' (but boing should always be vocally elongated – 'boo-oo-oo-ing') and accompanied with an exaggerated throwing action.

Fuzzy duck

Again, in a circle, students pass the cue 'fuzzy duck', followed by the response 'ducky fuzz' around in one direction. Any (unfortunate) slips of the tongue, hesitations, etc. mean that the utterer is eliminated. The cues and responses should get faster as the game progresses.

Chris Johnston's shoe game

The group sit in a circle.

Everyone takes off a shoe and holds it up in the air.

The facilitator needs to introduce a well-known tune or rhyming pattern which allows the game to be played.

Everyone sings the song.

At certain given words in the song – probably on the 'on' beat – players need to pass the shoe to their right and collect one from the left. The exercise is made more fun if on the other beats – the 'off' beats – the shoe is merely banged on the floor but not passed on.

(Continued)

(Continued)

> The aim is to try and keep the game/song going on without it all falling apart. If possible, up the tempo of the song as it goes on.
> The exercises develop ensemble, sense of rhythm, playfulness and verbal and physical co-ordination.
>
> (2012: 29)

These games also all develop ensemble, picking up cues, making fast responses and playing around with timing and rhythm.

While rhythmic clues may well be integrated into a scripted text it is, of course, how you, the performer, 'play' the text (in a similar way to how an orchestral player interprets a musical score) that is ultimately what is responsible for creating effective comic meaning.

In effect, timing and rhythm, as defined by performers, seem to refer to a mastery and exploitation of vocal and bodily performance techniques that, in turn, contain a satisfactory inevitability that is both meaningful and pleasurable to the spectator or auditor. Mastery of comic timing may indeed partly be systematic and technical – as in Brian O'Gorman's description of watching his father, the Variety comedian Joe O'Gorman, in action:

> It was an eye-opener to the comedian's timing, control of the voice and power to work on an audience. Interrupt too soon and the listener's

attention is divided, pitch the voice too low and the joke loses its punch ... sitting nearby that evening I appreciated as never before the need for utterances to be of the right number of words for impact and humour.

(1998: 48–49)

Or, as is the case with much 'craft' expertise in performance, comic timing can be seen as something that is only evident to the spectator when it is actually missing in a performance. Its very absence being what makes it overt. Remembering where the laugh should come, rather than timing it for the audience that is present, can be problematic:

When the remembered response of the audience becomes the principal sensation of doing the play, and one starts unconsciously to engineer the repetition of that response – stops, in fact, playing the truth, the character, the situation: starts in a word to ACT IN THE PAST, to recreate an effect. Then it stops being funny and one works harder and harder to bludgeon the audience into laughter.

(Callow, 1984: 169, emphases in the original)

Callow provides a useful illustration of how timing can simply be either 'right' or 'wrong'. Correctly timed performance will achieve the quality of laughter that you, the director, the author and the audience all seek, whereas incorrectly timed performance leaves all parties frustrated. The comedy principle of relief has not been enabled in the latter case. In Freudian terms, comic relief (the laughter of release) is 'an outlet for psychic or nervous energy' (1905, 1964: 111), and this outlet has to be properly triggered. The performers' use of timing signals the audience to laugh. This can seem overly manipulative at times – the critic Tom Sutcliffe refers to 'buttons being pressed' and refers to an instance of where 'the line had the shape and timing of a punchline and the audience understood what was expected of it' noting disapprovingly that 'they laughed because the play had instructed them to' (2011: 2)

Nonetheless, correct timing remains integral to the communicative act that is performing in comedy. 'Rhythm provides cohesion ... into communicative moves that propel the ... event forward' (Van Leeuwen, 2011: 169). The actress and director Maria Aitken notes that, simply, listening and breathing are the first steps to getting your timing right in performance:

If you don't anticipate, but allow your idea to form when you have heard enough data, then your breathing will assist your timing. You will never be artificially speedy; you will never tread on laughs. You will be able to pick up certain cues like lightning, well supported by breath, because you received all the information you needed to answer before the end of the other actor's line ... All of this matches an audience's rhythm of comprehension. You will never be too fast or too slow for them ... if you *listen*.

(1996: 67)

To practise your timing, below are some more ensemble exercises that are particularly useful when working with text:

GROUP EXERCISES

Cut up cues (see also 'Shakespeare's rolls' exercise in Chapter 5)

Cut up a scene from a play text – possibly one that you are working on – or use a poem. Re-number and distribute the speeches/lines. Students should read in their line according to the new order of the sequence that emerges.

Try to pre-empt the end of the previous speech/line (by guessing where this will land from the previous actor's use of rhythm in their reading) and come in directly 'on cue'. Also try and make each response sound as much as possible as if it is a logical answer to what has just gone before, no matter how much of a *non sequitur* it may actually be!

Wild emphases

Using a piece of text, vocally highlight any key words that offer satisfying sounds or powerful imagery. Practise giving these words a much greater emphasis to paint the picture with verbal gusto. You can always ease back on these emphases in actual performance while retaining some sense of any rhythmic possibilities that have been discovered through this practice.

As an example, see the highlighted words in the extract from James Bridie's 'lamentable comedy' *The Anatomist* (1931) below. Dr. Knox is addressing a group of anatomy students while dissecting a rhinoceros' heart. The emboldened words that he uses can be delivered with particular relish when you read them! Note Bridie's use of alliteration in words that begin with the 's' sound (i.e. 'sneaking, scribbler, smudge, scratch, citizens, scream, splutter, street, stream, surges, snout, such, sustained'). What does this tell us about the possibilities of Knox's anger, his venom, even his reptilian qualities that are being signified by his use of language?

> KNOX: And now, gentlemen, I should say ladies and gentlemen, I am humbly obliged to you. You are well aware that every **sneaking scribbler**

in this intellectual **Gomorrah**, who can **smudge** an un**grammatical sentence** employs his miserable talent to **scratch venom** on the public news-sheets; that, for the benefit of those worthy citizens who are unable to read, **gap-toothed mountebanks scream and splutter** at every street corner ... With you I shall take the liberty of discussing a weightier matter ... 'The Heart of the **Rhinoceros**'. This mighty organ, gentlemen, weighs full twenty-five pounds, a **fitting fountain-head** for the tumultuous **stream that surges** though the arteries of that prodigious monster. Clad in proof, gentlemen, and terribly armed as to his **snout**, the **rhinoceros buffets** his way through the **tangled verdure** engirdling his tropical habitat. Such **dreadful vigour**, gentlemen, such **ineluctable energy** requires to be sustained by no ordinary forces of nutrition ...

The repetitive friend

A fun exercise that contains comic potential in which one player becomes the 'repetitive friend'.

In this exercise one student articulates a scripted (or improvised) speech. The other student acts as the repetitive friend who randomly parrots parts (usually the ends of sentences) of the first student's speech.

The comedy and timing skills rely, firstly, on how expected and/or unexpected the repetitions are; secondly, on how seriously they are delivered; and, thirdly, on how the first speaker reacts or does not react to the verbal mirroring.

Generally speaking, the more 'truthfully' serious and unselfconscious that the second speaker is, and the more 'truthfully' the first speaker attempts to hide or mute any signs of irritation, the funnier it should prove.

Two touches – Augusto Boal

This exercise is modelled on a Brazilian football exercise. None of the players can keep possession of the ball for more than two kicks. They cannot stop the ball, and having touched it twice, they must pass it to their neighbour. The same here with the actors: this eliminates all 'empty' pauses ... Silence is also action.

(2002: 231)

These exercises develop timing in text, picking up cues, emphasis of key words and the use of rhythm in reactions.

Developing verbal timing

As we have seen, like all forms of comic meaning-making, timing is learned in early childhood communication activities and appears in the CDS interactions made between care-giver and child. The games and toys that are used in CDS, for example, rely on comic timing, and the surprise and repetitions that we experience early in life continue to influence comic response into adulthood, where, as Simon Critchley suggests in *On Humour*, we continue to 'laugh in a physiological squeal of transient delight like infant's "peek-a-boo"' (2002: 10).

Comic communication is hard-wired in CDS where the rhythm and metricality of 'the prosodic patterns of maternal speech serve psychobiological functions central to the development of communication in the first year of life' (Tafuri, 2008: 12). As the CDS engagement acts as a blueprint for understanding how comedy works, so the speech rhythms, repetitive engagement, singing and emphases in the 'melodies of maternal language' (ibid.) that the care-giver uses mean that in 'trans-generational communication – music may have originated as a useful mnemonic device for passing on information from generation to generation' (Hallam, 2006: 3). Babies themselves moreover, 'show sensitivity to musical phrase structures based on pitch and rhythmic patterns' (Tafuri, 2008: 11). In learning how musicality works, comic meaning and how timing and rhythm impels comic communication are all also learned during the process. As Sue Hallam notes:

> Infants have a predisposition for processing rhythm. Babies bounce
> and sway rhythmically in response to music up to the age of about six

months Infants can ... impose rhythmic groupings on tone sequences on the basis of pitch or timbre similarities. They are sensitive to changes in the relative temporal patterns of rhythm and at 2 months can detect a small change in tempo, are able to habituate to a particular tempo and react if there is a change of tempo ... From birth, infants have well developed capabilities for processing pitch, melody and rhythm, and enjoy musical stimulation – particularly interacting with caregivers.

(2006: 33, 43)

The performance of CDS is fundamentally comic in execution and this is the case even in the non-verbal communication that occurs. New mothers are specifically encouraged to engage in a basic form of comic acting with their babies in the first three to four months – 'put out your tongue and make funny faces. Your baby may even try to copy you! ... Your baby is learning all about expression, mood and communication' (Welford, 1999: 124).

CDS, just as comic timing and rhythm, often relies upon the deliberate use of repetitions. Roger Wilmut writes of the ways in which Variety double-acts consciously exploited rhythm for comic effect:

The straight man would question the statements made by the comic by repeating them and the comic would repeat them yet again ... it was an important comic device and a way of giving a rhythm to the delivery and making it flow better.

(1989: 55)

The repetitions used in CDS engagement, where 'vocalisation includes two-year olds' repetition of brief phrases with identifiable rhythmic and melodic contour patterns' (Dowling in Tafuri, 2008: xi), link to comedy's use of repetitions seen in, for example, basic joking structures ('I say, I say, I say, my dog's got no nose!' 'Your dog's got no nose? How does he smell?' 'Terrible!'). It is further linked in the use of catch phrases in sitcom and TV sketch programmes, e.g. in *The Fast Show* (BBC, 1994–1997), which is, arguably, little else but catch phrases! In writing of Phil Silvers' playing of Sergeant Bilko in *The Phil Silvers Show* (CBS, 1955–1959), David Everitt refers to Silvers' repetitions in his 'machine gun spiels ... [and] his ability to bark and growl in a series of commands that brings a platoon to attention without the benefit of a single word of English' (2001: 106). Repetitions often impel the timing and rhythm in comedy and are examples of how the 'rhymes, alliterations, refrains and other forms of repeating similar verbal sounds ... make use of the same source of pleasure – the rediscovery of something familiar' (Freud, 1905, 1964: 122).

Compare an example rhythm used in CDS with that employed in a comic performance. Take, firstly, Stephen Pinker's description of the CDS process (formerly called 'motherese'):

Motherese has interpretable melodies: a rise and fall contour for approving, a set of sharp, staccato bursts for prohibiting: a rise pattern for directing attention, and smooth, low legato murmurs for comforting. The psychologist Anne Fernald has shown that these patterns are very widespread across language communities and may be universal.

(1994: 279)

Contrast this with a transcript account of the comedian Frankie Howerd delivering a comic monologue during the BBC Festival of Variety in 1951. Note the use of rhythmic variations, repetitions, vocal inflexions, interlocutions that invite complicity and his use of vocal rise and fall to admonish and cajole the audience:

Today I'm going to tell you what happened to me in the Sahara desert. In the Sahara-ha-ra desert! And – ooh, no ... it was hot! Ooh, it was real hot! Even the Sphinx had sunglasses on ... No ... well ... you see ... I'd just settled back on a hummock, and it moved! ... I was up in the air! I was on top of a camel! (Falsetto voice). I was a-mazed! (Normal voice). I was way up in the air! But mind you ... mind you, high though I was, high though I was, the camel beat me. What a pong! Ooh! Ooh, and it knew you know – ooh, it knew! ... no, please, now ... now, control please, control ... now please control ... con-ever-so-trol!

(Frankie Howerd in Wilmut, 1989: 165)

Howerd's delivery of this routine closely mirrors CDS delivery, moreover, in:

The way that adults speak to small children is instinctively higher-pitched. It has an exaggerated modulation of intonation contour, moderate intensity and gentle sonority, syllabic and word repetition, with decelerated pronunciation.

(Tafuri, 2008: 12)

The following exercises use childhood games and playfulness and are designed to help you to get in touch with your inner child and to be playful. Trying out these verbal and physical rhythmic games and songs will also help you develop your comic timing.

GROUP EXERCISES

Below is a vocal and physical game that can be sung as a group, repeating the actions as described. It is also a good warm-up song that combines punchy words with physicality.

The Clap Clap Song by Shirley Ellis

Three, six nine,
The goose drank wine,
The monkey chewed tobacco on the street car line.
The line broke, the monkey got choked
And they all went to heaven in a little row-boat.
Clap Pat Clap Pat Clap Pat Slap! Clap Pat!
Clap your hand, Put it on your partner's hand ... Right Hand.
Clap Pat Clap your hand. Cross it with your left arm.
Pat your partner's left palm.
Clap Pat, Clap your hand. Pat your partner's right palm
With your right palm again.
Clap Slap, Clap your hand, Slap your thighs and sing a little song.
My mother told me
If I was goody
That she would buy me
A rubber dolly.
My aunty told her
I kissed a soldier,
Now she won't buy me a rubber dolly.

Repeat song with actions:

Clap Clap (clap your hands and prepare to pat)
Pat (with your right arm, pat your partner's right palm with your right palm)
Clap (hand back to clap)
Pat (with your right arm, cross your right arm with your left arm. Pat your
partner's left palm with your left palm.
Clap (hand back to clap)
Slap (slap your thighs with your palms)
Lyrics © Werner, Werner and Chase, Sony/ATV Music Publishing LLC

Hannigan's Hooley

Below is an Irish patter song that provides a great vocal warm up. It needs a
strong rhythmic emphasis on the names, accuracy in timing within the metre
and it also allows for some accent work.

Now Hannigan was an Irish man,
He came from Erin's Isle.

(Continued)

(Continued)

You'd hear for half a mile
When Hannigan throws a Hooley
Sure, the news soon gets about
Though you may be a stranger
If you're passin' by, he'll shout ...
Hey, come into the parlour, sure and make yourself at home.
Come into the parlour, sure you won't be on your own.
There's Mick McGee, and there's Rafferty, there's Murphy and Muldoon
They say McGilligan's daughter, doesn't know the taste of water
There's kegs of stout, just stickin' out,
Sure, there's grub for half the town
There's plenty of the potcheen if you want to wash it down
And if you're Irish, you're sure of a welcome
For there's a Hooley on at Hannigan's house tonight
Come into the parlour, you can make yourself at home
Come into the parlour, sure you won't be on your own
There's tons of ham and legs of lamb
If you look around the room
The knives and forks are flashin'
And there's nothing on the ration
There's quite a store of eggs galore, there's corned beef and there's veal
There's a sit down tea and a stand up fight at every bloomin' meal
So if you're Irish you're sure of a welcome
For there's a hooley on at Hannigan's house tonight
Meet Brannigan, Flannigan, Gilligan, Milligan,
Duffy, McCuffy, McLachie, Malone.
Rafferty, Cafferty, Donnelly, Connolly,
O'Dooley, O'Hooley, Muldooney, Malone.
Manahan, Canaghan, Lanahan, Fanahan,
Hagan, O'Kagan, O'Hollihan, Finn.
Shannihan, Fannihan, Fogarty, Gogarty,
Kelly, O'Kelly, McGuiness, McGinn.
And bring your mother ...
'Cos there's a Hooley on at Hannigan's house tonight!

Train opening song from *The Music Man* (Meredith Willson, 1950)

Learning this song (and getting the timing right) is a challenge! This group vocalisation requires accurately picking up cues and practising a distinct set of rhythms. For the full effect, the group's timing (in expression and picking up the cues) must be absolutely spot on.

The (numbered) salesmen's speeches vocally imitate the rhythm of the train at it starts, speeds up, rushes along and finally slows down again.

1 **Cash** for the mer-chan-dise. **Cash** for the but-ton hooks.
2 **Cash** for the cot-ton goods. **Cash** for the hard goods.
3 **Cash** for the soft goods. **Cash** for the fan-cy goods.
4 **Cash** for the nog-gins and the pig-gins and the fir-kins.
5 **Cash** for the hogs-heads, cask and demi-john. Cash for the crack-ers and the pickles and the fly-pap-er.
6 Look, whad-a-ya talk, whad-a-ya talk, whad-a-ya talk, whad-a-ya talk, whad-a-ya talk,
7 Where-da-ya get it?
8 Whad-a-ya talk?
9 Ya can talk, ya can talk, ya can bick-er, ya can talk, ya can bick-er, bick-er, bick-er, ya can talk, talk, talk, ya can talk, talk, talk, talk, bick-er, bick-er, bick-er, ya can talk all ya wanna, but it's dif-fer'nt than it was.
10 No it ain't, no it ain't, but ya got-ta know the ter-ri-tor-y.

... and so on. The lyrics mirror the 'train's' movement.

Audio visual

For YouTube video of *The Music Man*, search for 'Rock Island' or 'Music Man train song'.

Comic performance, in fact, does very often require the adoption of a slightly faster pace than 'straight' drama – the use of a 'quick tempo' (Chekhov, 2002: 127). David Everitt again describes Phil Silvers' 'quicksilver turns from one character to another, from one idea to the next' (2001: 106). Comedy can involve taking a slightly more energised pace (particularly in the playing of farce). Look at the speedy pace and dialogue of the 1930s' screwball comedies, or the madcap films of the Marx Brothers, Three Stooges or Abbot and Costello. Even today in stage, television and film comedies, witticisms fly back and forth, and reactions and responses clip along at a lick that is much faster than people actually tend to communicate in real life! As John Wright observes, 'rhythm is central to comedy: in drama as in life, rhythm encapsulates meaning, but in comedy, rhythm manipulates meaning ruthlessly' (2007: 130). Suzanne Langer, meantime, states 'the rhythm of felt life (is) the essential comic feeling' (Enck, 1960: 86).

GROUP EXERCISES

More rhythmic exercises to help you develop playfulness and rhythm. These childhood-related games will also help you develop your comic essence, expand your physicality and sharpen your timing.

Beans

Students move around the room. One student or the facilitator stands at the front and calls out commands which the students emulate.

'JUMPING BEAN' = jump around the room
'RUNNER BEAN' = run around the room
'BROAD BEAN' = move around, making yourself as wide as possible
'STRING BEAN' = move around making yourself as thin as possible
'JELLY BEAN' = move around on wobbly legs
'BAKED BEAN' = students huddle together

Different background music can be incorporated and players can move around the space accordingly in time to the varying rhythms. This exercise can be expanded to:

Strictly come acting

Students improvise or act out a scene from a play they are rehearsing. Different mood music (tango, cha cha cha, rumba, waltz, rock drum solo etc.) is randomly played in the background at intervals and the performers continue to act, incorporating each new rhythm into the playing out of the scene. How do the slower/faster tempi affect the performances?

The machine of rhythm – Augusto Boal

An actor goes into the middle and imagines that he is a moving part in a complex machine. He starts doing a movement with his body, a mechanical, rhythmic movement, and vocalising a sound to go with it. Everyone else watches and listens, in a circle around the machine. Another person goes up and adds another part (her own body) to this mechanical apparatus, with another movement and another sound. A third, watching the first two, goes in and does the same, so that eventually all the participants are integrated into this one machine, which is a synchronised, multiple machine.

> When everyone is part of the machine, the [facilitator] asks the first per-
> son to accelerate his rhythm – everyone else must follow this modification,
> since the machine is one entity. When the machine is near to explosion,
> the [facilitator] asks the first person to ease up, gradually to slow down,
> till in their own time the whole group ends together. It is not easy to end
> together, but it is possible.
>
> For everything to work well, each participant really does have to try
> and listen to everything he hears.
>
> (2002: 94)

Operatic musical chairs – Dymphna Callery

> Use opera as the music for the game – something like the 'three tenors' or
> Lesley Garret will do nicely. Play a game of musical chairs with the added
> proviso that when you lose your chair, i.e. when you are out, you sing an
> aria. Imitate the vigour and verve of the opera singers. You may be ecstatic
> or desperate that you've lost your chair.
>
> (2001: 136)

(You might also perform an over-dramatic or hammy death – as Bottom
playing Pyramus in A Midsummer Night's Dream, say!)

Accents and dialects

The actress and comic 'feed' (i.e. the vital performer who often sets up the
comedian's funny lines, acting as the 'straight-man' or sidekick to the humorous character) June Whitfield notes that 'all spoken words have a tune,
accents have a tune. If you can hear and reproduce it you're halfway there'
(2000: 224). Therefore, an important tool in the comic performer's kitbag is
to be able to hear and authentically reproduce accents and to exploit dialect
possibilities. Every accent and dialect has its own quirks and cadences which
can be practised. Listening closely to and really hearing (through your whole
body) the qualities and characteristics of localised speech, then internalising
these until the dialect becomes a sort of 'mind-worm', is the only real way
to be able, accurately and consistently, to reproduce accents. In this way,
as the percussionist Evelyn Glennie states, the whole body is 'a huge ear'
(Sturges, 2015: 39).

In the UK alone (a small country) there are a myriad of accents, each of
which is very different. Every accent or dialect brings with it a discrete and
varied sociocultural history behind every statement that is made in that voice.
If, say, you are speaking using Frank Gallagher's Mancunian underclass

estate twang (e.g. in *Shameless*, Channel 4, 2004–2013), then you are uttering a very different set of social and cultural 'truths' than if you are using, say, Smithy's Essex 'estuarine' in *Gavin and Stacey* (BBC, 2007–2010). Accents are cultural and class indicators. As Richard Hoggart noted, 'speech will indicate a great deal. In particular the host of phrases in common use. Manners of speaking, the use of urban dialects, accents and intonations, could probably indicate even more' (1960: 9). A Welsh burr, for example, will automatically imbue what you say with a certain lyricism and profundity (see Nessa's utterances in *Gavin and Stacey*); while the West Midlands accent, as used by the cast of *Raised by Wolves* (Channel 4, 2015–), affords a sort of off-key edginess to everything that is said. The way accents employ different elisions, glottal stops or unusual emphases can help tell the story being told and will impel the comic meaning-making. For example, Dolly Wells' use of the New Zealand rhythms in *Some Girls* (BBC, 2012–2014) or David Jason's Yorkshire accent in *Still Open All Hours* (BBC, 2013–) help to convey the full comic message (which includes the character's identity and any hidden sociocultural 'baggage' that they carry). Your character's mode of speech acts as a vocal 'fingerprint', fixing their identity within the time and place being portrayed. For example, although they are both 'locals' and share a time and place, the weaver Bottom's speech patterns and rhythms would be very different to that of the aristocratic Theseus in *A Midsummer Night's Dream*. The excellent Iranian comedian and actor Omid Djalili can play with comic meaning by switching from his 'original' Iranian accent to using the received pronunciation of the English upper middle class, in order to make satirical points about identity, class and cultural understandings and assumptions.

Audio visual

For the TV show references above, type in the programmes' titles.

For Omid Djalili, type in 'Omid Djalili accents' or 'Omid Djalili on Jack Dee Live at the Apollo'.

Of course, you must always be very careful not to slip into caricature or to reinforce any negative stereotypes when using accents and dialects. In the 1970s it was commonplace for stand-up comedians to try to make capital out of the ways of speaking that were employed by others – and those who were usually regarded as 'foreign' and thus, somehow, 'inferior' were specifically targeted. This so-called 'comedy' did not emerge from any sense of truth – no real people were being lampooned – only caricatures or lazy racial stereotypes. There was no affection, interest or understanding underpinning the performers' characterisations – only mockery. This was the most egregious and naked example of the superiority theory of comedy being employed. Especial care must therefore be exercised when using accents. There is a world of difference between a mocking caricature of someone speaking English with a 'funny' accent (cheap humour) and a serious and accurate portrayal of someone who speaks English with a genuine accent (real humour).

However, when studied, modelled on real individuals and duly internalised, a diligent approach to accent work in performance can tell an audience much about the character being portrayed. Different dialects, when replicated seriously and truthfully, can successfully impel comic meaning. As an example, a friend of mine, telling of a drunken evening she had had, once uttered the simple phrase, 'I was absolutely plastered'. The phrase seemed much funnier, simply because of the way she said it. She was a Scottish West Highlander and so it came out sounding something like 'I was aaaaahbsoluuuutely ppplas-turtt'. Similarly, an old back-and-white B-movie I once watched, whose title escapes me, featured a gloriously Bronx, New Yorkese coroner who was giving evidence in a courtroom scene. He uttered the immortal phrase that a cadaver showed 'con-too-sions of da second and thoid coivical voit-ebrae'. In neither of these examples were the speakers actually trying to be particularly funny. Nonetheless, their real modes of speaking helped to enhance or create a comic moment.

All accents and dialects have their own rhythmic clues, and accuracy in reproducing these quirks will help your comic performance to register. Noting the rhythmic clues that are inherent in any accent that you are required to use, reflecting on how these can work comically and what they might tell us about the speaker is recommended. Listen closely to any examples that you can find of the accents or dialects spoken by people similar to those whom you will play. Really try to absorb these ways of producing sounds into your own core (i.e. deeply), rather than trying to replicate them purely aurally and orally (i.e. on the surface). Like a singer, you need to have use of both 'head' voice and 'chest' voice to internalise and then to externalise your vocal effects. As well as any geographical facets of your character, study their temporal, social and cultural background for clues to their 'true' identity. And, of course, practise the performance of the character – including their accent or dialect – as much as possible!

EXERCISES

Reflect upon what the way the following characters speak tells us about them. How do their accents, inflections and vocal rhythms enhance the comedy?

Find examples of people who speak in a similar way to the characters below (perhaps from the Internet). Study the speakers closely and really try to absorb

(Continued)

(Continued)

their accents/dialects. Practise your accent work, attempting to speak the words using the various characters' voices as accurately as you can:

1. The Northern British accent

The character of Elsie in John Christopher-Wood's spoof version of Shakespeare's *Macbeth* – *Elsie and Norm's 'Macbeth'* (1977, 1990) – is a middle-aged, working-class Northern woman. In the play, Elsie enters as Lady Macbeth; 'she wears a housecoat not dissimilar from Elsie's own, except its tartan'. She has received a postcard from Norm/Macbeth telling her of the witches' prophecy that he will become Thane of Cawdor, then King of Scotland:

> Elsie/lady Macbeth: Ooooh! Thane of Cawdor! That's nice. I suppose I'm the Thaness then. But if he's going to be King, that means I'll be Queen Macbeth! That's more like it! We'll be able to move out of this dump, and live in a proper detached palace at Dunsinane. Actually I think I'll change it to Dunromin. And we'll have a low-level avocado toilet suite and room dividers everywhere! Oooh, I can hardly wait! All he's got to do is kill King Duncan and get Malcolm out of the way. Mind you, I bet he doesn't want to do it, the big soft bugger! I can see I'm going to have to give him a good talking to when he gets home!
>
> (Act 1:7)

Elsie speaks with flat, Northern vowels. Comic capital can be achieved through her articulation of the 'oo' sound found in the Yorkshire accent; in her initial 'Oooh' which is then echoed in 'dump/doomp'; 'Dunsinane/Doonsinane'; 'Dunromin/Doonromin'; 'Duncan/Dooncan'; and 'bugger/boogger'. The phrase 'low level avocado toilet suite' has much potential for dialect comedy. Note too the alliterations in the last sentence of the speech – four words begin with 'g', interspersed with four words beginning with 'h' – allowing the last line to become a rhythmic coda.

2. The Glasgow accent

This example of a Scottish accent is even based on its own language form – what Albert Mackie terms 'Glesceranto' (1973: 100). Glesceranto can be heard as an inherently comical language. There is a tendency to a preponderant use of lively imagery, as Michael Munro notes in his book *The Complete Patter*:

> Someone who is very nervous or on tenterhooks may have it said of him that his *arse is nippin buttons* ... Whit d'ye want me to dae ... *burst out in fairy*

lights? Said by someone refusing to be as excited or impressed as a person making some kind of announcement thinks it should be.

(1999: 4, 196)

In delivery, Glesceranto has an abrasively comic (often nasal) undulating rhythm with the intervention of a throaty glottal stop. As Charles Jennings notes:

Glasgow English likes to keep a certain dance-band swing, the front half of the sentence getting a little beat going before the second half closes (ideally) with a stress followed by an unstressed syllable, to lead the speaker back out into space ... two CHANcers and a DANcer.

(2001: 232; emphases as in the original)

In Iain Heggie's play *A Wholly Healthy Glasgow* (1988), the venal health centre worker Charlie Hood is speaking about reduced footfall into the club during the summer months.

And. Who's Bobby think he's kidding? Because I says to Bobby. I says: 'No chance breaking even in August, Bobby. Glasgow's evacuated to the Costa Brava. Glasgow's eyeing up talent out a hotel balcony telescope at Corfu. Glasgow's chucking up paella down a Majorcan stank'.

(1988: 7–8)

Each sentence is short, punchy and ends on a satisfyingly curt and quirky drum-beat scansion ' ... **think** he's **kid/ding**', ' ... **Cos-ta Bra-va**', ' ... **Cor/fu**' leading up to the 'punchline' with its final monosyllabic beat on '**Ma/jor-can stank**'. Note too the use of repetitions in this short extract – 'Bobby', 'I says' and 'Glasgow' – which give the speech a rhythmic impetus.

Hearing the Glaswegian accent might evoke a list of words that tell us something about the speaker – these might include, for example, 'working class', 'proud', 'indomitable', 'assertive', 'intelligent' and 'humorous'. A good example of the comic use of rhythmic Glaswegian is to be found in *Rab C. Nesbitt* (BBC, 1988–1999, 2008–2014) or *Chewin' the Fat* (BBC, 1999–2002).

3. The American accent

There is, of course, like the 'Scottish' or 'English' accent actually no such thing as an 'American' accent! There is, however, a general US accent which is often employed by performers, but because it is inauthentic it provides limited comic potential. In fact,

(Continued)

(Continued)

in lots of American films and comedies, even the genuinely American performers tend to employ a general, homogenised US accent, irrespective of wherever and whenever their play film or sitcom is actually set! But 'American' actually covers hundreds if not thousands of local variations and specificities. Take the Boston blue collar accent (as used by John Ratzenberger as Cliff Clavin in *Cheers*; NBC, 1982–1993) and contrast it with the Boston blue blood accent used by David Ogden Stiers as Charles Emerson Winchester III in *M*A*S*H* (CBS, 1972–1983). Similarly, a Californian 'slacker' drawl is a world away from an East Coast, fast-taking patter mode of speech. Again, these ways of speaking tell us much about the character's attitude to life along with any comic potential that they contain. When we hear an 'American' accent we may perhaps think of terms such as 'confident', 'self-assured', 'relatively wealthy', 'educated'; perhaps, more negatively, words such as 'brash' or 'modern' may crop up in association with the character who is speaking.

Because of the myriad of great Jewish American comedy writers (from S. J. Perelman, Mel Brooks, Woody Allen, to Larry David), you may be called upon to replicate a New York accent. In this extract from Neil Simon's *The Odd Couple* (1966), living with his over-fastidious and neurotic friend, Felix Unger, has brought Oscar Madison to breaking point:

> Oscar: Good. Because now I'm going to tell *you* off ... For six months I lived alone in this apartment. All alone in eight rooms ... I was dejected, despondent and disgusted ... Then *you* moved in. My dearest and closest friend ... And after three weeks of close personal contact – I am about to have a nervous breakdown! ... Do me a favour. Move into the kitchen. Live with your pots, your pans, your ladle and your meat thermometer ... when you want to come out, ring a bell and I'll run into the bedroom ... I'm asking you nicely, Felix ... As a friend ... Stay out of my way!
>
> (Act III: 79)

Note the emphases, the alliterations ('dejected', 'despondent', 'disgusted'); the way the speech builds to a crescendo; the wonderful image of the 'meat thermometer'. Note also the comic potential of Oscar's New York accent for the words 'personal' and 'nervous'. These would, respectively, be authentically rendered as 'poisonal' and 'noivous' – allowing genuine 'extra' comic potential through the authentic reproduction of dialect.

4. The standard English accent

Finally, standard English, sometimes known as 'received pronunciation', is, again, an inauthentic and increasingly elusive dialect, even though it remains a common accent choice for performers to use when playing 'upper class' or quintessentially 'English' characters. It is usually the accent favoured when playing in period pieces. It has clipped qualities and substitutes vowel sounds, for example, 'eh' for ah 'ah' (as in 'absolutely/ebsolutely') and ah for eeh (as in 'really/rahlly').

Extremes of this accent for comic effect include Paul Whitehouse reproducing Rowley Birkin QC's incomprehensible drawl in *The Fast Show* (BBC, 1994–1997); Stephen Fry's barking and baa-ing General Melchett in the fourth series of *Blackadder* (BBC, 1983–1989); or Matt Lacey's 2010 YouTube phenomenon *Gap Yah* guy. We may tend to think of words such as 'privileged', 'old fashioned', 'eccentric', even 'caddish' in association with this accent.

Received pronunciation would also be used when playing the actress Judith Bliss in Noel Coward's *Hay Fever* (1925, 1949):

> Judith: I'm much more dignified on the stage than in the country – it's my *milieu*. I've tried terribly hard to be 'landed gentry,' but without any real success ... I long for excitement and glamour ... Think of the thrill of a first night; all those ardent playgoers willing one to succeed; the critics all leaning forward with glowing faces, receptive and exultant – emitting queer little inarticulate noises as some witty line tickles their fancy. The satisfied grunt of the *Daily Mail*, the abandoned gurgle of the *Sunday Times*, and the shrill, enthusiastic scream of the *Daily Express*! I can distinguish them all.
>
> (Act I: 266)

Note the character's ability to speak in perfect, albeit over-lyrical, sentences; her use of clipped four- or five-syllable constructs in 'terribly hard', 'landed gentry', 'ardent playgoers', 'glowing faces', 'satisfied grunt' and 'abandoned gurgle'; and the repetition of the 's' sound in the penultimate sentence – conjuring up an underlying echo of an (audience) hiss which undercuts her hyperbolic boasts about her theatrical successes!

Developing physical timing

The most basic unit of physical timing could simply be seen as an instance of someone falling over. How truthfully and expertly this action registers to the spectators dictates the success, or otherwise, of the action as a piece of comic performance. As Susan Purdie notes, 'at the simplest level, performers themselves "utter" the pratfalls or gaffes which make us laugh' (1993: 15). Performing a safe but authentic 'pratfall' certainly needs to be properly timed to be fully effective. It also has to be read by the audience as something that is possible, realistic and true within the context in which it is presented to them. A pratfall caused by, say, a person slipping and falling on a banana skin has become an almost proverbial piece of comic 'business' even though this is something per se that rarely happens in real life! In the case of the pratfall as a basic comic 'utterance', even this apparently simple action contains deeper implications that have to be resolved for the action ultimately to be read as comical.

On the surface, a pratfall may enable audience laughter in relief (as a purely biological response caused by the element of surprise, or shock, inherent in the sheer unexpectedness of the event). The fall is more likely to trigger the sudden reaction of the laughter of release in the onlooker if the faller is a stranger and is otherwise emotionally unconnected to the spectator. The apperception of the painfulness of the situation moderates our response to the incident. As William Hazlitt wrote:

> As long as the disagreeableness of the consequences of a sudden disaster is kept out of sight by the immediate oddity of the circumstances, and the absurdity or unaccountableness of a foolish action is the most striking thing in it, the ludicrous prevails over the pathetic, and we receive pleasure instead of pain from the farce of life which is played before us.
>
> (1885: 66)

Laughter may, alternatively, be cued through inducing a 'schadenfreude' feeling of superiority, in which the spectators take some delight in the fact that the fall has happened to someone else and not to themselves. Laughter may, alternatively, result from the fact that it is a 'high status' individual who has fallen, and then there may be some rejoicing in the puncturing of dignity that the fall affords. The spectator may enjoy the discomfort of another while feeling superior for managing the simple task of remaining upright when the other has failed. Apperceptions of superiority may ensue through loss of face and the lowering of status – two potential features of the comic 'business' which may, on this occasion, cue audience laughter.

As the event unfolds – and, in retrospect, perhaps even if the faller *is* known to the audience or has, indeed, sustained an injury – the spectators may still be able to conceive the sheer incongruity of the spectacle as being funny. The incongruity in the event is caused through violation of expectation and, again, through the perception of thwarted dignity to create a comic effect. In perceiving the event as incongruous, two opposing phenomena clash, that is, the upright individual moving along pavement is the acceptable, 'correct' normal situation, whereas the person sprawled on the street is abnormal, out-of-place and inappropriate. It is here in this 'gap' (a literal 'slippage') that amusement through awareness of the contradictory nature of the absurdity may arise. Here, it may be the incongruity of the event that the audience identifies as being the primary cause of what cues its laughter.

In creating a 'pratfall' as a deliberate piece of manufactured comic business, you, the comic performer, have to remain fully aware of the deeper significances of the seemingly superficial action. What are the wider implications of the activity? What is its full cause and effect? What potential comic meaning is contained in that particular character, in those particular circumstances, falling over in front of that particular audience on that particular night? Further, the simplest of falls must also demonstrate performative craft skills and expertise in its execution. The manner in which the fall is set up, presented and performed is crucial for the spectator to find it funny. The action must be made to seem entirely plausible in context. It must either build to a comic inevitability or be so surprisingly sudden, that the conclusion comprehensively confounds the audience's expectations. Alternatively, the act must be done in such a way that the spectators believe that the expectation of the *actor* has been confounded in a manner that conveys the fall as being truthful.

In a similar way, a single, verbal joke can work like a 'pratfall'. Craft skills are required in the communicative act of the telling of the joke, just as physical expertise is necessary in the performance of the pratfall. In the successful telling of a joke, the *way* it is told – the manner in which the action is executed – is vitally important. Just as a joke must be uttered effectively, the pratfall needs to be set up and executed as an enjoyable narrative for the audience – one that builds to a punch line. To quote the catchphrase of the stand-up comic Frank Carson (1926–2012), 'it's the way I tell 'em' – and the way the 'story' is told is a major imperative in the effective signalling and reception of all forms of comic expression. So, in the case of the pratfall, someone familiar to the audience as, for example, a habitually well-dressed, refined and high-status individual slipping gracefully into a pile of mud may be very funny indeed, for example, Penelope Keith's Margot Leadbetter (Penelope Keith) falling backwards in the rain-soaked neighbour's garden in *The Good Life* (BBC, 1975–1978). Similarly, someone jumping joyously into a puddle and suddenly plunging neck-deep into it – Dawn French in *The Vicar of Dibley* (BBC, 1994–2006); staggering drunkenly into a hedge or grave – Jennifer Saunders in *Absolutely Fabulous* (BBC, 1992–1996, 2001–2005); executing an acrobatically implausible, straight-legged, backward keel-over in the street – Buster Keaton in *The Cameraman* (Keaton, 1928); undertaking athletically undignified pratfalls as the 'remarkable pantomimist' (Quinlan, 1992: 237) Martha Raye did in 1930–1940s' Hollywood comedies; or falling non-chalantly sideways through an open bar hatch – David Jason in *Only Fools and Horses* (BBC, 1981–2003) – all these exemplify the craft/expertise skills of the comic performer at work. (The last of these examples, indeed, was once voted as one of the top three in the 'most paused TV moments' 2010 survey.) An audience's apperception of the comedian's expertise will link directly to their recognition of a situation that displays a sense of comic 'truth'. While an obviously faked and 'inexpert' fall, as is often seen (and in many cases are deliberately showcased for being phoney) in viewer-made 'camcorder disaster' programmes such as *You've Been Framed* (Granada, 1990–), is immediately obvious and crass, it creates a feeling in the spectator of having been somehow cheated. Such scenarios simply disappoint as they lack either timing or expertise in their execution and are thus devoid of any sense of comic 'truth'. As a comic performance it reveals the difference between that which is merely contrived and unconvincing and something which registers as somehow convincing and plausible.

From practising something as simple as a pratfall as a unit of physical comedy, it is possible to hone your physical comic performance skills and your basic timing. Please remain safe – use of a crash mat and (at least) knee and elbow pads for this exercise come highly recommended! From this basis you can work together on developing increasingly complex pieces of business (such as the 'hats' routine as outlined in Chapters 2 and 3). You can also develop your physical timing though practise of games and exercises similar to those listed below. Wherever possible, it is most useful to do these exercises as group activities and as part of the ensemble preparation work.

GROUP AND INDIVIDUAL EXERCISES

These exercises will develop your physical dexterity and timing. As with verbal timing, picking up on cues is vitally important.

Counting actions

Count to 50 adding (or substituting) a nod of the head for any mention of the word 'three'; a handclap for any mention of the word 'five'; and a stamp of the right foot for any mention of the word 'nine'.

Further additions/substitutions can be added.

This exercise can also be adapted to involve the substitution of an action each time certain words are mentioned in a speech.

'Captains coming'!

The facilitator randomly issues a series of commands to the players, who have to perform the actions immediately. Eliminations of the slowest person to complete any of the actions can be enforced.

If the facilitator calls out 'Bow', everyone has to run to the front of the space.
'Stern' means that everyone instantly rushes to the back of the space.
'Starboard' – people rush to the right of the space.
'Port' – all rush to the left.
'Captain's coming' all stop, salute and shout, 'Aye, aye Cap'n'.
'Captain's wife' – all curtsey.

'Scrub the decks' – all mime scrubbing action on hands and knees.

'Climb the rigging' – all mime climbing a rope ladder.

'Man overboard'! – players must find a partner and huddle together. Anyone without a partner is out.

'Sharks'! – Players lie on their backs and stick one leg up in the air.

Mechanical band

Players mimic the different actions performed by members of a musical band.

Each player mimes one action of their chosen band member, for example, sliding the trombone, hitting a drum, bending sideways to scrape the violin with the bow, bending forward to play a saxophone, etc. Once everyone has their repetitive action in place, the band is put together so that everyone is playing simultaneously in an amorphous blob. The actions of the group must interlace closely without any member of the band actually touching another member.

Once the band are playing together at different levels and are (just) managing to avoid contacting each other, music – either 'sung' live or imported as background noise – can be added to accompany the activity.

Commedia lazzi

The first professional company of actors in the early years of the sixteenth century was the Commedia dell'arte. These performers played semi-improvised comedies based on the plots of classical comic dramatists such as Plautus and Terence.

Commedia's staple characters included old men, lovers, servants, soldiers and Arlecchino or Harlequin who was both the wise fool and the interlocutor figure. In *One Man, Two Guvnors*, Richard Bean's update of the Goldoni play, Francis Henshall identifies himself as the Harlequin figure and, speaking directly to the audience, explicitly invites them to consider, 'what will his [i.e. me as Harlequin's] motivation be in the second act'? (2011:73).

Think of the Marx Brothers' films in terms of the Commedia's zany plots, fast-paced slapstick and anarchic feel.

Commedia comprised of 'lazzi' or 'tricks' or 'turns' which can be practised as physical routines:

> The scenes consisted of comic interludes played in pantomime, among the most famous being Harlequin eating a hat full of cherries, or catching flies ... [or] where Pierrot and Burratino express their sorrow at an accident

(Continued)

(Continued)

which has happened to Pierrot's wife by eating a large dish of macaroni with tears streaming down their cheeks.

(Mawer, 1932: 63)

In British pantomime, many of these physical routines survive – in the slapstick scenes, set, for instance, in the palace kitchen where the routine might end with a custard pie to the face. These routines require physical dexterity and split-second timing from all involved to work to their maximum comic potential. Below is an account of the 'brokers men' routine taken from *Henry Marshall's Gag Book*:

Ugly sisters entertaining Vicar. Cinderella serving, Brokers keep taking chairs away just as people are going to sit down on them. Trolley for tea wheeled in. tea pot taken below by one of Brokers men sitting concealed under curtain below trolley. Cinders sent for another one. Vicar in big chair. One BM puts arms through hole in chair and they become Vicar's arms. Business while he is having tea, eating and drinking etc. strawberries and cream. Cream in Vicar's hat. He goes not to put it on at first, but gets or is given tea cosy by mistake. When he does put it on it has a hole in top so cream squirts straight up.

(Abbott, 2012: 305)

These exercises will help you practise responsiveness; plus a sense of reflexivity and awareness of what your fellow performers are doing within the comic whole. These examples will help you hone your bodily expertise and timing. It is important to keep relatively fit and agile to be able to perform physical comedy to its full potential.

In practicing these pieces, firstly, try to make the physical characteristics of your essential Commedia character overt – and then repeat the scene trying to keep the characteristics hidden. Which is 'realer' and ultimately funnier? Remember, when you play these characters you should still attempt to inhabit 'real' people as much as possible. Remember, it is all about how you subvert the stereotype.

Suggested further study

Reading

Aitken, Maria (1996) *Style: Acting in High Comedy*, London: Applause. A practitioner illustrates approaches to playing in a more verbally rhythmic style of comedy.
Boal, Augusto (2002) *Games for Actors and Non-Actors*, London: Routledge. Contains excellent ensemble exercises, many of which allow practise of movement

and vocal skills and that also contain wider implications for personal and socio-cultural development.

Johnston, Chris (2012) *Drama Games for Those Who Like To Say No*, London: Nick Hern Books. There are valuable studio exercises to build ensemble in this handy book, some of which involve rhythmic interplay.

Muir, Frank and Brett, Simon (eds) (1992) *The Penguin Book of Comedy Sketches*, Harmondsworth: Penguin. Some great material for short, comic performances can be found here. Many require use of correct verbal emphasis and an awareness of incongruities in text for achieving their maximum comic effect.

Audio Visual

Type 'hand clap skit-the original' into the search box for an excellent example of physical and rhythmical ensemble expertise that manages to be both funny and admirable.

Also see the work of 'The Three Stooges', 'Laurel and Hardy', 'Buster Keaton' or 'Bottom' starring Ade Edmondson and Rik Mayall (BBC, 1991–1995) for examples of physical comedy.

Examples

Verbal timing

In 1966, Alan Bennett performed a monologue on a telephone in which his character attempted to narrate the contents of a telegram to be sent to the object of his affection:

> Hello, I want to send a telegram please ... Yes my name is Pratt, Charles Pratt ... Yes, 68 Chalfont Square ... Yes, and its going to a Miss Edith Harness ... yes 87 Fitzroy Road. Yes ... right, well the telegram, uh, right ... No 'right' is not the telegram, no. I will say, uh, this is the telegram, and whatever comes after that is the telegram ... yes. This is the telegram ... are you still there? No, sorry, that's not it, no, no, well, um um, well it's, 'Bless your little' ... yes ... 'bless your little ... bottibooes'. Ah, well, I have never been called upon to spell it actually. Ah, that's your job. Yes, I will hazard a guess and say B-O-T-T-I-B-O-O-E-S. I don't think that the last E is statutory ...
>
> (Muir and Brett, 1992: 220)

Note the use of verbal timing in the pauses, hesitations and emphases that occur in the performance. Note, too, the manner of speaking in the 'posh' accent that Bennett uses to delineate character and to make the loss of dignity in the embarrassing situation that the speaker finds himself become even more acute.

> **Audio visual**
>
> Type in Alan Bennett 'The Telegram' for the above example.
>
> See also 'Shelley Berman telephone', 'Bob Newhart telephone' or 'Carol Burnett telephone' for similar examples of comic performers using (predominantly) vocal and verbal timing to create comic effect.

Physical timing

The physical comic expertise of an artist like Buster Keaton is worth studying. His timing, command of his body and awareness of how to use physical effects to induce laughter all provide a master-class in comic performance. This really is comic artistry at its height and was recognised as such by contemporary artists, even those working in other disciplines.

Indeed, it is worth noting that, in the twentieth century, interest in comedians working in music hall, variety and vaudeville is apparent across the creative arts disciplines. T. S. Eliot wrote about Marie Lloyd in his *Collected Essays*: 'the working man who went to the music-hall and saw Marie Lloyd ... was engaged in that collaboration of the audience and artist which is necessary in all art' (1923, 1953: 239–240). The absurdist playwright Ionesco referred to the influence of the Marx Brothers in his work (1960, 2013: 59), while Samuel Beckett was an *aficianado* of both 'vaudeville at the Olympia and the Theatre Royal in Dublin and "never missed" a Chaplin or a Laurel and Hardy film' (Robinson, 1993: 157).

Artists were similarly influenced by comedians. Suzi Gablik notes that René Magritte 'followed the comedies of Mack Sennett and Charlie Chaplin' (1992: 189), suggesting that his recurrent muse 'the bowler-hatted man is a perfect vehicle for our projections' (ibid.: 168). Magritte's depiction of the bowler, 'the comic hat of modernity' (Robinson, 1993: 82), also being, as the comedian Stan Laurel (a comedian Magritte 'admired'; Robinson, 1993: 141) 'part of a comic's make up for as far back as I remember. I'm sure that's why Charlie [Chaplin] wore one' (McCabe, 1966: 91). Magritte's bowler hatted man may 'suggest ... a man compelled to live against his own grain, although he lets himself drift along without any constraint' (Gablik, 1992: 162). He is also symbolic of Chaplin's tramp character, a beleaguered fool reacting to events which can threaten to overwhelm him, or of Laurel and Hardy's 'innocents ... children in a grown-up world' (Halliwell, 1987: 126).

Salvador Dali too 'was influenced by the silent, slapstick comedy of Buster Keaton, Charlie Chaplin and Harry Langdon ... he admired the inventiveness of slapstick' (Akbar, 2007: 20).

The silent screen comedians were mainly products of the Vaudeville/music hall circuit and their work has also influenced artists. Steve McQueen reconstructed a scene from 'deadpan' comic Buster Keaton's *Steamboat Bill Jr.* (Reiner and Keaton, 1928) in his video short *Deadpan* (1997). As Tom Dardis describes the original sequence in the Keaton film:

> One of Buster's most celebrated stunts occurs in *Steamboat Bill*. Standing in stunned disbelief on the empty street, staring at the ravages of the cyclone roaring around him, Buster is not aware that the entire façade of the house behind him is about to fall on him. It does, but he is saved by the fact that a tall window frame at the top of the house passes safely over his body, leaving him perfectly unharmed. In order to accomplish this feat without trickery, it was necessary for extremely accurate measurements to be taken of both Buster and the window above him; a mistake of an inch or so would have proved fatal, for the façade weighed over a ton.
>
> (1979: 155)

McQueen's sequence copies the essential shots but, arguably, with more serious 'artistic' intent and effect – that is, 'presenting us with a gag and a compelling study in purgatory' (Gellatly, 1999). Similarly, the artist Gordon Matta-Clark 'borrowed' a comic sequence and in his filmed performance *Clockshower* (1973) quoted the classic 'Safety Last' (1923) with Harold Lloyd. For this Matta-Clark hung from the clock of a skyscraper in New York, where, at a dizzying height, he brushed his teeth, shaved and washed (Martin, 2006: 21).

Meanwhile, a contemporary artist, Bruce McLean, draws on the sketch form for his *Soup (A Concept Consomme)* (2010) in which he draws on the classic dinner set-up of, say, Freddie Frinton's *Dinner for One* (Dunkhase, 1963), or the Two Ronnie's *The New Rook Restaurant* sketch (1975) or Victoria Wood's sketch *Two Soups?* (1985).

Thus we see that comic expertise – and perfect physical timing – is, arguably, an art in itself!

Audio visual

Any of the 'silent film clowns' – 'Keaton', 'Chaplin' or 'Harold Lloyd' – are worth studying.

Photograph © David Curtis (2014)

Chapter 5

Working with text

> It is the writer's job to make the play interesting. It is the *actor's* job to make the performance truthful.
>
> (David Mamet, 1998: 410; italics in original)

Text, theory and the world of comedy

When comic dramatists write texts they do so with the expectation that at least some of their material will make the audience laugh. When you work with these texts you are interpreting the comic potential of the play or script and it is important to recognise where Tom Sutcliffe's comic 'buttons' occur in the writing. Comic texts often present a skewed world of 'improbable fiction' (Gay, 2008: 138) in which the mechanisms of superiority, incongruity and release are at the forefront of the play. As Geoff King writes in *Film Comedy*:

> A comedy might initially be defined as a work that is designed in some way to provoke laughter or humour on the part of the viewer ... it is a relative rather than absolute phenomenon, dependent on a range of specific, contextual factors.
>
> (2006: 2)

He further notes that:

> All comedy is founded on assumptions of existing in-group knowledge; the background against which comedy works its disruptions, inversions or exaggerations.
>
> (Ibid.: 121–122)

As the performer of comic text, your role is to illustrate, implicitly rather than explicitly, those mechanisms in action through the precision of your acting. As Eric Weitz notes, 'a printed dramatic text ... cannot be fully considered without some acknowledgement of the enactment ... for which it is conceived' (2009: ix), and the crucial part that you, the performer, play in bringing a text to life therefore cannot be underestimated.

Comic text – and the world of comedy that is conjured therein – stems in the West from three essential main original sources. Firstly there is the well-spring of ritual. The first of these – early church liturgy – allowed for scenes of comic relief – usually intended to be of an 'improving' nature – in which some comic expression and the license to perform material intended to be funny was allowed. Naturally, over time, these officially sanctioned comic interludes became the most popular elements of the liturgies with the populace. When the interludes were seen to threaten or overwhelm the more serious messages of the rituals, the authorities were forced to clamp down on the seemingly unfavourable and 'unserious' elements of the ceremonies. This rejection has, in its turn, contributed to comedy's lower status in society and culture (despite those prominent twentieth-century artists who celebrated it and the heavyweight philosophers who have championed it)! It has also meant that, although comedy has always been a tool for satirising and poking fun at authority, it is something that, at the same time, has had to operate within the bounds of official sanction, usually allowed to flourish only within rather strictly defined parameters. Comedy must, in other words, toe the line while, often covertly, still endeavour to make its satirical presence felt in the mainstream. Contemporaneously, the 'moral panics' that ensue every so often over the jokes that comedians make – or the media storms created by satirical programmes such as Chris Morris's *Brass Eye* (Channel 4, 1997–2001) – can also be seen as an indication of the legacy of tension that comic expression still inspires within mainstream society and culture.

The second origin of comic text emanates from (similarly officially licensed) revelry and festivity that is 'carnival', the Bahktinian 'phenomenon of mediaeval carnival as an officially sanctioned holiday from the usual order of things' (Weitz, 2009: 186). Carnival was (and is) a celebratory rite involving large-scale partying with drink, merriment, sexualised interplay, burlesque and satirical expression as its constituents – all being temporarily licensed and sanctioned by the church or state power-brokers concerned. This permissive (and permitted) revelry gave life to the 'the Italian professional comedy' (Banks, 1998: 101) of the Commedia delle' arte, which emerged from Italy in the middle ages which was, in turn, a formalisation of the clowning scenarios that had been evident in classical old comedy's pantomimic satires. The routines and status play that emerged from Commedia dell'arte from the late sixteenth century onwards have, in turn, proved hugely influential on Western comic texts.

The third and most influential force on comic textual formalisation came from the extraordinarily influential cultural age of classical civilisation. From the fifth century Athens BC (and through the cruder facsimile that emerged during the Roman Empire) Western democratic politics, society, philosophy and aesthetics were codified and comic drama, text and characterisation were subject to definition by the philosophers of this age. So, in the satiric drama 'the kind of comic drama natural to tragic poet ... moral law was suspended, or inverted; cowardice, drunkenness and lechery became normal, heroism a thing to laugh at' (Kitto, 1971: 228). Western comic text's foundations were laid in the structure and archetypal characterisations evident in the work of classical Greek and Roman comic authors and, particularly, in the 'new comedy' formulae of Plautus and Terence. While non-comic theatre forms might be seen to emanate more directly from the dramatic unities and conventions found in Aristotle's theories, models of comic text reveal such constituent elements as 'plot', 'lexis' (popular language) and the rhythmic 'melos' (musical rules) which are 'found in all comedies' (Cooper, 1943: 790).

Classical comic drama also often featured an interlocutor figure (who spoke directly to the audience). Indeed, there was often a direct interplay prologue in the plays. Further direct interplay with the audience featured asides and the use of local language to develop complicity. The texts often contained complications, misunderstandings, disguises, characters in hiding and subplots. The staple themes established such tropes as pairs of young lovers, being helped by a slave or servant, being disguised, in order to outwit the older, higher status figures in the plays.

In short, the oldest comic forms that we know about established the same tropes that inform contemporary comic texts. For example, the theme of the bad teacher that Aristophanes introduces in his lampoon of Socrates in *The Clouds* (*c.* 423 BC) is echoed in the 'dottore' of the Commedia, recurs in the character of Holofornes in Shakespeare's *Loves Labours Lost* (*c.* 1595) and is evident today in characters in the sitcoms *Bad Education* (BBC Three, 2012–2014), *Big School* (BBC, 2013–2014) and *Bad Teacher* (CBS, 2014). The theme of the battle of the sexes in Aristophanes' *Lysistrata* (411 BC) is not too dissimilar a theme to that of the Commedia-inspired *The Mistress of the Inn* of Carlo Goldoni (1751); is to be found in Shakespeare's *The Taming of the Shrew* (*c.* 1590); and is explored more contemporaneously in sitcoms such as *Everybody Loves Raymond* (CBS, 1996–2005) or *Bluestone 42* (BBC Three, 2013–). The plots, twists and characters that you are likely to encounter in comic text and scripts will often reflect their early origins. For example, Terence's *The Brothers* (*c.* 160 BC) relies on misunderstandings arising between country and the city ways – another staple plot theme of comic text – see the TV shows *Green Acres* (CBS, 1965–1971), *Corner Gas* (CTV, 2004–2009) or *The Vicar of Dibley* (BBC, 1994–2007). *The Brothers* similarly contains the systematic acts, scenes, unities of time and place and resolution of a happy ending that were the hallmark constituents of earliest comic text.

The excessive individual

To take another ancient comic theme, perhaps the most extreme example of a comic figure is that of the drunkard. Originating in earliest drama it is hardly surprising that this figure of license, excess and revelry represents the comic ... ahem ... spirit. Alcohol, literally and metaphorically, enables comic relief, while the loss of corporal and moral control that it allows presents us, in the drunkard, with a physical metaphor of Bergson's theory of comic momentum being all about mismanagement of the bodily mechanism.

The Ancient Greek Dorian farces feature a figure of humour who steals wine. This is a character that embodies temporary comic license and is also someone whose excesses and folly we can enjoy through the lens of superiority. He (and is usually a male figure) follows in a tradition of staple comic antecedents, from representations of Noah in certain mediaeval Morality plays; through Sir Toby Belch and Falstaff in Shakespeare's plays; to Captain Boyle and Joxer Daly in *Juno and the Paycock* (O'Casey, 1924). More recently the drunkard character can be traced through the work of Jimmy James (1892–1965); or Gregor Fisher as Rab C. Nesbitt; or seen in the work of Foster Brooks (1912–2001) in the US; or in the early stand-up work of Johnny Vegas in the UK.

The drunkard is a mainstay of comedy. He embodies (limited) excess, disorder and misrule. The incongruity of his behaviour and his off-kilter utterances are deep-seamed, larger-than-life comic themes. As Peter Watts notes, 'it is interesting how frequently drunks crop up in cartoons' (2011: 21).

Drunken comedy is a keystone of the British tradition. The comic drunk acts of, say, Frank Randle, Freddie Frinton or Dickie Henderson follow a tradition that can be traced back throughout the history of UK comedy. There is a lineage discernable from Noah and his wife (providing the comic relief) in the mediaeval Miracle Play cycles (Banks, 1998: 76–84); through the routines of such performers as John Harper (an eighteenth-century Falstaff) who 'first made his name with a drunken man dance at Southwark Fair in 1715' (Thomson, 2000: 49); to the antics of (notable female exceptions) Jennifer Saunders and Joanna Lumley as Edina and Pasty in *Absolutely Fabulous* (BBC, 1992–2002). It is a deeply embedded cultural phenomenon. Of the complex and differentiated British attitude to drink, Edwin Muir noted:

> Scottish people drink spasmodically and intensely for the sake of a momentary but complete release, whereas the English like to bathe and paddle about bucolically in a mild puddle of beer.
>
> (Finlayson, 1987: 203)

As Finlayson observes about the Scots, 'their reputation as hard and purposeful drinkers exceeds the merely recreational' (ibid.: 204), and, inevitably, perhaps, the comic drunk often emerges as a staple of Scottish comedy. This is evident from Harry Lauder's singing of a 'Just a wee Deoch and Doris'; through Will Fyffe's 'I'm fu the Noo' and 'He's Been on the Bottle Since a Baby'; to Rab C. Nesbitt's defiant alcoholism.

The ambivalence of Scottish attitudes to alcohol is indicated in the comedy of the stand-up comic Arnold Brown, 'we had the shame in Glasgow of my father being a teetotaller, and the disgrace on Saturday nights of him being thrown into pubs' (O'Brien, 2006: 71).

Scottish comic performers make capital out of the drunken, excessive individual. Expertise, including a superb use of comic timing, and interplay are evident in a *Scotch and Wry* (BBC, 1978–1992) performance in which Rikki Fulton plays the Reverend David Goodchild in a parody of a then well-known STV short, religious, epilogue, sign-off broadcast entitled *Late Call* (STV, 1960–1975). Certainly, recognition and familiarity are evident in the use of the format in which, nightly, different ministers and priests would deliver five-minute homilies. In the set-up to his late-night televised sermon, in the sketch 'Last Call', Fulton plays an otherwise respectable, mild-mannered minister (a more affable forerunner of his later minister character I. M. Jolly) who is inadvertently supplied with alcohol, instead of water, in his carafe. As he sips the liquid during the transmission of the religious broadcast, Fulton's character becomes increasingly drunk, more confused, conspiratorial, indiscreet and giggly as the sermon unfolds. The sketch is a master-class in comic expertise and timing. There is also

0133

FOU THE NOO.

CHORUS.

And I'm fou the noo !   Absolutely fou !
     But I adore the country I was born in.
My name is Jock McGraw, and I dinna care a straw,
     For I've somethin' in the bottle for the mornin' !

By arrangement with Harry Lauder, Gerald Grafton, and Francis, Day and Hunter.

© I. Wilkie Collection

incongruity to be found in the mismatch of dignified preacher with naughty drunk. There is release afforded from the superiority play of what Walter Humes terms the 'tensions, conflicts and contradictions' (1983: 133) of guilt and licensed celebration that are depicted within the comedy. There is also pastiche of Hume's 'maudlin sentimentality' (ibid.) in Fulton's performance of clichéd drunken behaviour.

Audio visual

For the Rikki Fulton clip, type in 'Rikki Fulton'/'Last Call'/'Reverend David Goodchild'.

Type in 'Jimmy James' 'drunk' and/or 'Foster Brooks' 'drunk' or 'laughing gas'/ 'Cicely Courtneidge' for comic scenes and sketches that show drunkenness, excessive and inappropriate behaviours being played out within otherwise serious situations.

GROUP EXERCISES

Trying not to laugh

Imagine you are all at a funeral.

One person comes to the front and tries to deliver a eulogy to the 'dead' person (perhaps this is about someone else in the group) which is intended to make the rest laugh through the use of inappropriate means – by pulling funny faces, adding ludicrous gestures to accompany the speech, making ridiculous statements about the imaginary dead person, etc. The main object of the exercise, however, is for the group *not* to laugh, with them bearing in mind the seriousness of the situation.

How tempting is it to laugh inappropriately? How infectious is the group's 'forbidden' laughter?

Inappropriate levels

Try performing a scene – either scripted or improvised – which varies in levels of intensity as numbers are allocated at intervals (with 1 being the lowest and most muted level and 10 being the most energised). This will replicate and demonstrate the inappropriateness, unpredictability and excess of drunken behaviour.

Cross purposes

The facilitator gives out indications of a character and situation. Each character and situation should have a simple, single intention (e.g. a pet shop owner trying to sell an animal, a traffic policeman who has stopped a driver for speeding, an actor making a speech at an awards ceremony, a chicken who is trying to cross a road, a footballer celebrating a goal, a lion tamer trying to train a lion; a schoolteacher trying to teach subtraction, a steward/ess demonstrating an airline safety drill etc.)

Characters are then randomly paired off and should attempt to play out their conflicting scenarios and intentions. Each participant must hold onto their belief of their character and situation and their own intention throughout the scene and, as much as possible, make no acknowledgement of recognising the other player's intention or acknowledging their seemingly inappropriate behaviour in the given circumstances.

The improvised scenes which occur as a result of the above exercises will reproduce themes that recur in comic texts where license, inappropriateness and excessive behaviours prefigure. They demonstrate 'wrongness', incongruity and events spiralling out of control, all of which are staple ingredients of comic text.

Buttons in text

Try to identify any comic buttons in the scenes, scripts and plays that you work on.

Just as age-old dramatic theories, plots and characterisations recur in comic text, so too do elements of all the three 'principles' of comedy – that is, superiority, incongruity and relief. Superiority became most evident as a concept in Classical comic drama formulations. Thus, Plato delineated the characters in a comedy as being 'such persons ... when their conceit is not backed by power so as to make them formidable and hateful ... are merely ridiculous' (Morreall, 1987: 12). Aristotle saw comedy as a mode that places the characters in a position of inferiority. Ancient Greek and Roman comedy often contained caricatures of the leading figures of the day. The superiority theory requires 'the butt' (Purdie, 1993: 58), that is, 'laughing at someone or something ... that ... has been "brought" low, *degraded*' (ibid.: 59; italics in original). Thus, today we can still find humour in the comedy of embarrassment as specialised in by Ricky Gervais or Larry David. Similarly, the action of superiority is apparent in the thwarting of the lofty aspirations of, say, Sergeant Bilko, Lucille Ball, Captain Mainwaring or *Citizen Khan* (BBC, 2012–) or seen simply in the villain getting their come-uppance at the end of a British pantomime.

Just as the superiority theory originates from classical models, so too does the incongruity principle, where comedy was seen to foreground what Aristotle termed the 'ludicrous' (1997: 9). Over time, the theory of superiority became superseded by that of incongruity. In Britain, by the eighteenth century, Henry Fielding wrote that 'the only source of the true Ridiculous ... is affectation ... from the discovery of this affectation arises the Ridiculous, which always strikes the reader with surprise and pleasure' (1742: 2). George Santayana similarly sought to qualify the implicit cruelty and the imposition of oppressive status play that was presupposed in a theorising of comedy that was built on notions of superiority, 'it is never the incongruity or the degradation itself that gives us pleasure; it is rather the stimulation and excitement caused by our perception of those things' (1896: 90).

British comedy, in particular, is certainly rife with the absurd and incongruous. From the Elizabethan 'star' comic William Kemp's nine-day Morris dance, in which 'in 1599 Shakespearean comic actor William Kemp attracted much attention by dancing the Morris from London to Norwich' (Dyce, 1860: vii), there is evidence of a strain of incongruity which borders on a form of surrealism. Take the ramblings of Victorian comedian Dan Leno:

> Eventually I reached Japan ... I settled down there as a rhubarb merchant, and the next place to mine was a ginger beer plantation. He was a very nice fellow, the owner; he used to throw all the broken bottles into my garden. One morning when I was weeding the glass I happened to look up, and there I saw a woman trying to attract my attention. She winked at me with her ear – not her eye ... so I walked over to her – I walked backwards to make people think I was coming away – and soon we were married.
>
> (1968: 46)

Incongruity can also be seen as a form of 'comic surrealism' – a staple of British comedy, as evident in the comedy of the Goons – for example, 'The Dreaded Batter Pudding Hurler' or 'The Affair of the Lone Banana' (Milligan, 1973); Monty Python ('Crossing the Atlantic on a Tricycle', 'Exploding Version of "The Blue Danube"' or 'A Doctor whose Patients are Stabbed by a Nurse') (Chapman, Cleese, Gilliam *et al.*, 1989); Reeves and Mortimer ('the enigmatic Man with the Stick, whose amusing helmet is decorated with cartoons of [1980's British pop group] Spandau Ballet laughing at an orphan who's fallen off his bike' or 'Milli Vanilli trying to create negative energy in their tights') (Thompson, 2004: 18–19); or *The Mighty Boosh's* 'talking animals, including a lecherous yeti, boxing kangaroos, a wolfman who sounds like Clint Eastwood and so on' (Hall, 2006: 82).

In essence, incongruity in comedy is something that:

> Does not match up with what we expect things of that kind to be, or because it is out of place in the setting in which we find it. Something amuses us if it somehow violates our picture of the way things are supposed to be, and if we enjoy this violation.
>
> (Morreall, 1987: 216)

The mixture of superiority and incongruity is present in much comic text – and these are comic buttons that can be pressed, worth identifying in the plays or scripts that you work on. A fundamental of comedy that is easy to find in any comic script is in the depiction of a set social situation where someone 'gets it wrong', as, for example, occurs in this description of inappropriateness of behaviour of a group member 'getting it wrong' during a ritual ceremony, found in Margaret Mead's seminal, cultural anthropological observation, *Growing Up in New Guinea*:

> Now it was the turn of Ngatchumu, another aunt. Ngatchumu was unaccustomed to the ceremony. She stumbled and halted, and was prompted by Kiteni's grandmother. Half-way through, she paused and said hopefully, 'Is that all?' … The hilarity occasioned by Ngatchumu's ignorance continued. Women began to feed each other taro and utter mock incantations; a most unusual good humour prevailed.
>
> (1963: 139–140)

As a simple case of cause and effect, comic superiority and incongruity can thus manifest themselves in simple loss of face or the lowering of status due to a social transgression. Such reductions of human dignity presume comic outcomes, and it is in how these scenes are played that comic performers' meat and drink are to be found within comic texts. Take this example from the BBC sitcom *Only Fools and Horses* (BBC, 1981–2003). The scene is from the first part of the 1996 Christmas Special trilogy entitled *Heroes and Villains* that was first screened on 25 December 1996. This episode attracted a record UK television audience of 21.3 million and topped the viewers' poll for the favourite 1990s' TV programme in *When Were We Funniest?* (Gold, 2008) first shown in March 2008.

The protagonists Del Boy (David Jason) and Rodney (Nicholas Lyndhurst), by then well established as popular and likeable comic characters, are incongruously dressed up as Batman and Robin in this episode. They think they are about to attend a fancy dress party and burst into what turns out to be a solemn wake for a deceased neighbour. Incongruity in their choice of costume is further enhanced by their activity – they enter the room full of mourners, noisily and enthusiastically spraying silly string and singing the 'Batman' theme tune.

The performance contains apperceptions of superiority through our knowledge that the characters are experiencing loss of face and lowering of dignity. Jason and Lyndhurst's expertise in playing the comedy of embarrassment is also apparent. There is skill in the truthfulness of Jason's performance of 'embarrassed apology' for their mistake and his conveyance of their evident acceptance of the inappropriateness of their actions. Comedy (excess and inappropriateness) intruding incongruously on the taboo of death and mourning (seriousness and decorum) affords comic release.

Note, too, that there is use of repetition within the scene in the other regular characters' reactions. Trigger (Roger Lloyd Pack) articulates his established catch phrase as he reacts to Rodney, characteristically referring to him, wrongly, as 'Dave', while Boycie (John Challis), equally characteristically, revels in point scoring over Del Boy. Interplay and complicity are achieved by tight two and three medium close-up reaction shots on Del and Rodney, while Rodney's bemused reaction to Trigger's assumption that they have come dressed as the 'Lone Ranger and Tonto' is framed on a single medium close-up on Lyndhurst. The interplay and complicity ensures that we, the viewers, are included in knowing what Rodney is thinking, while, once again, our superiority, in this case, over Trigger's 'getting it wrong', is achieved.

Finally, in identifying potential comic buttons in text, class preoccupations often appear as the drivers of sociocultural exchange in much comic writing, certainly in that which emanates from the UK. As Andy Medhurst suggests, 'class has always been a central theme of English comedy' (2003: 48). The principle of social status play has certainly proved a ripe source for performance and laughter throughout historical genres, cultures and societies, most clearly evident in the master–servant routines that originated in classical dramatic text. It is a theme which continues to preoccupy British comic writers as in, for instance, the sitcoms *Plebs* (ITV, 2013–2014), *Radges* (BBC Three, 2015–) or in the film *Dad's Army* (Parker, 2016).

Audio visual

Type in 'Only Fools and Horses' and 'funeral scene'.

For similar transgressions in comic scenes, see also 'Mrs Brown's Boys' and 'funeral scene'; 'Anchorman 2' and 'funeral scene'.

The third of the traditional philosophies of comedy is relief (also interchangeably referred to as 'release'). This principle appears to have a more straightforwardly physiological origin. Aristotle's notion of catharsis as a 'purgation of ... emotions' (1997: 10) was not linked by him to comedy per se, although Richard Janko argues in *Aristotle on Comedy* that:

> Catharsis applied as much to epic and comedy as to tragedy, as to be linked with Aristotle's central concept of mimesis ... 'pleasure and laughter' given moderate expression by mimesis relieve one's impulses to the immoderate display of these emotions in everyday life, and in so doing, produce pleasure.
>
> (2002: 82–83)

Janko also contends that Aristotle posited that 'laughter is one of the emotions to be purged' (ibid.: 143). Geoff King resumes the idea of relief in comedy as being an expression of a physiological manifestation:

> A fear of the kind of loss of bodily control manifested ... that was a driving force behind the denigration of laughter-creating forms of comedy in neoclassical debate in the sixteenth century, a tradition dating back to the writings of Plato and Aristotle ... the physiological act of laughter itself constitutes an upsurge of bodily response
>
> (2006: 88)

The concept of 'comic relief' also appears as a form of escapism, enabling a deviation from, rather than a complete subversion of, the norm. This is most apparent in the context of literature where 'comic relief' means a scene or character devised to be a tension breaker and deliberately inserted into a tragic or serious themed play (such as the Gravedigger in Shakespeare's *Hamlet* or the Porter in *Macbeth*). Moelwyn Merchant defines this idea of comic relief as 'an occasion ... for the physical release of tension in laughter' (1972: 16–17). In comic performance, as Geoff King notes,

> Comedy can offer a form of escape or 'release', of one kind or another, from the pressures or norms of everyday life, whether understood at the social or social-psychological level.
>
> (2006: 17)

In cueing laughter (or pressing the comic 'buttons'), comic relief or 'release' is afforded, in its most basic manifestation, as a physiological response – that is, the involuntary explosion that might be triggered simply by, for instance, Bergson's 'jack-in-the-box' effect. Laughter is 'released' in response to comic stimuli. Albert Mackie in *The Scotch Comedians* refers to 'the humour of release, to which a pent-up audience suffering from all the stresses of the social system immediately responds' (1973: 93). As the Scottish comedian Lex McLean observed, 'you've got to hit them with the pail to make them forget their problems' (ibid.: 26). In its most extreme form, comic release can be achieved in activating Jeff Nuttall and Rodick Carmichael's concept of 'survival laughter' (Medhurst, 2003: 65). Here, the 'liberating' function of the comedian's jokes (Mellencamp, 1986: 93) also enhances complicity and collusion, establishing a sense of shared community.

Take, for example, this description of the laughter of release in wartime. It can clearly be imagined in reviewer Jack House's description of a 1940/41 Scottish pantomime sketch:

> If you haven't observed the funny side of an air-raid warning, I recommend a visit to the Queen's Theatre at Glasgow Cross, where the city's first panto has just opened. Scene is a kitchen, complete with recess-bed, occupied by Doris Droy and 'child'. Off go the sirens; out of bed leaps Doris; struggles into her stays and other garments, and then outside to shelter. There's no room for faither (Billy Fields). Doris is unconcerned about him, except for the sudden thought: 'Whit wid we dae for the buroo money if ye wir killt?' *[What would we do for welfare payments if you were killed]*. Sam Murray (dame) remarks that when her hoose was bombed she and her old man were blown into a field – 'first time we've been oot thegither *[out together]* for 30 years'.
>
> (House in Bruce, 2000: 68)

Allowing comic relief – where the audience's laughter is visceral – is what the comic performer strives for. In this sense, the audience's laughter becomes like Northrop Frye's 'reflex' (Enck, 1960: 88). Prompting visceral laughter through a 'belly laugh' is described by the comedian Freddie Sales in his report of an audience's response to a (admittedly unintentional) piece of comic performance involving a troupe of incontinent elephants at the Tivoli Theatre, Melbourne:

> It was then I witnessed the phenomena all comedy entertainers want to achieve. The audience were literally out of their seats and were on their hands and knees, rolling in the aisles!! Some banging the floor with their hands – rolling onto their backs, screaming with laughter – they were helpless.
>
> (Hudd, 1993: 151)

To prompt the deep laughter of relief or release is the comic performer's job to press the button which will enable this to happen, all the while still maintaining the 'essential comic integrity' (Weitz, 2009: 119) of the text and character. By plotting in advance where the superiority, incongruity and – in the case of a potential visceral laugh – the relief occurs in the comic text can help you to prepare your performance to fully underscore and support such scripted moments.

INDIVIDUAL EXERCISES

Plotting the buttons in the text

Identify examples of 'classic' comic themes, characterisation and where the principles of superiority, incongruity and relief arise in the texts that you are working on. These are the comic mechanisms that contain potential buttons for helping you to plan how you perform the scenes.

The following extracts contain examples of the comic theories and of classical themes in scripted comic texts. The first is from an ancient writer, the second from a mediaeval piece and the last is taken from a more modern source.

Firstly, note the themes of confusion, mixed-up twins, status play, characterisations and audience interplay that occur in this extract from *The Prisoners* by Plautus (*c.* 200–190 BC):

Prologue

See these two prisoners standing here,
Standing by on their own two feet as it were?
Well, they're *standing* on them, not sitting – ha ha ha! ...
(*His laugh trails away at the conspicuous lack of response*)
At least you can see I'm not lying
(*Resumes briskly*)
Hegio, the old man who lives here, is the father of *that* one.
(*Jerks a thumb toward TYNDARUS. Frowns*)
What! Father's son a slave? How come?
Listen and I'll tell you.
(*Takes a step towards the audience*)
The old gentleman had two sons.
One of them when four years old was stolen by a slave,
Who took to his heels and sold him;
Yes, sold him in the in the country of Elis to the father of *that* one
(*Indicates PHILOCRATES*)
Get me? ... Fine ... Oh, dear
There's a man at the back shaking his head
(*Waves to him*)

(*Continued*)

(Continued)

> Come nearer, sir.
> *(Waits, but there is apparently no move)*
> Take a seat, for god's sake, or take a stroll.
> You're reducing an honest actor to a beggar.

In this second example from the Commedia delle 'arte, note the themes of young lovers, incongruity of behaviour and the use of direct interplay found in this extract from *Harlequin, Emperor of the Moon* (1684) by Gherardi:

> HARLEQUIN: Ah, unfortunate that I am! The doctor wants to marry Columbine to a farmer, and how can I live without Columbine I shall die! O ignorant doctor! O inconstant Columbine! O knavish farmer! O extremely miserable Harlequin! Let me hasten to die … sirs, if any amongst you would be so good as to die so as to afford me a model, I should be infinitely obliged … Faith, I have it! We read in history that there are people who have been killed by laughter – I am most sensitive to tickling. If someone were to tickle me for long they would make me die of laughter – I shall go and tickle myself, and thus I shall die (He tickles himself until he falls down with laughter).
>
> (Mawer, 1932: 62–63)

Finally incongruity to the point of absurdity and status play in superiority shown by the 'bad teacher' is evident in this extract from Vaclav Havel's *The Memorandum* (1965).

LEAR: Mr Thumb! Mr Thumb! Yipee!

THUMB: We haven't learned yippee yet, sir.

LEAR: Don't try to excuse yourself. You simply don't know it. Hurrah!

THUMB: Frnygko jefr dabux altep dy savarub gop texeres.

LEAR: Goz texeres!!

THUMB: I mean, goz texeres.

LEAR: Such an important word! No, no. Mr Thumb! It won't work this way. I've placed so many hopes in you, and you have done what? Well? You have disappointed me! Yes disappointed! No, no, this way we can't do what? Well? Carry on. Certainly not. This way our class would soon turn into what? Well? Go on, answer me!

THUMB: I don't know.

LEAR: Then try.

THUMB: A kindergarten?

LEAR: No.

THUMB: A borstal?

LEAR: No.

THUMB: Bedlam?

LEAR: Quite correct! Bedlam! No no! Under these circumstances I can't let
          you carry on with your studies. You'd only slow down the class and
          hold up the other students. Please leave the classroom!
          (THUMB takes his briefcase and sadly leaves by B.D.)

LEAR: *(addressing the empty classroom)*. Let us proceed. 'Hallo!' becomes
          'trevunt', 'gosh!' is translated as 'kavlyz ubahaj kupit'. The American
          'gee!' becomes 'hofro gaborte', 'pooh!' is translated as –

Creating a comic text

Try creating your own short comic text – a sketch or monologue – using the
following stimulus as a start:

Photo © I. Wilkie 2012

Evaluate what buttons – basic comic tropes (principles, plots, themes, characters or devices) – you have incorporated within your own written version
of this scene.

Working through the text – finding interplay

Aston and Savona note that 'the spectator...is engaged in a project of creative collaboration with the dramatist and actor in the interest of a more complete realisation of the performance' (Aston and Savona, 1991: 160) and, as we saw in Chapter 2, interplay is important in establishing comic meaning. Sometimes it is clear where you, as a performer, can directly transgress the fourth wall. Perhaps by referring to the audience, in cases where the author makes it overt that audience interplay is allowed as, for example, in this moment in Ian Hay and P. G. Wodehouse's comedy *A Damsel in Distress* (1928) in which a butler leads a group of paying visitors around a stately home:

> Keggs (*coming C. and pointing out to audience*): I should next like to draw your attention to this truly colossal group by an unknown artist, representing an assemblage of old English comedy types. Note the gargoyle-like effect of the faces in the foreground and the wide open mouths in the middle distance.
>
> (Act 1, Scene 2)

A similar gag, where the audience is directly acknowledged, appears in Beckett's *Waiting for Godot*:

> Vladimir: We're surrounded! (*Estragon makes a rush towards back*). Imbecile! There's no way out there. (*He takes Estragon by the arm and drags him towards front*). There! Not a soul in sight! Off you go. Quick! (*He pushes Estragon towards auditorium. Estragon recoils in horror*). You won't? (*He contemplates auditorium*). Well, I can understand that.

Indirect interplay – that is, where the performer is aware of, and responsive to, the audience's laughter reaction but makes no reference to this fact – is not usually scripted in comic texts. It is a purely performer-driven link made between you and audience, and the author plays no part in the process at these points. Comedy as a live event is, nonetheless, reliant on the interplay of reciprocated audience response and reaction as a gauge of the effectiveness of the engagement. Comedian Stephen Fry refers to this phenomenon (from the transmitter's perspective) as:

> The almost hyperaesthetical way in which one was aware of each microsecond on stage, of how one could detect precisely where an audience's focus was at any time, I loved the thrill of knowing that I was carrying hundreds of people with me.
>
> (2010: 109)

The phenomenon of simultaneously 'doing and awareness' is most acute for the comic performer who must, in live-time, stimulate, monitor and reflexively respond to the cues that are supplied by the audience's continuing laughter. Doing this may be problematic if you have been taught performance in a purely Stanislavsky-influenced context, as you may feel that you have to break certain habits. As Sonia Moore notes in *The Stanislavski System*, his teachings have encouraged modern performers to access 'conscious means to the subconscious' (1974: 12), while affording the actor a creative role in interpreting the text in the formation of 'a character [as] a new human being, born of the elements of the actor himself united with those of the character conceived by the playwright' (ibid.: 17). The modern actor has become central to the meaning-making process in theatre where 'it is the truth of the actor's behaviour that will keep the audience's attention' (ibid.: 18). The Stanislavski system's terminologies of 'super-objective, logic of actions, given circumstances, communion, subtext, images, tempo-rhythm' (ibid.: 9) have become the lingua franca of Westernised performance. As John Miles-Brown notes:

> Stanislavski required actors to ... develop powers of imagination ... to believe in the characters within the stage situation; to work from conscious techniques in order to liberate subconscious reactions (the psycho-technique).
>
> (2006: 12)

All these techniques are massively useful (and are, arguably, even more necessary) for developing truthful and real comic performance. However, such an inward-looking, intra-psychological way of approaching performance generally may run counterintuitively to the Stanislavskian precept that requires the performer to remain fully in character at all times. In performing comedy, being in character while remaining alert and aware to the audience's reactions in real time is vital. As William Gruber notes:

> Even during the performance of a comedy, which necessitates frequent pauses for the audience to laugh, that 'acknowledgement' constitutes no acknowledgement ... the representational frame demands that the actors always be 'in character'.
>
> (1986: 132)

Nonetheless, eminent Stanislavskians such as Lee Strasberg acknowledge that the performer's role in the overall intercommunicative process of performance requires some degree of interplay:

> On stage the actor ... must be ninety nine per cent actor and a little bit critic and a little bit audience ... acting is a profession where the doing

and the awareness of doing go hand in hand – and not after the doing but during the moment of doing.

(Hethmon, 1966: 84)

Comedy requires the adoption of a more reflexive approach (and certainly more than one per cent!) in its requirement of the performers' constant monitoring of the audience's response. This is rarely something that is ever made explicit in comic text. In this aspect, the writer devolves responsibility to the performer. The responsiveness of the audience is a vital ingredient of the live play, where in a very real sense 'the audience "makes" the comedy' (Greig, 1969: 221). Here, 'an audience is both shaped by the talk it is attending' and through its responses 'help shape what will be made of that talk' (Goodwin, 1986: 311). The audience, as Peter Brook notes of all forms of theatrical exchange, provides:

> The true function of the spectator, there and not there, ignored and yet needed. The actors work is never for an audience, yet always is for one ... this implies a sharing of experience, once contact is made.
>
> (1968: 57)

Audience contact is crucial to performing comedy. In *The Craft of Comedy* (1943), her reflective meditation on the subject from the performer's perspective, the actress Athene Seyler advocates a Stanislavksian route to discovering characterisation from within, while acknowledging that comedy relies on adopting a more explicitly interactive process with the audience than non-comic forms of drama:

> In playing comedy I am sure one has to rely first on the subconscious or inspirational method of reading a part by sinking oneself in the character, and then check the results consciously from outside oneself and keep what seems good, and discard what is overdone or what misses fire. It's a kind of dual control of one's performance.
>
> (Ibid.: 52)

Here, interplay in the 'checking of results from outside oneself' is a defining feature of performing comedy. An audience's response through laughter, moreover, 'is the only immediate way in which a performer can test, gauge and establish audience approval' (McIlvenny, Mettovaara and Tapio, 1993: 230).

Performing Shakespearean comedy

Many types of comic text require mastery of direct interplay. Classical comic drama relies on much direct address to the audience in the prologues, exhortations and appeals that feature in the texts. Many early forms of comic text use an interlocutor figure – often an 'Everyman' type of figure (albeit in many instances a character who is also a trickster or rogue) who assumes the role of the eyes and ears of the audience and personifies the one with whom we are most expected to identify. Often this character will place the other characters under scrutiny from a position of superiority as he (and, again, it is usually a he) comments unfavourably on his peers' foibles and idiosyncrasies. This type of interplay continued throughout the Middle Ages and is found in the work of Shakespeare – 'all of the characters in Shakespeare's comedies are easily to be placed by a popular audience, although their full depth is only to be appreciated by readers' or actors' study' (Bradbrook, 1963: 88). Thus, in performing Shakespeare's comic characters, keeping an awareness of their functionality in context is important, but so too is maintaining knowledge of where the potential for expressing truthful and believable performance continues to be fully realisable.

R. P. Draper usefully categorises the comic character types in Shakespeare's works to 'dupes', 'clever fools', 'manlike women' and 'odd men out' (2000: viii–ix). Very broadly speaking, you are likely to play one or another of two distinct types of comic figure in Shakespearean comedy. There are the clever clowns who emerge from the interlocutor figure traditions of early drama and who commentate on the events that are unfolding (Feste, Touchstone or The Fool in the tragedy *King Lear*). These also include Draper's 'manlike women', that is, women who are normally wise characters who can (at least eventually) see the truth of what is going on. The most extreme examples of the clever clown may indeed be directly depicted as licensed jesters or jokers in the plays and, in this sense, are somewhat akin to modern stand-up comedians, in that they comment on the folly and foibles of the other characters and so are designed to be laughed *with*. In contrast, there are the dupes (and the 'odd men out'). These characters are more akin to the buffoonish clown of antiquity. They appear as figures of ridicule (drawing upon the superiority principle of comedy) and are designed to be laughed *at* (e.g. Malvolio, Bottom or Dogberry). Obviously, much leeway is permitted in how you, the performer, might play the different roles, and retaining some degree of ambivalence or detachment from the sheer functionality of the role will, in turn, affect how, say, sympathetically, knowingly, boldly, timidly, sardonically, violently or wryly that you imbue the part. Thus, in essence, how sympathetic, funny or real these characters appear comes down to your performance. As the American actor F. Murray Abraham notes of playing Bottom in *A Midsummer Night's Dream*, 'truth is always the touchstone ... Shakespeare ... makes an actor feel he wrote the part specifically for him' (2005: 88–89).

In much comic drama, there exist two types of comic performance – to repeat the American comedian and actor Ed Wynn's definition – someone who 'does funny things' or someone who 'does things funny' (Marowitz, 1996: 117). Shakespeare's comedy is particularly satisfying to play in that the characters often contain both possibilities – they do funny things and they do things funny. The role of Launce in *Two Gentlemen of Verona* (*c.* 1590), Shakespeare's 'early attempt' at romantic comedy (Draper, 2000: 247), for instance, provides both opportunities for the performer. Launce has a dually functional role in the play – he says funny things as he 'provide[s] a satirical perspective on the behaviour of conventional lovers' (Gay, 2008: 38) through his wit and powers of observation. Here, he is a clever fool to be laughed with. He also provides a catalyst for comedy to arise in that he 'does' funny things. In his speech to his dog, Crab, he becomes a figure to be laughed at. In his incongruous manipulation of his shoes in a puppet show and in being upstaged by his dog, he also becomes the dupe:

LAUNCE: Nay, 'twill be this hour ere I have done weeping. All the kind of the Launces have this very fault. I have received my proportion, like the prodigious son, and am going with Sir Proteus to the Imperial's court. I think Crab, my dog, be the sourest-natured dog that lives. My mother weeping, my father wailing, my sister crying, our maid howling, our cat wringing her hands, and all our house in a great perplexity, yet did not this cruel-hearted cur shed one tear … Nay, I'll show you the manner of it. [*taking off shoes*] This shoe is my father. No, this left shoe is my father. No, no, this left shoe is my mother. Nay, that cannot be so neither. Yes, it is so, it is so – it hath the worser sole. This shoe with the hole in it is my mother, and this my father. A vengeance on't! There 'tis. Now, sir, this staff is my sister, for, look you, she is as white as a lily and as small as a wand. This hat is Nan, our maid. I am the dog. No, the dog is himself, and I am the dog – O, the dog is me, and I am myself. Ay, so, so. Now come I to my father: 'Father, your blessing'. Now should not the shoe speak a word for weeping. Now should I kiss my father – well, he weeps on. Now come I to my mother. O, that she could speak now like a wood woman! Well, I kiss her – why, there 'tis: here's my mother's breath up and down. Now come I to my sister; mark the moan she makes. Now the dog all this while sheds not a tear nor speaks a word!

(Act 2, Scene 3)

The routine that Launce performs belongs in a long tradition of comic business. Phil Silvers, for example, made great success with an upstaging dog companion in his playing of the part of Jerry Biffle in the musical *Top Banana* (Mercer, 1951) performing a 'duet' with the canine in a song entitled *A Dog Is a Man's Best Friend*. In a similar way, Charlie Chaplin performed a table-top piece of puppetry using forks and bread rolls in *The Gold Rush* (Chaplin, 1925). The funny things that Launce does in the routine are dependent on the comic performer's craft and expertise skills which, in turn, dictate how these actions can become sure-fire comic effects.

Audio visual

Type in 'Top Banana' and 'A dog is man's best friend' for audio of the routine.

Also, 'Chaplin' and 'fork ballet' for the video of the scene from *The Gold Rush*.

Interplay in Shakespeare's comedies is achieved through the 'rapport with the audience which is denied to the "serious" actor' (Thomson, 2002: 139) and is also managed through the performers' 'running commentaries ... on the behaviour of [others which] set up a confidential relationship between the clown and the audience' (Gay, 2008: 40). It is also achieved, however, through finding something likeable about your character that will, in turn, register with the audience. The audience must somehow like your character no matter how villainous or unappealing their functionality within the play might superficially render them. Take, for example, the playing of such a seemingly non-comic Shakespearean role as Richard III. As Antony Sher notes:

> I got some great laughs as Macbeth, Leontes, Titus, even Prospero, and as for Richard III, he brought the house down when at the end of the Lady Anne scene, he turned to the audience, and asked, 'was ever woman in this humour wooed?'
>
> (2015: 65)

The play itself is actually a 'hybrid form' (Walsh, 2013: 109) of tragi-comedy in which the character of Richard achieves complicity with the audience through his direct interplay. In this way, Richard draws the audience into his intentions through inviting them to laugh at, say, his outrageous humiliation/seduction of Lady Anne (Act I, Scene 2), or to cheer on his openly professed villainies. Through his honest addresses in soliloquy about his unashamed dishonesty he makes us complicit. It is, frankly, disarming to be taken into confidence by a character who openly confides what he intends to do. Such frank admission also raises our status as the audience, as, at the expense of the other characters in the play, we know more than they do. Despite Richard's out-and-out villainy, we cannot help but rather like, even admire him, for his overt interplay. Here, as Walsh notes, 'it is the *performance* elements of *Richard III* that, I think, best help us to see around the play's providential façade to some of its other connotations' (ibid.: 110; italics in original).

Unalloyed comic Shakespearean scenes, 'whether solo pieces or double acts' (Thomson, 2002: 142), can be played in a variety of different ways and it is the performance elements that bring out the comedy. Take for example this short master–servant exchange between the Lady Olivia from *Twelfth*

Night (a witty, manlike woman) and her steward Malvolio (a serious-minded 'dupe' and 'odd man out'). Olivia is curious about an emissary (Cesario), seemingly sent by her would-be admirer (Count Orsino).

Olivia:	What kind o' man is he?
Malvolio:	Why, of mankind.
Olivia:	What manner of man?
Malvolio:	Of very ill manner. He'll speak with you, will you or no?
Olivia:	Of what personage and years is he?
Malvolio:	Not yet old enough for a man, nor young enough for a boy ... he is very well-favoured and he speaks very shrewishly. One would think his mother's milk were scarce out of him.

(Act 1, Scene V)

It is possible for the actor playing Olivia to perform the lines in a variety of ways – in a bored manner; or distractedly, teasingly, pedantically or flirtatiously (i.e. consciously within Cesario's hearing) – or in any combination thereof – to comic effect. It is similarly possible for the performer playing Malvolio to respond to Olivia's questions variously – in a bored manner; or with confusion, or pedantically, conspiratorially or judgmentally (i.e. consciously within Cesario's hearing) – or in any combination thereof – to equal comic effect. As long as the character's intention is clear and the performer plays the 'truthful' state of mind that lies behind their utterances, then the comedy will work.

There is, furthermore, an even purer interplay format of performing this particular scene which establishes complicity with the audience and which gives the reading an immediacy and knowingness. This manner of playing the scene would make more sense in the original. In the Elizabethan version, Lady Olivia would have been played by an adolescent boy and Cesario/ Viola would have been played by an adolescent boy playing a young woman playing a young man! Malvolio, conversely, would have been played by an experienced 'star' comic actor of the company. Thus, for the original audience, the scene could play out as a series of knowing 'in' jokes that are more of a (possibly semi-improvised) interchange between the actors, specifically designed for the audience's benefit, rather than being the strictly scripted intervention that might appear from the evidence of the text alone:

Olivia:	What kind o' man is he? *[Subtext for the contemporary audience's benefit – 'go on then, old man, explain this one. Describe a young man playing a young woman playing a young man to us ... '!]*
Malvolio:	Why, of mankind. *['Don't try and be funny, sonny. That's my job'].*
Olivia:	What manner of man? *['No, go on then. Explain it'].*

Malvolio: Of very ill manner. *['Like you! Impertinent!']* He'll speak with
            you, will you or no? *['Get back to the script'].*
Olivia: Of what personage and years is he? *['This is fun. I'm winning this
            challenge of making things awkward for you and so I'm going to
            press you to describe him. Let's hear the full details about him'].*
Malvolio: Not yet old enough for a man, nor young enough for a boy ...
            ['Like you! I'm warning you!'] He is very well-favoured and
            he speaks very shrewishly. *['Just like you!']* One would think
            his mother's milk were scarce out of him. *['You cheeky young
            upstart. Take that! Don't try and best the old man, laddie!')*

                                                          (Act 1, Scene V)

Shakespeare highly valued the comedians in his theatre companies and
what they could bring to the stage in terms of their performative expertise
and craft skills. He fully appreciated their ability to please an audience and
to bring comic relief to the plays. In fact, as John Russell Brown notes,
contemporary leading comic performers (Sincklo, Cowley and Kemp) were
specifically mentioned by name by Shakespeare in his original play texts
while 'none of the straight actors of the company ever crept into the stage
directions in the same way' (1993: 87). These were 'the kind of virtuoso
comedian for whom Shakespeare created [roles] ... the crowd puller[s]'
(Thomson, 2002: 139, 142). Shakespeare may also have particularly appreciated the tragi-comic potential that comic characterisations can bring. As
Friedrich Durrenmatt notes, 'we can achieve the tragic out of comedy ...
indeed many of Shakespeare's tragedies are already comedies out of which
the tragic arises' (Corrigan and Rosenberg, 1964: 267).

GROUP EXERCISES

The Seven Ages of Man

One actor reads Jacques' speech from *As You Like It*, while the other performers take it in turn to act out the different ages described. Note how using a
Commedia (or Brechtian archetype) way of quickly and simply embodying each
of the different ages works well:

JACQUES:
All the world's a stage,
And all the men and women merely players;
They have their exits and their entrances;

(Continued)

(Continued)

His act being seven ages.
At first the infant,
Mewling and puking in the nurse's arms.
Then the whining schoolboy, with his satchel
And shining morning face, creeping like snail
Unwillingly to school.
And then the lover,
Sighing like a furnace, with woeful ballad
Made to his mistress' eyebrow.
Then a soldier
Full of strange oaths, and bearded like the pard,
Jealous in honour, sudden and quick in quarrel,
Seeking the bubble reputation,
Even in the cannon's mouth.
And then the justice,
In fair round belly with good capon lin'd
With eyes severe and beard of formal cut,
And so he plays his part.
The sixth age shifts
Into the lean and slipper'd pantaloons,
With spectacles on nose and pouch on side;
His youthful hose, well sav'd, a world too wide
For his shrunk shrank; and his big manly voice,
Turning again to childish treble, pipes
And whistles in his sound.
Last scene of all,
That ends this strange eventful history,
Is second childishness and mere oblivion;
Sans teeth, sans eyes, sans taste, sans everything.

                              (Act II, Scene VII)

Shakespearean insults

Use these insults from Shakespeare's texts as the starting points or first lines
to create improvised scenes:

> "Thou damned and luxurious mountain goat" (*Henry V*).
> "This sanguine coward, this bed-presser, this horseback-breaker, this huge
> hill of flesh!" (*Henry IV*).

"Away you three-inch fool!" (*The Taming of the Shrew*).

"You scullion. You rampallian. You fustilarian. I'll tickle your catastrophe" (*Henry IV, 2*)

"Away you moldy rogue, away!" (*Henry IV, 2*).

"Zounds, ye fat paunch, an ye call me coward, I'll stab thee" (*Henry V*).

This can be extended to:

Kent's rant

The insults are split up into component parts and allocated out. Students stand in a circle and add their insult in order. This should build to a crescendo.

KENT: A knave, a rascal, an eater of broken meats; a base, proud, shallow, beggarly, three-suited, hundred pound, filthy, worsted-stocking knave; lily liver'd, action taking knave, a whoreson, glass-gazing, super-serviceable, finical rogue; one-trunk-inheriting slave; one that wouldst be a bawd, in way of good service, and art nothing but the composition of a knave, beggar, coward, pander, and the son and heir of a mongrel bitch.

(*King Lear*, II, ii)

Shakespeare's rolls (a variation of the cut up clues exercise from Chapter 4)

Cut up a scene from a Shakespeare play text. Randomly renumber the speeches/lines and distribute. Students should read their line into the new ordered sequence as their numbers are called out.

Players should try to preempt the end of the previous speech/line (guessing from the previous actor's use of rhythm in their reading) and come in directly 'on cue'. You should also try and make each consecutive addition sound as much as possible as if it is a logical progression to what has just gone before.

In some ways, this actually mimics how Elizabethan actors would have delivered their lines! They would only have been given the three cue words of the previous character's dialogue in the dispersal of their 'parts' or 'rolls' of text, so they had to listen very intently to hear their vocal cue or clue to know exactly when it was their turn to speak. Their live responses would, accordingly, have had the semblance of spontaneity that this exercise demonstrates!

Later comic texts

The Restoration comedy that followed the Elizabethan period similarly demanded interplay between the comic performer and the spectators.

As Simon Callow notes, in his book *Acting in Restoration Comedy*, 'the plays ... demand a special complicity between the actor and audience' (1991: 12). Despite the conception of a fourth wall being in place, some form of acknowledgement and intercommunication between performer and spectator that the enterprise being mutually undertaken was intended to be received as funny still remained possible. Take for example Congreve's *The Way of the World*, in which the character Lady Wisfort, whom we first met in a master–servant routine, disparages her servant, Peg:

> *LADY WISHFORT:* Ratafia, fool! No, fool! Not the ratafia, fool – grant me patience! I mean the Spanish paper, idiot! Complexion, darling. Paint, paint, paint! Dost thou understand that, changeling? Dangling thy hands like bobbins before thee! Why dost thou not stir, puppet? Thou wooden thing upon wires.
>
> (Act III, Scene i)

This is a scene intended to be performed behind the fourth wall, but Lady Wishfort elsewhere indulges in conspiratorial direct address with the audience:

> *LADY WISHFORT (Aside):* Oh he has witchcraft in his eyes and tongue! When I did not see him I could have bribed a villain to his assassination; but his appearance rakes the embers which have so long lain smothered in my breast.
>
> (Act V, Scene i)

In her text *Style: Acting in High Comedy*, the actress Maria Aitken acknowledges the Stanislavskian, mediator role that the performer must play between audience and writer, describing comedians as 'the middlemen: the actors who have to catch the comic spark from the playwright and pass it on to the audience' (1996: 4). Aitken also notes the extra performative layers that comic performance requires – 'the words demand display as well as truthfulness' (ibid.: 5) – all the while also emphasising the necessity for maintaining a duality of focus – 'we actors experience simultaneous connection and disconnection with our character. Comedy requires a parallel universe' (ibid.: 9).

In some ways, adopting a more Brechtian stance in approaching comedy (at least in the early stages of rehearsal) can be helpful. Whereas Stanislavsky's approach, to put it somewhat crudely, is partially about internalisation and taking a more overtly inside-to-outside performance stance, a Brechtian style requires you to adopt a more externalised, outside-to-inside approach. This resonates more with the performance of comedy – a mode that requires Brechtian precision and clarity in expressing a character's role within the whole and which establishes the making of connections with the audience. Brecht was interested in the functionality of characters – what they represented and what baggage they might bring – and this is also true of a lot of comic characterisation in text. Brecht scripted archetypal characters (such as the Mother, the Peasant, the Soldier or the Worker), partly for establishing simplicity through the role's essential signification for the purpose of his 'political' or 'solemn' clowning (Schechter, 1994: 68). Similar stock characterisations generally abound in comedy. An element of incongruity too is evident in absurdist texts, such as those by Pirandello or Ionesco, where, again, the characters are often 'types', as, say, the Father, Mother, Producer, Leading Actress and so on (in Pirandello's *Six Characters in Search of an Author*); the 1st and 2nd Drunk (in *The Rules of the Game*); or The Old Gentleman, The Housewife, The Logician (in Ionesco's *Rhinoceros*); and Old Man, Old Woman (in his *The Chairs*). Brechtian comic types can be found in these absurdist texts, which take as their essential themes such matters as life, art, sanity, being and death. Brecht's 'gestus', albeit a 'difficult term' (Unwin, 2005: 61), is basically all about the 'detailed relationship to social relationships and a commitment to expressing them in three dimensions ... [and to] telling the story' (ibid.: 62). This manner of meaning-making is basically similar to all comic text which requires externally realised role-play in its wish to bring about a change in the audience, that is, in its fundamental aim to make the spectators laugh.

As previously discussed, subverting the stereotype is an important stage in creating comic performance, and it is after establishing the Brechtian potentialities of your character that the introduction of Stanislavskian techniques to uncover their essential, individual, inner truths can be what that make your performance of the role become fully rounded, real, interesting and, ultimately, funny. As Margaret Eddershaw notes, 'the Brechtian performer, while not avoiding psychology, places more emphasis on the role's social interaction and behaviour ... [and] to find ways of highlighting key moments of decision' (1994: 271). The Brechtian/Stanislavskian performer makes those 'key moments of decision' appear instinctive, believable and natural to the character.

In working with comic text, the following exercises will help you to find occasions where some kind of interplay with the audience is possible (without necessarily breaking through the 'fourth wall') and to practise interplay. These exercises also focus on using archetypal or 'stock' characterisations to help you, firstly, to develop Brechtian, externalised techniques to performance in which your character's functionality in the scene is centralised while, secondly, also allowing you to experiment with finding 'that special collusion upon which comedy bases its conversation with an audience' (Weitz, 2009: 88).

GROUP AND INDIVIDUAL EXERCISES

Part 1: Finding the comic archetype

Pick a character from a comic text from any age – for example, a role from, for example, a classical Greek or Roman comedy, Commedia; Shakespeare or Ben Jonson; a Restoration comedy; Oscar Wilde; Shaw; Gilbert and Sullivan; Brecht; Ionesco; Joe Orton, Alan Ayckbourn or a Patrick Marber comedy.

The exercises on text that follow offer you the opportunity to discover, then to work around, the tendency towards the presentation of stock characters in comedy whose functionality in the play could threaten to overwhelm their humanity, individuality and believability. In the first part of this exercise you will take a Brechtian approach to the character.

Once you have chosen your character (say the Nurse in *Romeo in Juliet*), ask yourself the following questions about her. Who is – or was – she? What was her society like? What aspects of society might have shaped her? What class does she belong to? What would her clothes be like and why would she have chosen what she is wearing? How were her attitudes, beliefs, prejudices, securities and insecurities formed by her society?

Wordlessly mime her going about her work and daily business according to the textual clues and instructions that you can find at the various points in the play. What outer behaviours does she manifest? Introduce the miming of her interactions with other characters in the play. How does your character present herself? Also observe where your character displays any superiority and incongruity in her actions. Try to identify if, and where, any areas of implicit interplay with the audience may be found. To do this, temporarily abandon any fourth wall considerations.

What does your character's external life look like?

Part 2: Subverting the stereotype

Once you have explored the outer-to-inner journey of your character, in order to subvert the stereotype, you should now imagine what has made your character become the way she is. In this way, you will start the process of discovering the individual 'truth' of what may be even the most extreme stock character. Having established your character's function in energising the comedy, you will now be taking a Stanislavskian approach to discovering your role's inner life.

Again, ask yourself the same questions who is – or was – she? What was her society like? What aspects of society might have shaped her? What class does she belong to? What would her clothes be like and why would she have chosen what she is wearing? How were her attitudes, beliefs, prejudices, securities, and insecurities formed by her society, background, family, relationships and social interactions?

Also, how does she express herself? Where was her language and way of speaking formulated?

Use these questions to investigate your character's inner life. But keep these psychological motivations firmly hidden behind the fourth wall.

What does your character's internal and external life look like?

Taken together, these Brechtian/Stanislavskian approaches and decisions will help you shape your role. You will make choices that create believability in your character while retaining the comic truth of the role. Working in this way, using both outside-to-inside and inside-to-outside approaches will help you build up your performance to establish a real, living and breathing person who reacts credibly at all times within the comic world of the text.

Telling the story

Brecht was keen on the important story being told in the most efficient and effective way possible. Comic texts in general also rely on their comic tale being well told with humorous characters being well expressed by their performers.

(Continued)

(Continued)

In this ensemble exercise, the group will perform a fairy tale, perhaps from the Grimm canon, or will play out a fable from, perhaps, Aesop, or will enact a folk-legend. Having chosen the source text, one performer will narrate the story while the others will play out all the allocated roles as the narrative progresses, for example, the wood cutter, wolf, prince, princess, old woman, miser, etc. If the story calls for a forest, a mountain or a river, the performers will also work together to enact these pieces of scene setting. Each scene or tableau should help to move the story forward.

This exercise encourages creating instant characterisation, practicing Brechtian outer-to-inner techniques, and builds the ensemble skills of listening, responding to the narrative and clear telling of the story.

One question that may come up in rehearsal is whether you should play something 'for laughs' or should keep it 'real' or 'truthful'. The correct answer is, of course, both! It is a trap to think of such performance choices as being contradictory. As long as the truthful intention, motivation and expression are firmly in place in the playing of the moment, the comedy will register and the story being told will fully resonate with the audience. In talking of comic texts, Eric Weitz notes 'for the student of comedy it is always worth unravelling ... to inspect beneath the surface of clever contrivance: how do character, relationship and circumstance support humorous effect, and what possibilities are created for performance?' (2009: 75). Your approach to comic performance should encompass recognition of any comic buttons that are embedded in the text. If you are fully familiar with the tropes and principles which impel comedy generally and you can draw upon the repertoire of craft skills that you have practised, you will be able to create a fully rounded realisation of your scripted character.

INDIVIDUAL EXERCISES

Characters in text

Study these roles. Once you have identified the comic buttons in the speeches and have considered the outer-to-inner repercussions that these roles offer, it is suggested that you then look for the inner-to-outer aspects and decide on the characters' possible motivations. These parts are also worth performing in front of the group for you to gauge any live response to the comic moments and to gain any post-performance peer feedback.

The first text exercise is for a female actor. The extract is from Tom Stoppard's *The Real Inspector Hound* (1968) which, on one level, depicts a parody of stage thriller conventions. The character is Mrs Drudge, a stereotypical housekeeper figure, typical of the genre, whose functions are to explain the set-up of the plot and to embody a parody of thriller play elements and conventions.

Practise this exercise using a prop or imaginary phone to enable direct audience address and breaking down of the fourth wall. Note how the comic performance changes from being presentational in the first half of the speech, whereas in the second part (where the second character enters), your performance approach will require a more traditional, fourth wall framing.

> [*The phone rings. MRS DRUDGE seems to have been waiting for it do so and for the last few seconds has been dusting it with an intense concentration. She snatches it up.*]
>
> MRS. DRUDGE [*Into phone:* Hello, the drawing-room of Lady Muldoon's country residence one morning in early spring? ... *Hello!*-the draw – Who? Who did you wish to speak to? I'm afraid there is no one of that name here, this is all very mysterious and I'm sure it's leading up to something, I hope nothing is amiss for we, that is Lady Muldoon and her houseguests, are here cut off from the world, including Magnus, the wheelchair-ridden half-brother of her ladyship's husband Lord Albert Muldoon who ten years ago went out for a walk on the cliffs and was never seen again-and all alone, for they had no children ... Should a stranger enter our midst, which I very much doubt, I will tell him you called. Good-bye.
>
> [*She puts down the phone and catches sight of the previously seen suspicious character who has now entered again, more suspiciously than ever, through the French windows. [To him:]]*
>
> I'm Mrs Drudge. I don't live in but I pop in on my bicycle when the weather allows to help in the running of charming though somewhat isolated Muldoon Manor. Judging by the time [*she glances at the clock*] you did well to get here before high water cut us off for all practical purposes from the outside world ... Yes, many visitors have remarked

(Continued)

(Continued)

on the topographical quirk in the local strata whereby there are no roads leading from the Manor, though there *are* ways of getting *to* it, weather allowing ... The fog is very treacherous around here-it rolls off the sea without warning, shrouding the cliffs in a deadly mantle of blind man's buff. I've known whole week-ends when Muldoon Manor, as this lovely old Queen Anne House is called, might as well have been floating on the pack ice for all the good it would have done phoning the police.

The second exercise is for a male actor and is taken from Alan Bennett's *Forty Years On* (1968). Here, the interplay convention is that the character of the headmaster is directly addressing the audience in the pretext of them being a school assembly. Use the convention of the lecture presentation – along with the direct addresses to individuals contained within the speech – to practise interplay with the audience.

HEADMASTER: Members of Albion House, past and present. Parents and Old Boys ... It is a sad occasion, but it is a proud occasion too ... None of you boys are old enough to remember [the] Second War, nor even some of you masters. Yet I remember them both ... Those times left their mark on Albion House. Some of the older ones among you will remember Bombardier Tiffin, our Corps Commandant and Gym Instructor, lately retired. The more observant ones among you will have noticed that one of Bombardier Tiffin's legs was not his own. The other one, God bless him, was lost in the Great War. Some people lost other things, less tangible than legs but no less worthwhile – they lost illusions, they lost hope, they lost faith. That is why...chewing, Charteris. That is why the twenties and thirties were such a muddled and grubby time, for lack of all the hopes and ideals that perished on the fields of France. And don't put it in your handkerchief.

The third exercise is for a female actor and is taken from John Godber's *Shakers Restirred* (1991). The character of Mel is impersonating a rough, male chef (and carrying an imaginary pizza) at this point in the play as part of the telling of the story. Here, use the audience as Mel's unseen kitchen worker to practise interplay and the breaking down of the fourth wall.

MEL: Can you shout up when you make a bloody order, I can't hear you. Shout up. You're bloody useless. What you think I like making pizzas in public? You must be bloody joking kiddo. This place is crap. I should have stayed on North Sea Ferries if you ask me. And the waitresses are bloody useless. [*Shouts*]. There's a steak burning here. Get your arse round here. I'll tell you what, they bring the food back all the time, I've had seafood pasta coming back here all the night. What I do is this, they bring it back, all coy and helpful, I slap it in the microwave pour some sauce over it and call it a brand new dish. If they bring a steak back complaining that it's not done, I turn it over slap two bits of parsley on it, three more chips, half a tomato and it's ready to go. [*Shouts*]. Steak Diane ready to go. God. I'll tell you this, when I'm feeling really vindictive I put things from my nose in the Pizza Margarita ... Spices it up a bit. One Pizza Margarita ready to go!

The fourth exercise is taken, again, from Alan Bennett, this time from *Habeas Corpus* (1973).

Here, the middle-aged doctor Wicksteed imagines a scene between himself and the focus of his lustful attentions, the younger female character, Felicity Rumpers. To practise interplay, imagine that the character is facing out front and speaking into a shaving mirror while he impersonates both Felicity, the object of his attraction, and his imagined self in this invented 'dialogue'.

WICKSTEED: [Alone] Break, break, break,
On thy cold grey stones, O sea
And would that my tongue could utter
The thoughts that arise in me.
Would that it could, but you see, Felicity I'm rather a shy
person.
Are you Doctor?
Don't call me Doctor. Call me Arthur.
Are you Arthur?
Now you mention it, Felicity, I suppose I am. But you
Felicity ... you somehow restore my faith in human kind,
remind me of what perfection the human body is capable.
And spirit, of yes, and spirit, Felicity. To think I was
already qualified when you were born. I might have
brought you into the world, felt the first flutter of your

(Continued)

(Continued)

> fragrant life. I could have cradled you in my arms, touched
> your little face …
> Arthur.
> Yes, Felicity?
> Arthur, you could still.
> Could I? Oh, Felicity.

The fifth exercise is taken from John Byrne's *Cuttin' a Rug*. Sadie is a middle-aged, world weary, working-class Glaswegian woman. There is comic truth to be found in telling of her potentially tragic tale. The incongruity of the morbid story being told at a social occasion (a staff dance) is also central to the comedy:

> *SADIE:* That's the age my mother was when she was took … fifty one …
> coming up the stairs with the message bags … wee insurance man had to
> side-step her corpse to collect her premiums … we got a lend of the one
> and six from the woman down the stair. All Tommy got in his Christmas
> stocking that year was a nut and that fell through the hole in the toe … it
> was one of my mammy's … the stocking, not the nut … She hated nuts.
>
> (Act 1:60)

Extracts taken from:

Bennett, Alan (1985) *Forty Years On and Other Plays*, London: Faber & Faber

Byrne, John (1987) *Cuttin' a Rug: The Slab Boys Trilogy*, Harmondsworth: Penguin

Godber, John (2001) *Plays: 1*, London: Methuen

Stoppard, Tom (1968) *The Real Inspector Hound*, London: Samuel French.

In dealing with comic text, your role as a performer is paramount in ensuring that the whole comic story is as well told as it can be. As Eric Weitz notes, 'when reading a comic text, we should ask ourselves not only, 'What does it *ask* the performer(s) to do?', but 'What does it *allow* them to do?' (2009: 110; italics in original). Creating a comic role allows for discovery and creativity and places you, as performer, at the intersection of where the author and the audience converge.

Suggested further study

Reading

Below are valuable works, both for identifying and for unpacking the comic principles and buttons and for illustrating how these apply in practice within specific literary forms:

Aristotle (1997) *Poetics*, London: Dover Publications.

Beckett, Samuel (1956) *Waiting for Godot*, London: Faber & Faber

Draper, R. P. (2000) *Shakespeare: The Comedies*, Basingstoke: Macmillan Press. Textual and character analysis of the comedies

Gay, Penny (2008) *The Cambridge Introduction to Shakespeare's Comedies*, Cambridge: Cambridge University Press. Gay looks at plots, language and characters in the comedies.

Weitz, Eric (2009) *The Cambridge Introduction to Comedy*, Cambridge: Cambridge University Press

Example

Take a piece of comic text such as Samuel Beckett's *Waiting for Godot*, what Lawrence Graves terms as 'one of the most widely discussed, influential literary landmarks of the twentieth century' (2004: 1). Note how it contains superiority in the classic master–servant relationship and Commedia-style slapstick comedy in the scene in which Estragon attacks Lucky, 'kicking [and] hurling abuse at him', in Act II. Compare this with an old Vaudeville routine 'Slowly I turned' (sometimes known as 'Niagara Falls'). The routine features one actor reliving an account of taking revenge on an enemy. In the routine the actor becomes so involved in the story that he is telling that he recreates his attacks on the innocent listener to whom he is speaking. Each time the attacker comes to his senses, only to go berserk again when the listener repeats the trigger words, for example, 'Niagara Falls' that sets off the account – and the attacks – once again, starting with the words 'slowly, I turned ...'. The routine relies on repetitions that build in the scene played out; 'truthfulness' in the performances of the storyteller; in the believability of the slapstick attack and in the accuracy of the response of the victim; superiority in our realization that the victim continually prompts the attack through his/her own folly in repeating the trigger word; and the incongruity in the sheer over-the-top ridiculousness of the storyteller's actions.

These are clear examples of comic buttons (if somewhat cruel ones in this case) that might exist within a comic text. The potential for the performers is in how they recreate the scene to prompt comic release in the audience.

Audio visual

Type in 'The Three Stooges' or 'Abbot and Costello' and 'Niagara Falls' or 'Slowly I Turned' for versions of the routine.

Finally, when using text, reflect on how the physical actions (using performance skills as their basis) differ from the purely scripted descriptions. How do the performance elements improve the comedy?

Chapter 6

Comic performance in television and film

Screen acting is about absolute sincerity.
(Mala Powers, *To the Actor* 2002: xliii)

In this chapter we will look in more detail at comic performance in television and film. Brett Mills notes that for the success of sitcom as a genre, 'acting clearly plays a significant part in the ways in which comedy is made to make sense' (2005: 68), and so the comic performance craft skills that you have developed, along with your knowledge of the buttons or mechanisms for provoking laughter, need to be in place. These expertise skills, however, must then be sublimated and made less explicit for screen performance. Performing – or acting for comedy – on screen might (crudely) be described as all about 'being', or at least replicating 'being'. Put simply, reacting with 'sincerity', within the admittedly heightened context, is what is required. All your comic expertise skills need to be at your disposal, but these must be deployed in a more muted and nuanced way. Your performance skills need to be rendered less obvious, as the camera lens tends to pick up, magnify and overblow any presentational emphases. Playing up the comic reference points and showcasing the funny moments, so necessary for establishing and maintaining interplay in live stage situations, also need to be tempered for screen depictions. Any overemphatic comic performance can be read as 'telegraphing' and ends up appearing as merely excessive or indulgent.

However the simple 'being' that is often seen as the requisite for television and film performance/acting is also something of a red herring, in that performing screen comedy still requires the performers to possess expertise and performance abilities in order for the scenes to be rendered as funny as is possible. But on the other hand, the 'truthfulness', 'believability' and 'subtlety' of simple 'being' are also vital to the process – that is, Bella Merlin's 'absolute sincerity' (2010: 146). Luckily, sincere 'being' is an innate skill that we all have anyway (see Erving Goffman's ideas in *The Presentation of Self in Everyday Life* (1959) on the concept of how we are all 'acting' at all times):

By behaving in particular ways the person 'gives off', to use Goffman's terms, personal cues about the social role performances one is making and thus indexes these invisible psychological and sociocultural states … Ambiguity arises, of course where the non-normative occurs.

(Scollon and Scollon, 2003: 203)

The effective comedy performer also knows how to impersonate or reproduce someone else's 'being' and to make it appear to be utterly authentic, irrespective of the comic frame or however outrageous the premise is that surrounds and informs their actions. They know how to give their characters' actions and behaviours a still believable 'twist'. The philosopher Jean Paul Sartre observed, 'consider this waiter in the café … he is playing … But what is he playing? … he is playing at *being* a waiter in a café' (1957: 59; italics in original). The same thing holds true for comic performance on screen. In a way, it is a case of authentically impersonating people who are already busy impersonating their own roles in society! Everyone is playing 'being' in different roles in different contexts. The same person might assume the 'being', say, of a motorist and, at different times, of 'being' a pedestrian. Under different circumstances we all perform different displays of 'being'. That same person is also different when being a 'son' as opposed to being a 'father'; or when being a 'shop assistant' as opposed to being a 'customer'. Each state of being is played out differently and is entirely fluid according to the situation that the person finds himself in. The same holds true for playing comic characters on screen. Your job as a comic performer is to realistically impersonate the person who is impersonating their own 'role', while ensuring that the underlying comic potential of your character is not overlooked. Given the necessity to make less explicit the craft skills of performance (as required for the stage) and to represent these as the skills of appearing to 'be', a useful way of thinking about performance for the screen is, as the film director Patrick Tucker suggests, that 'screen acting is as much about **reacting** as it is about **acting**' (2015: 57, bold in original). Just as the person reacts to the situation or context he is faced with in order to authentically 'be', so is performance for the screen a question of authentic reaction to the situation, or to the actions of the other characters in the scene.

It is, perhaps, no surprise that the earliest screen comedy was a short scene showing a (real) human acting out a piece of involuntary and apparently inappropriate action. In 1894, Thomas Edison recorded on film a piece known as 'Fred Ott's sneeze' which showed one of his assistants sneezing. Thus 'the first movie gag' (McCabe, 2005: 3) was born and it is no coincidence that what made the earliest viewers laugh was the surprise of seeing 'being', that is, a real person performing a recognisably human reaction. The reality of (literal) release, performed with absolute sincerity, was the key to the comic effect.

Audio visual

Search for 'Fred Ott's sneeze' for the early short video of basic human transgression appearing as the beginning of screen comedy.

Type in 'fails' for videos of 'real' people falling over, breaking things and acting inappropriately. The comedy is in the social transgressions of people 'getting it wrong' (i.e. showing the principle of incongruity). As the actions are often cause-and-effect mechanisms occasioned through heedlessness, the superiority theory of comedy also applies. The videos will show you how real people (both perpetrators and spectators) authentically react to fundamentally comic events.

My own favourites fails include anything involving someone attempting a seemingly simple activity (e.g. boarding a boat that is on the water, preparing to sit on a deck-chair or to lie down on a hammock) where the inevitable spectacle of an inanimate object conspiring to scupper a human performing a basic movement task is funny in a truly Bergsonian sense!

GROUP EXERCISES

Being

Act out a waiter and customer scene – firstly make the waiter and customer 'generic'. What essential behaviours does a 'waiter' exhibit? What actions do 'customers' manifest? In what ways are these characters just 'being'? What actions and behaviours represent their essential 'waiter-ness' and their 'customer-ness'?

To add layers of comedy, incorporate incongruous elements of behaviour. Make the waiter too unctuous, slovenly, distracted or overzealous. Make the customer impatient, suspicious, indecisive or drunk. How do these layers change the characters' 'being'?

Reacting

This is a variation on the party game where you are given the name of a famous person written on a post-it note which is stuck onto your forehead. You cannot see who you are representing, but everyone else can. The object of the game is to ask questions of the group (ones that can prompt only yes-or-no answers) to establish who you 'are'. The winner is the first to correctly work out the identity of their allocated person.

In this variation of the game, you are given an unseen post-it note with an archetypal role, for example, king, peasant, tramp, soldier, priest – or with a comic stock character-type – 'the bossy mother-in-law', 'the officious civil servant', 'the domineering boss', etc. – written on it. The exercise is non-verbal. You have to work out your archetype or stock comic character by seeing how other people react to you as you move around the space. What does the way they react to 'you' tell you about your role? How do the others' reactions to the different characters and their social 'being' change your own 'being'? In what ways does your 'being' change in accordance with how others react to 'you'?

Reflect afterwards, as a group, on what came out of this exercise.

Performing with sincerity

This is a twist on the 'can I have this chair?' exercise in which students enter one by one and ask the group if they can have an empty chair to take away. The group decides yes or no to the removal of the chair depending upon how believably the request was communicated.

The sincerity of the request is everything.

To add a layer of comic impetus, the student making the request should improvise the chair as representing something else. Thus, they ask if they can take away the imaginary 'hovercraft', 'octopus', 'mess of potage', 'Archbishop of Canterbury', or whatever. Again, if the request is delivered with sufficient sincerity, the group should allow the questioner to remove the object.

Audio visual

For a selection of comic television scenes involving waiters and customers, type in 'Julie Walters'/'Two Soups'; 'The Two Ronnies'/'Complete Rook'; 'Catherine Tate'/'Restaurant' or 'Amanda'.

For film scenes type in 'The Meaning of Life' (1983) and 'Mr Creosote' for a wonderful but gross out comedy scene; or for the extended sequence in the 1968 film *The Party*, type in 'Drunk Waiter' or 'Dinner Party Scene'.

(Interestingly, if you type in 'Rowan Atkinson' – 'The Waiter' and 'The Drunken Waiter', you will find a deconstruction of the waiter role in physical comedy.)

As we saw when considering comic text in the previous chapter, the conditions for comic performance involve you operating within a skewed reality or within a heightened world. In performing in television and film the same principles and buttons that impel comic the text apply. Television and film comedies are reliant on the all same mechanisms and tropes. Take a film such as *Some Like It Hot* (Wilder, 1959) – which 'the American Film Institute voted ... the number one comedy movie of all time, a position it often occupies whenever such lists are drawn up' (McCabe, 2005: 140). The film features comic, stock devices that would not have seemed out of place in an Aristophanic, Shakespearean or Commedia dell'arte piece. Incongruities such as cross dressing, misunderstandings and mistaken identities abound; superiority features in the status play that occurs between the different characters; stock characters appear (such as the young lovers, the dizzy young female, the old man or the villain who wishes to impose a repressive regime). Music, escape and play jostle with death and repression in the skewed comic world of the film. Similarly, many of the typical comedic devices can be traced in screen comedies, through early silent films of Chaplin or Fatty Arbuckle to those of the Marx Brothers, through the Ealing comedies, to the films of Woody Allen. Screen comedies usually feature familiar performers (as Sante and Holbrook's 'semiotic markers') with star comic performers performing in the main roles. In television and film comedy the scripts may have been especially tailored to suit the abilities of a 'star' comedian's established persona as, for example, in the case of Richard Curtis' writing for Rowan Atkinson or Nat Hiken's for Phil Silvers. Silvers, an ex-Vaudeville American comedian, starred in the seminal 1950s' US sitcom *The Phil Silvers Show* (a.k.a. *Sergeant Bilko*) (CBS, 1955–1959). As David Everitt notes in his biography of the American 'Golden Age' TV sitcom writer, Nat Hiken:

> Sergeant Bilko was the ultimate Silvers rogue, a character that allowed him to use every technique he had mastered in his twenty-five years of comedy experience ... the wonderfully agile takes; and, perhaps his greatest comic weapon of all, his brilliant, dimpled smile, dazzling with insincerity.
>
> (2001: 106)

The Bilko character, in turn, drew from ancient comic stock character models of the conniving chiseller figure, defined by Chris Ritchie as they appeared in classical comedy, as 'the professional flatterers ... the professional joker ... the soldier's satellite ... the agreeable parasite ... the social handyman or fixer' (Ritchie, 2006: 26). In drawing on this classical comic type and by appropriating many of Silvers' own characteristics, between them, Silvers and producer/writer Nat Hiken created the comic character of Sergeant Ernie Bilko. In so doing, they also influenced a sitcom formula that is traceable in the US, through sitcoms such as *Barney Miller* (ABC, 1974–1982), *Taxi* (ABC/NBC, 1978–1983) and *Frasier* (NBC, 1993–2004). Jim Burrows, the director of *Cheers* (NBC, 1982–1993) and *Friends* (NBC, 1994–2004) described Nat Hiken as 'a founding father of the situation comedy' (Everitt, 2001: xiii). In the UK, the sitcoms of Jimmy Perry and David Croft and Ben Elton can be seen to follow the *Bilko* format, where a central manipulator is surrounded by a put-upon ensemble comprising a gallery of comedic feeds, patsys and co-conspirators who attempt to best authority and to improve their lot through, often, nefarious means. *The Phil Silvers Show* ran for 142 episodes between 1955 and 1959, was internationally syndicated and, ironically, became a victim of its own success, with the CBS network finding it cheaper to syndicate the numerous reruns rather than to make any new programmes after 1959.

On screen, in a comedy, you may be called upon to play a supporting (i.e. a much more reactive) role and, given the prevalence of stock characterisations in film and television you may be performing much more of an ensemble function in realising the comedy as a whole.

Furthermore, the tendency to present stock characters in comedies means that, as a performer, in terms of casting, the way you look can affect the roles you are offered (i.e. if you are not already a star performer)! Your gender, age, height, weight, hair colour or facial characteristics, even your previous screen work, might prove significant in how you find yourself being cast. Your appearance is a more significant indicator of your likely contribution to the comic effect. For example, the British comedy actress Pat Coombs (1926–2002) was highly familiar to her contemporary screen audience as a player of specific, comic 'types'. Her career started on radio with Arthur Askey and Irene Handl as the downtrodden daughter Nola in *Hello Playmates* (BBC, 1954–1955). From then on, Coombs became a well-known face in British television comedy, carving a niche as an endearingly dotty character and comic feed. As Anthony and Deborah Hayward note:

> Whenever a dithering, giggling slice of the female race was needed in British TV comedy, Pat Coombs would be there. She was a foil to comedians such as Eric Barker, Eric Sykes, Terry Scott, Marty Feldman, Reg Varney and Dick Emery, before moving on to more restrained, elderly characters.
>
> (1993: 64)

Familiarity with the type of persona that Coombs performed in her previous character work signalled some of the comic meaning within her subsequent performances. In TV sitcom, as Casey *et al.* note, 'the stereotype is used as an economical way of establishing character types' (2008: 269). Regrettably, perhaps, therefore, you might find that your perceived casting bracket as a *purely* comedy performer might render you more limited in the types of roles you are offered.

At any rate, in order to be an effective performer in on-screen comic roles, your craft or expertise skills will still play a large part in acting for the screen. The comic performer's interpretive input thus remains a crucial facet in supporting or, in many cases, improving the script. As the actor and comedy feed Nicholas Parsons states, 'any inventive performer will always try to improve the comic potential of the part he is playing' (1994: 192). Conversely, a good television or film script requires less performer 'assistance'. The actor Nigel Hawthorne, for example, referred to the performer's response to a 'good' script, in this case, that of the sitcom *Yes Minister* (BBC, 1980–1984):

> 'Surely the script's funny enough in itself, we don't have to try to make it funny'. We solemnly agreed there and then that come what may, we would play it for real – with a comic awareness of course.
>
> (2002: 248)

The performer's input, nevertheless, is always the most vital element in making the comedy come to life. Compare, for example, Basil Fawlty's goosestep (as executed by John Cleese the performer) in the transmitted episode of *Fawlty Towers* (BBC, 1975: Episode 6, Series 1), as opposed to the rather bland and bald scripted 'stage direction' version (as suggested by John Cleese the writer):

> He places his finger across his upper lip and does his Fuhrer party piece ... he performs an exaggerated goose-step out into the lobby, does an about-turn and marches back into the dining room.
>
> (Cleese and Booth, 1988: 156)

Just as for stage, the performance elevates the written text and is what 'makes' the comedy.

Comedian Bob Monkhouse spoke thusly of John Cleese's characterisation of Basil Fawlty in *Fawlty Towers* (BBC, 1975, 1979):

> All [was] rendered joyous to behold by Cleese with more than just precise timing, energy and originality. The man invested more than his skills in bringing Fawlty to life: he put himself in.
>
> (1993: 47)

In some cases, then, the performance is everything, as, for example, the television reviewer Tom Sutcliffe notes of the contemporary BBC sitcom *The Persuasionists* (BBC, 2010):

> Comedies like this don't require subtle acting skills so much as inspired clowns. What the jokes need to work isn't emotional or psychological nuance (that sense of truth) but exuberant comic salesmanship.
>
> (2010: 19)

In instances like this, your comic craft skills remain particularly important.

Audio visual

For John Cleese's goosestep, type in 'Fawlty Towers'/'Don't Mention the War'.

Similarly, it is difficult to equate the bald stage directions in the significantly titled script version of *Monty Python's Flying Circus – Just the Words* (Chapman *et al.*, 1989: 183) with the ultimate performance in, say, Cleese's 'Ministry of Silly Walks'. Type in 'Monty Python', 'Ministry of Silly Walks'.

Achieving interplay

The element of interplay which is so important to comic performance is, obviously, almost impossible to achieve in film and television scenarios when there is no live audience present as is the case in a theatre setting. Here too, however, as Andy Medhurst notes, 'the core mission of all ... comedy (is) the eliciting of complicity' (2003: 140), but interplay and complicity are extremely difficult for comic performers to achieve when working within the media of television and film. In television comedy, especially in sitcom, the presence of a studio audience is, accordingly, common practice, in order to recreate impressions of immediacy, communality and rapport. Where no live studio audience is diegetically included as part of the finished product, the solution is often artificial. As 'TV comedy without a studio audience is ... problematic. [So] a CBS executive, named Charlie Douglass, invented canned laughter' (Carr and Greeves, 2006: 118). Charles Douglass (1910–2003) invented the 'Laff Box' in 1953 to create (and later to augment) the laughter track for television comedy programmes. His *Guardian* obituarist Christopher Reed notes that Douglass' invention, for American popular culture academic Robert Thompson, 'is the "rhythm, syntax and grammar of comedy, which depends on pauses supplied by people laughing"' (Reed, 2003: 39).

As a tool for shaping comic response to televised comedy, studio audiences have provided a vital element, to an extent that the Scottish comic actor Rikki Fulton noted on his visit to the US, 'what interested me was that they brought in two audiences for the shows and could put right any problems in the second sitting' (1999: 282).

In contemporary British television comedy, the presence of a studio audience is still a vital signifier of intended comic response. A lack of audience or canned laughter often signifies comedy that presumes towards realism or more satirical aims, for example, *The Office* (BBC, 2001–2003); *The Thick of It* (BBC, 2005–present); *The Royle Family* (BBC, 1998–2006); while the presence of a studio audience or the use of a laughter track depicts more traditional, populist aspirations, for example, *The IT Crowd* (Channel 4, 2006–); *My Family* (BBC, 2000–) or *Two Pints of Lager and a Packet of Crisps* (BBC, 2001–2009). As the British stand-up comic and actor Chris Addison noticed, apropos of US sitcom:

> Have you noticed that all the Monday-night sitcoms on CBS are studio-audience sitcoms and all of NBC's Thursday night sitcoms are single-camera sitcoms? The NBC ones get all the good reviews and the CBS ones get all the ratings!
>
> (Hall, 2008: 24)

More recently, a multi-camera, live-audience approach has been taken by the award-winning but 'stagy and stylised' (Gilbert, 2011: 22) sitcom *Miranda* (BBC, 2010–2014). Writer/performer Miranda Hart stated, 'I want to do looks to camera. I want a studio audience. And I want each episode to end with a musical number' (Walker, 2011: 12).

The intention behind such complicity-generating features is that the viewer at home is made to feel that s/he is participating in appreciating the comedy as a communal activity. This overt attempt to make the viewer feel like an extended audience member equates to David Marc's dictum that 'all forms of TV comedy are video approximations of theatre' (Mills, 2005: 38). An audience for a comic 'spectacle' can attain some form of 'membership' through ongoing, acknowledged, joint participation in an event where their laughter, as a response to comic stimuli, unifies them as a (mainly) 'like-minded' audience for that period they exist as an entity.

The actor David Jason refers to the presence of a studio audience while playing comedy as 'intrusive' (Taylor, 1994: 119) and the same sense of discordance can also hold equally true for the viewer, who may feel alienated by what s/he perceives as disproportionate or undeserved 'live' laughter from the invited studio audience. As J. B. Priestley states, they laugh too easily and loudly at bad jokes and give the performer nothing 'to play against – bouncing the ball of comedy against a wall and not into – a heap of slush' (1976: 158–160).

For the performer, in practice, when working in recorded forms of television comedy, there is always the problem of which audience to play to – to communicate with. Should you pitch your performance at a 'larger' and 'broader' performance level more appropriate for the live studio audience? Or should you deliver a more muted performance that translates more effectively through the medium of the television?

> The actor is faced with a dilemma if he goes for a full-bloodied [*sic*] performance – he may be much appreciated by the studio audience,

and raise the laughs they are there to provide; too muted a performance won't raise a titter but may be acclaimed by the television critics (who may be surprised by the lack of audience response).

(Taylor, 1994: 118)

It is also illuminating to watch, for example, again a classic sitcom such as *Fawlty Towers* (BBC, 1975, 1979) and note where the studio audience does NOT laugh – for example, it is noticeable that the more surrealistic whimsicalities of the Major (played by the splendid character actor Ballard Berkeley) often pass in silence by the studio audience who are presumably more receptive to responding to the broader, farcical elements of the overall comic narrative and tone of the comedy.

Martin Jarvis refers to 'the seductive presence of the studio audience ... it's essential to be real for the cameras, while timing laughs that come from the three hundred people watching the recording' (1999: 133). Certain famous comedy performers were in no doubt as to which audience to play to. For example, Arthur Askey was 'always playing to the camera' (Jimmy Grafton in Wilmut, 1989: 212), while Morecambe and Wise had special rostra built within the TV studios so that they 'could work over the camera to the (live, studio) audience' (ibid.: 225). The 'Two Ronnies', Barker and Corbett, in *The Two Ronnies* (BBC, 1971–1987) differentiated their playing between the present, live audience and the audience at home:

We did everything to keep the audience warm – you'd pull silly faces, shove your glasses up your nose, anything, right up to the opening word of the next sketch.

(Barker, 1988: 114)

And:

Ronnie C and I used to psych each other up during filming for the *Two Ronnies*; you had to be about twenty per cent higher to make up for having no audience, 'Energy, energy, energy' we'd tell each other, just before each take.

(Ibid.: 120)

Many otherwise successful live comedy performers, such as Scots comedienne Renee Houston or the variety superstars the 'Crazy Gang', never mastered the exigencies required in the transition of their comic interplay from stage to television – 'I didn't care for television much ... I always felt terribly shut in' (Houston, 1974: 119); And, 'that ugly little eye isn't kind ... we need a happy laughing crowd out front and not the clinical atmosphere of a studio and a specially invited audience' (Flanagan, 1961: 196).

The difficulties that the comic performer experiences in establishing interplay while working within the different media is perhaps best summed up by the American actor Jack Lemmon:

> Live in front of a theatre audience, you depend on the feedback. Occasionally you set up the joke, do it and nothing happens, they don't react. And there you are, you and the audience, both a little bit embarrassed. You've misfired somehow and they know it ... You signalled to them that you expected a laugh and they're aware that they didn't. There's a loss of mutual confidence. It can take you five minutes to get them back. But it's different with a dramatic scene when it goes adrift. You can hear them moving around a little bit, that tight wire between you and the audience may have a little slack in it, but what you're doing still holds a little interest so it works. That fact alone makes drama less complicated ... Early on, I learned from a few films that were not cut well, poorly edited, that you cannot count on a laugh and you cannot time a laugh on film.
>
> (Monkhouse, 1998: 128)

In cinematic forms, where, overwhelmingly, there is no studio audience or canned laughter, comic performers lose the potential for establishing complicity even more comprehensively. Comedians surrender their transmission of interplay to the director and editor. As the filmmaker and director Dusan Makavejev expresses this, 'director and editor produce a certain amount of "acting" for each actor ... selecting and improving what was originally done' (Callow, 1992: 99). On film, the comic performer is further distanced from exercising h/er control of complicity with the audience. As Simon Callow, on working with Makavejev, laments:

> [It is] one of the passive elements of being an actor in a film. You can give rise to extraordinary images which are absolutely nothing to do with you. You don't really know what the image you're part of is like. You can't see it ... it really does mean that you become completely passive ... you have to become living furniture.
>
> (Ibid.: 208–209)

Makers of comic film can be alive to the need for interplay in their work. As Fiona Gordon remarked during a question-and-answer session, after a showing of their film *Rumba* (Abel and Gordon, 2008) at the ICA London in July 2009:

> What's important to us was to keep the theatre in the cinema ... we wanted to keep this idea of having with the audience a sort of complicity and you use your imagination ... you know it's false and we know it's false – and we hope you take part in the make-believe.
>
> (*Rumba*, 2008: DVD Extras)

However, it is also apparent that some degree of interplay/complicity can still be realised by certain comic performers on film, in highly individual ways. Interplay can be perceived, even in the form of sitcom where the 'live' audience is normally 'unacknowledged' – sometimes overtly, as in the device of Frankie Howerd's complicity-inducing, direct audience address 'prologues' in *Up Pompeii* (BBC, 1969–1970); or in Miranda Hart's self-aware direct addresses to camera in *Miranda* (BBC, 2010–2014); or in Ricky Gervais' rather less self-aware significations of his 'playing' to the camera as David Brent in *The Office* (BBC, 2001–2003).

Moreover, Roger Wilmut claims that George Formby's 'combination of innocence and knowingness … gave him an appeal which is strong even for a modern audience seeing his films' (1989: 78). Milling and Barnham concur:

> The spirit of Formby is in the eyes. There is a smile in them that can turn to the most touching pathos, like the eyes of a spaniel. There is also in them an unquenchable optimism that sums up the very essence of his character.
>
> (2004: 144)

Here, Raymond Durgnat's observation in *A Mirror for England* resonates, 'the English comedians have a homely, hot-oven intimacy whose artistic quality becomes more apparent as time passes' (1971: 172). Similarly, in his tribute to the 'Carry-On' film actor Charles Hawtrey, Roger Lewis notes:

> Whenever he is situated in a scene that he'll continue to glance or stare into the camera – or perhaps it's more accurate to say that he's gazing into the audience. He catches your eye; there's a collusion as he pirouettes into place and gives his secret smile.
>
> (2001: 15)

Furthermore familiarity, likeability and some degree of interplay may be signalled by the experienced comic performer, even in the playing of stock comic characters (recognisable stereotypes all) – such as the domineering, older female 'battle-axe' figure, for example, Doris Ewell (Joan Sanderson) in *Please Sir!* (LWT, 1968–1972); Grace Riggs (Rosemary Leach) the 'difficult' mother in law figure in *My Family* (BBC, 2000–2011); or, in corollary, the comic staple of the hen-pecked husband – George Roper (Brian Murphy) in *George and Mildred* (ITV, 1976–1979), or, once again, Basil Fawlty (John Cleese) in *Fawlty Towers* (BBC, 1975, 1979). There is also the 'quirky neighbour' character – Dorian Green (Lesley Joseph) in *Birds of a Feather* (BBC, 1989–1998); Doris (Margaret John) in *Gavin and Stacey* (BBC, 2007–2010); Mary Carroll (Doreen Keogh) in *The Royle Family* (BBC, 1998–2000, 2006, 2010).

To achieve interplay in screen performance it is necessary to have an idea in your mind as to who the audience is that you are performing for. Through 'the device of … the imaginary … ideal audience' (Chekhov, 2002: 146 and 151) you can develop awareness of what Robert Allen terms an 'implied, fictional reader' (1987: 88). It is usually best to conjure this imagined audience in your mind as being one particularly discriminating viewer or reader whom you are trying to communicate with through your performance. As the psychologist Sigmund Freud noted, 'the comic is content with only two persons, one who finds the comical, and one in whom it is found' (1905, 1964: 70) and your implied, imaginary viewer should be thought of as someone who is open and alive to appreciating your performance effects. But they should also be imagined as someone of taste, intelligence and discrimination who will not be fobbed off with any cheap tricks or inauthenticity!

Another way to think of achieving interplay in onscreen comic performance is to erect your own internal fourth wall – but thinking of it as one that is transparent (so, in effect, actually more like a 'fourth window'). When you are performing, imagine that your fictional viewer can see your innermost thoughts, reactions and motivations through this window. This will have the effect of you communicating sincerely and authentically without resorting to over emphasis which can be a big danger in filmed comedy. Screen comedy often works best when we know what the character is thinking (even if it is in opposition to what she or he is doing or 'being'). Ricky Gervais as David Brent is an excellent example of a performer whose 'window' is easy to see through – his insecurities and sudden doubts are clear to see yet may be hidden – even from himself – by the comically presented front of 'being' that he displays.

Audio visual

For a fascinating display of how our 'being' bleeds through, see an astute reader of human behaviour, actions and motivations in action. The illusionist and human psychology exponent Derren Brown can tell all sorts of things about people from what we exude from behind our 'fourth windows'. Type in 'Derren Brown guesses professions' for an amazing demonstration of one spectator's ability to read clues about characters and roles from the outer-to-inner states that are presented to him.

Type in 'David Brent', 'The Office', 'life philosophy', for a good scene which shows Gervais (as Brent) and his 'fourth window' in action. As he talks to the camera about his beliefs, Brent cannot see himself as we see him, and his confident, inappropriate, cringe-worthy remarks are at odds with his real inner insecurities. We can see right through his words to the real character beneath.

For some great reaction shots, see Bea Arthur as Dorothy Zbornak in *The Golden Girls* (NBC, 1985–1992). Note how we can read what Dorothy is thinking about, say, Rose's interminable stories, even when she is not speaking. Type in 'Golden Girls'/'Rose Nylund'/'St. Olaf stories'.

GROUP EXERCISES

These exercises are designed to help you develop the skills of collusion and building complicity for screen performance.

Behind the eyes

In this exercise, students convey messages only through their eyes. The rest of the group sit close up and study the performer's eyes. Firstly, the performer should try to convey an emotion through their 'fourth window'. As subtly as possible, the performer indicates through their eyes whatever it is that they are feeling or experiencing. Can the rest of the group identify the correct reaction that has been conveyed?

Then the performer should try only to 'leak' what they are actually and genuinely feeling in the moment. Can the rest of the group accurately read those emotions?

In a further extension to this exercise, the student performer may think through one of the speeches or scenes from a comic text that they have been working on. They should 'live' the emotions and motivations of the piece, conveying these only through their eyes. Again, is it possible for the spectators to read correctly the 'being' that they are seeing?

Thought policing

Students are given a secret instruction which they must convey to the rest of the group non-verbally. Again, the rest of the group must get near to the student performer and read the clues from their eyes and face. An instruction might be something like, 'get the rest of the group to leave the room/to move a chair/to sing a song/ to join hands' etc. The performer should intimately convey the thought process to the rest, allowing the force of the thought to be read rather than using any physical clues as to the intended action. How accurately does the group interpret the silent command? What does this tell us about how readable motivations and intentions can be in close-up?

Gives and tics

Following on from Derren Brown's 'guessing the professions' video (above), in this exercise, three students are instructed to tell stories about themselves, interspersed with the odd (plausible) lie. Again, while scrutinising the

(Continued)

(Continued)

performers as close up as possible, the rest of the group must decide which versions were told in the most 'truthful' way and which were less so. Were there any surprises about how easily 'sincerity' can be faked? (There is a joke saying, often attributed to the American comedian George Burns, that goes 'acting is all about honesty. If you can fake that, you've got it made'!)

A variation on this exercise is for the three performers to collaborate beforehand, deciding on a story which happened to one of them and then each retelling it as if it had happened to them. Once more, the spectators must decide which student was telling the truth and which was not. Note whether there were any giveaways – little tics or 'gives' – which supplied any clues as to the truth or fakery of the account.

Technical considerations

The way that scenes are filmed for screen means that your performance will be almost certainly contained within a long shot (LS), medium shot (MS), medium close up (MCU) and, very occasionally, a big close up (BCU). This is, of course, very different to theatre performances where the 'viewfinder' is normally rather more fixed and where each spectator will decide for themselves what they will look at in the *mise en scene* at any given moment. The distance between viewer and performer on stage is much greater and therefore performance in theatre needs, generally speaking, to be larger in scale and in comedy, as we have seen, is more mimetically interpretative of the text, requiring audience–performer intercommunicative awareness. The camera tends to pick up every nuance of your performance, so it is a case of selecting your performative effects more carefully and tailoring the scale of your performance to be readable within the frame. In filming, the way in which each scene is being shot is usually evident during the process from the way the camera is positioned (unless you find yourself in an old-fashioned three camera studio sitcom set-up, which is increasingly rare). Normally, the scenes will be captured in different variations of shot size to give the director and editor the options of how the scene will cut together and be presented in the final version. Given that comedy often relies on others' reaction (to the inappropriate behaviour, the loss of face or to the outrageous activity that is being presented), some of your performance may even be captured as a pure reaction shot. As the director Patrick Tucker notes, 'on screen … we will concentrate on the main unknown – what the **listener** is thinking – and that means watching her **reactions** … the listener is often reflecting what **we** the audience should be thinking and feeling' (Tucker, 2015: 57; bold in original).

Tucker also notes that 'you must change your performance **according to the size of shot**' – a long shot requires a 'large, melodramatic style of acting'; medium shot an 'intimate' theatre style; medium close up needs 'reality' while a big close up is 'pillow talk' (ibid.: 10; bold in original).

While Tucker's description of adopting a 'melodramatic' style in long shot is too overstated and would only look odd, the 'intimacy' and 'reality' that he advocates for the closer shot choices are helpful. Practising the appropriate 'size' of your performance for comedy purposes is, therefore, highly recommended and with the modern technology that we have readily available, it is now a simple matter to film yourself, to experiment with performing within different frame sizes and then to download the results to study and evaluate. Practicing which performance levels work best with different sizes of shot is very informative. On the one hand, you may find there is, occasionally, some value in employing a 'broader' performance in a shot – for example, executing a larger-than-life reaction that is guaranteed to cue a laugh, like comedian James Finlayson's previously mentioned 'double take and fade away' (Halliwell, 1987: 309) in the Laurel and Hardy films. Indeed, John McCabe tells of Finlayson's 'most superb double take and fade away' in the film *Big Business* (James W. Horne, 1929):

> As the cameras started to whirr, he went into what he meant to be his most spectacular fade-away ever. It was. On the snapping back his head struck the brick portal of the doorway knocking him cold – a notable example of giving one's all for one's art.
>
> (1966: 100)

On the other hand, as stated, more subtlety generally works better for screen performance. This is partly because we know that the audience will read and supply much of the interpretation for itself, given the visual clues which they are directed to see. Lev Kuleshov, an early Soviet filmmaker, experimented with a montage technique in which he cut different images together in sequence with the same, expressionless, face of an actor. The juxtaposition of each image – a woman, a coffin, plate of soup – shown in conjunction with the actor's face was then evaluated by audiences as to what they read the actor to be 'thinking'. Audiences reported the immobile actor's gaze to be reacting with very different emotions – for example, love, sadness, hunger and so on – according to the preceding image. This indicates that an audience will attach a specific meaning to an actor's 'reaction', ascribing an emotion to an otherwise expressionless face when given other filmic information.

Effective comic performance on screen exists, then, somewhere between the excessive reaction shot and doing absolutely nothing. In essence, however, these reactions are tools within your skills set to be called upon and to be used accordingly. The performance choice that you make will depend on the 'type' of comedy (e.g. is it a broadly farcical piece or intended as a 'slice of life' presentation?). Furthermore, depending on the size and scale of the actions required at different points within the film or television narrative, you may be called upon to make your performance more, or less, explicit. You may well find that keeping it more contained is what generally works best.

But do remember that you will be guided by the director in this. They will be able to see the scale of your performance and how this reads within each shot and can monitor how your performance will fit in with the rest of the piece. Nonetheless, if you, the performer – have an awareness of the scene and how it interconnects with and furthers the entire story; you know what your character's intentions, motivations are; understand what the comic buttons are that needed to be pressed within the scene; can work in conjunction with the other performers and the director to ensure that the scene reads as effectively as possible; and are able to make informed choices about how to use your comic performance skills to best advantage – then you will be doing your job well. Bear in mind that some of your performance on screen might be filmed in close-ups which are:

> The fruits of film, and they reveal the characters' inner thoughts and feelings ... In film, learning the thought processes is vital, as these thoughts are exactly what the director captures in the close-ups. In many ways, film is the ultimate medium for subtext and inner monologues.
>
> (Merlin, 2010: 148)

For this reason, knowing your character's intentions and motivations are essential as, if you intimately know them, these should be readable too by the audience through your 'fourth window'. Thus, the route to discovering your character's psychology through the use of Stanislavskian means to explore inner truths suits television and film performance particularly well. But, in comedy, it is an inner truth that still contains a comic twist. Comic characters are (almost always) seriously true to themselves and remember that this is what you are trying to convey.

Practice makes perfect and the key thing is to experiment. Record and film yourself to see what works.

Audio visual

Reaction shots

To note how much we imbue the emotion to the reaction shot, type in 'Kuleshov effect' to see this early experiment in cinematography.

Type in 'Punch and Judy' to see how we can know what the puppet Mr. Punch is thinking at various points in the narrative, even though he has only one painted expression! Similarly, animated characters often 'convey' much reaction through very simple redrawing of the facial features – see, for example, 'Family Guy', 'Stewie and Brian' 'songs named after a girl'.

Comic performers range from using minimal reactions – see, for instance, 'Buster Keaton' in the boxing match in 'The Battling Butler' (Keaton, 1926) or Jacques Tati's reactions to modern architecture in 'Play Time' (Tati, 1967).

Contrastingly, for larger reactions, see 'James Finlayson', 'double take' or Oliver Hardy's looks to camera in 'chimney bricks'/'Dirty work' (French, 1933).

Ricky Gervais parodies the overdone comic reactions (and other comic performative excess) in his spoof sitcom 'When the Whistle Blows' in 'Extras' (BBC, 2005–2007).

EXERCISES

These exercises should be filmed, downloaded and evaluated. What is too much, what size and scale works best?

Kuleshov reactions experiment

As in the famous experiment, film yourself expressionless and juxtapose images (perhaps photos from your phone of family, friends, or favourite pictures you have taken). What do you 'read' into your own reactions to each image? What is the overall effect of the finished montage?

Monologue

Pick a comic text – or narrate a funny story, that is, something that happened to you (or to someone else). Perform the monologue in different sizes for long shot, medium close up, close up and big close up. Review the footage – what levels and intensity of performance work best? Re-edit the results to see which size of shot moves the story along most effectively.

Monologue reactions

Try the same exercise but film yourself reacting to the monologue or story. Either have another student play it out – or record your reactions to the filmed version of yourself performing the monologue. Focus only on the reactions.

(Continued)

(Continued)

Where might it be useful to intercut a reaction shot into your filmed monologue (above) to further the story or to heighten the comic effect of the moment?

One key thing is not to show you know you are being funny when you perform your monologue as this will be readable by the audience. Concentrate, nonetheless, on allowing the audience in – through interplay – from behind your 'fourth window'.

These clips may provide material for your showreel. A montage of different levels, types of shot, actions and reactions displays your abilities in working for screen better than any solo, 'fixed' piece to camera.

YouTube references

For monologue ideas type in 'Gerard Hoffnung', 'Address to the Oxford Union', 'Bricklayer';

'Anna Russell', 'The Ring der Nibelungen'; 'Joyce Grenfell Monologues'; 'Comedy roasts', 'Jonathan Winters', 'Foster Brooks'

(Seemingly truthful 'screen' reactions while performing comedy seen above, while, probably best to be avoided when performing for the screen below ... !):

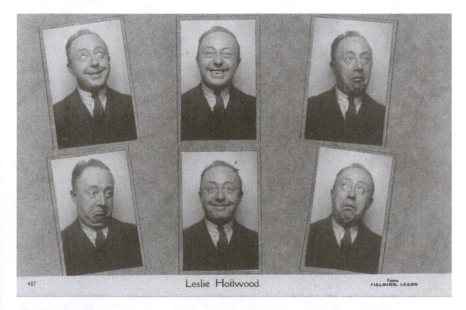

Leslie Hoilwood.

Online comedy

When it comes to recording comic performance, everyone can now be a film maker. New media thrives on 'user generated content [which] brings within our reach the possibility of being producers in our own right' (Lister et al, 2009: 221). Making your own work provides excellent performance practice opportunities and is, potentially, a useful calling card for the creative industries. If you can write, produce and perform good comedy, there is an international audience for your work. There is still an appetite for real people doing real things (just like the early twentieth century film showing 'Fred Ott's Sneeze') that press the spectators' comic buttons following the same age-old comic principles. For example, the notorious and popular YouTube video posting of the 'Star Wars Kid' (in which a well-upholstered Canadian youth cavorts with a golf ball retriever that doubles as a makeshift light sabre in homage to his cinematic heroes) comes complete with comic buttons and principles at play. There is the protagonist's (unwitting) expertise in the manner in which he performs the actions. His serious demeanour and his direct interplay in 'playing' to the camera underlines and counterpoints the essentially skilful way in which he executes the routine. It is possible to marvel at his thoroughness and dedication to the task. The unlikeliness of the performer – he is, perhaps, far from being ideal casting as an action hero on account of his age and size – adds incongruity to the overall comic meaning. There is superiority to be found in the interpretation and response to the performance from the audience's perspective – potential mockery of the boy's 'inappropriate' behaviour and in his failure to bridge Callow's 'gap between the way the character sees himself and the way the audience sees him' (1991: 36). In an essential reading of the comic cause and effect, the universality of the clip's appeal is underlined by its notoriety and ubiquity.

Similarly, another comic performance viral hit (reportedly at around 700 million hits at the time of writing) is the viral video of the 'Numa Numa Guy'. This is, again, a self-recorded sequence, and, in this instance, a similarly unlikely (young, male, large, geekish) individual gurningly lip-synchs and waves his arms about to a Moldovian pop song. Comic expertise is evident (performative accuracy and detail), and incongruity, superiority and interplay are, once again, all apparent. The 'Numa Numa Guy' may be a particularly unlikely boy band lover but he uses virtual technology to communicate a different – and comic - message to an international audience.

Given that Marshall McLuhan's notion of a 'global village' (1962) has become a reality in the early twenty-first century, comic communication will continue to be achieved through emerging technologies in which 'today, the status of the visual is on the rise' (Van Leeuwen, 2005: 52) and you can harness this technology to spread your own comic performance. As Kevin Williams states:

New media technologies such as satellites and the Internet represent 'a quantum leap' forward in the capacity of the media to bring people closer together.

(2003: 223)

For comic performance and response, the 'shared' 'laughter' of 'recognition' (Wright, 2007: 11; Lau, 1998: 24) will, in the new media formulae, be achieved through Auslander's notion of 'liveness', that is, that the 'virtual' community will drive the comic communication mode and content, 'from the specific audience situation, not from the spectacle for which that audience has gathered' (2008: 65). The Internet as a global forum for the creation and reception of comic significations in particular is increasingly evident. The YouTube 'rich list' of 2010 reveals that 'nine of those that appeared in the top ten are comics' (Brown, 2010: 16), while 'webisodes' are becoming of interest to British comic production companies such as 'Baby Cow' (Burrell, 2010a: 12). In emerging media, specific comedy download sites have sprung up, including Log.tv (Bownass, 2008: 13) or:

Funny Or Die, which is essentially a version of YouTube for comedy ... [it] has become the 'go to' venue for film and TV producers searching for new talent, or interesting fresh material. In the eyes of some experts, it could be a blue print for the future of television [it] contains thousands of short, comic video clips

(Adams, 2009: 23)

Writing in 2013, Adam Gray reported that 'YouTube has 800 million unique viewers per month' (145). British comedians (including Ricky Gervais) use 'podcast' to broadcast their performances (Whitehouse, 2009: 36) or, like Stephen Fry, use *Twitter* for 'road testing one-liners and even putting on stand-up gigs' (Hall, 2009: 40; Akbar, 2010: 9)). Gray noted 'Twitter now has more than 500 million users who currently send over 200 million tweets every day' (113) and for comedy audiences, Twitter is an ideal marketing tool in its approach. Tweets, moreover, can be constructed like concise mini-jokes. When using Twitter for publicising your work, 'be audience driven' (Kawasaki and Fitzpatrick, 2014: 126) but heed the comedian Dave Gorman's advice when he warns against Twitter becoming a forum for 'mass platitudes' (2014: 193). Webcasts and video sharing sites are, it would appear, the new lingua franca of performance modes. 'YouTube (created in 2005) is the variety show writ large' (Walker, 2009: 12). It is clear that the web will continue to provide the likely forum for continuing presentations of comedy. In doing so, it follows on in a tradition that harks back to comic performance's locus in variety and vaudeville formulae of Anglo-American, popular, modern entertainment, in which 'even though much modern comedy has sprung from other roots there runs through it the tradition of music-hall and Variety humour' (Wilmut, 1989: 226). This tradition seems equally true in comedy's early twenty-first century cyberspace manifestations. One of the top ten YouTube 'hits' according to www.readwriteweb. com, with, allegedly, over 134 million worldwide viewings, is a video of an American comedian named Judson Laipply performing an extended eccentric dance routine, exhibiting physical incongruity and a comic expertise that is directly in the tradition of Max Wall – or even, of William Kemp.

Even in traditional media, comic output is in demand. Channel 4 reported that 'a yearly spend of £11m in 2009, generating 24 hours of comedy programming, will grow to an annual budget of £20.25m next year [2011] and 57 hours of television' (Burrell, 2010b).

So, taken altogether, with the advent of mobile phone video functionality, easy upload to YouTube and similar media sharing sites, podcasting and the emergence of other new digital technologies, it is easier than ever to test your skills in front of the camera. Use the media to experiment with levels of performance, with building your 'fourth window' and for trying out reactions. Film producers are increasingly asking for self-filmed audition pieces and Skype interviews are also becoming more common. Potential employers want to test how comfortable you are in front of the camera and whether you can convey truthful and real performance on film. Confidence, but never overplaying, in front of the camera is a skill that can be practised and perfected. Contemporaneously, the fashion for 'real' people doing real things on television and in film is what you should aim to replicate. It is worth looking at the 'reality' of action and reaction when 'normal' people get things wrong and to attempt to reproduce these 'truthful' behaviours. Here, as mentioned, online videos of 'fails' can be illuminating. Note how much funnier it is when the protagonist of the 'fail' doesn't know that they are being funny. Through testing yourself by filming your comic performance, furthermore, you will accumulate material for a showreel which is, in many ways, your CV entry into the industry.

YouTube references

For the above-mentioned videos type in 'Star Wars Kid'; 'Numa Numa Guy' and 'Justin Laipply', 'The Evolution of Dance'.

GROUP EXERCISES

Interviews

Film an improvised interview in two-shot (two talking heads in frame) where one performer is introduced (without them being told in advance) as an expert on something ridiculous, for example, the history of the phrase 'willy-nilly'; being Cher's stunt double; owning a talking grizzly bear; being the world's leading distance asparagus thrower, etc.

Download and watch the film back – where does the interviewer's reaction to what the interviewee says strengthen the comic effect?

The exercise can be re-filmed as a close up on the interviewee followed by a continuous take of the interviewer's questions and reactions and the two can then be edited together to create a comic sketch.

Make a podcast

As a 'roving reporter', deliver an improvised 'story' to camera as you move through the space. Objects in the room, people who appear in shot and any random activities that appear in the frame should be incorporated into the fictional narrative that is being told to camera. The more sensational and ridiculous the story and, in contrast, the more banal and innocent what is being described actually appears – the funnier this will be.

This exercise will make you more comfortable on camera and will help sharpen your reaction shots.

Showreel

Practise and record a finished monologue. This should be filmed as broadcast quality, so borrow or hire a good-quality camera. Pick a comic piece – again, an excerpt from, say, an Alan Bennett monologue or a Shakespearean direct address comic speech. Experiment with delivering it to the camera to test levels of performance and to see whether what you are thinking comes across. The finished film should be something that you are happy with and which shows off your expertise in the best possible light.

This exercise also provides you with practice of a speech that might be useful for any live theatre auditions that you will have.

Suggested further study

Reading

These texts consider performing on screen and in new media:

King, Geoff (2006) *Film Comedy*, London: Wallflower
Kunze, Peter (ed.) (2015) *Comedy Studies: Online and Digital Edition*, Vol. 6, No. 1, Spring

Mills, Brett (2005) *Television Sitcom*, London: BFI Publishing
Tucker, Patrick (2015) *Secrets of Screen Acting*, 3rd edition, London: Routledge

Examples

One example of a comic performer who created his own work from originally self-broadcasting on the Web is the Scottish comedian and actor Brian 'Limmy' Limond (b. 1974). Starting as a blogger, Limmy's daily comic podcasts, entitled *Limmy's World of Glasgow*, began in 2006 and featured him playing a range of comic characters. Emerging as the 'new king of angry comedy' (Hankinson, 2011: 36), the success of the sketches interest came to the attention of the mainstream UK media, and in 2010 his work was commissioned as a series by BBC Scotland, broadcast as *Limmy's Show* (BBC Scotland, 2010–2013).

Limmy invented various running characters for the podcasts and subsequent TV show. One character self-consciously and pretentiously utters phrases in the Scots' vernacular ('that's pure bampot', 'you're so 'steesher', 'why the gallas', etc. – translating as 'that's absolutely mad', 'you are so stunning' and 'why the attitude', respectively). Displaying 'otherness' through his demeanour and his use of a Glasgow 'university student' accent, the character gets promptly punched in the face by an unseen assailant. Superiority, incongruity and 'someone getting it wrong' are all evident in an example of one, five-second-long comic performance.

Another recurring Limmy character is 'Falconhoof', the presenter of a televised, premium-rate phone-in adventure game show which purports to lead callers through to winning cash prizes by participating in a 'dragons and dungeons' type quest that is narrated by Falconhoof. The comedy resides in the flamboyantly made up and ludicrously attired Falconhoof's attempts to maintain the integrity of the bombastic and fantastical scenario while taking calls from an assortment of emphatically down-to-earth, real-world subversives, for example, Glaswegian wide-boys, disgruntled ex-callers to the show or old school friends with embarrassing recollections. Pretentiousness clashes with the prosaic to incongruous comic effect. A side-swipe of superiority is also signalled in Falconhoof's inevitable come-uppance and the callers' besting and exposure of the falseness and exploitative nature of the televised 'game'.

Similarly, *Gap Yah* is a popular comedy sketch which originally appeared on YouTube in 2010. It became a viral hit and 'calling card' material for the live sketch comedy group *The Unexpected Items*, the performers who were behind the broadcast. In the sketch (and the follow-up versions), another posh, university student-type, this time named Orlando, relates his gap year adventures to a friend, Tarquin. Orlando's adventures all result in the student inappropriately 'chundering' at various points on the international historically and culturally significant heritage trail. Superiority, incongruity, repetition, excess and inappropriateness all feature in the comic message and the sketch also shows how a simple performance idea (i.e. a comic monologue) can be easily filmed, uploaded and then have mass appeal to a potential global audience.

Audio visual

For the Limmy examples, type in 'Limmy's Show', 'That's pure bampot', 'You're so steesher', 'Why the gallas?' and 'Falconhoof'.
  For *Gap Yah* type in 'Gap Yah'.

Chapter 7

Advice from practitioners

> The definition of a dramatic actor is a comedian who is not getting any laughs.
>
> (Dickie Henderson in Cotes, 1989: 55–56)

Is the comedian Dickie Henderson's joke above really the only difference there is to comic performance? The real question is how do you get the laugh while still retaining the truth of the character and plot?

This chapter consists of suggestions culled from a series of interviews (both formal and informal) which have been undertaken over the last ten years with working performers who do both comic and non-comic acting. The performers were all asked about performing comedy and whether they felt there were any 'differences' in the execution of comic performance as opposed to the more widely discussed and analysed phenomenon of 'straight' acting and, if so, what these were. In this, the performers were behaving as 'reflective practitioners', articulating what worked, what did not – and what lessons they learned for their future performance of comedy.

Firstly, it was evident that some degree of wariness in attempting analysis of something that it often seen as 'instinctual' was initially present in

Figure 7.1

some cases. As Geoff King notes, for some performers, evaluation of practice methods might actually appear to be a threatening or destabilising activity. Such performers may ascribe to a belief that what they do is, of necessity, subconscious and so dependent on intuitive processes that execution of their practice is utterly antithetical to conscious analysis. King refers to such informants as 'practitioners for whom excessive analytical probing might threaten a form of creativity that draws on a range of unstated and unselfconscious assumptions' (2006: 4). This found expression in some of the interviews with practitioners. Julian Protheroe pointed out to me that 'there is an element that is indefinable and "mysterious" – something about that is to do with being human, that is not necessarily approachable through rational enquiry'.

Some of the performers I spoke to even took the view that analysis is detrimental to the intuitive process of performance creativity. Antipathy towards reflection-on-practice is evident in some performer autobiography too. Michael Hordern expressed this reserve, 'it scares the shit out of me, my view being that an actor should learn the lines without too much cerebral interference' (1993: 162), while Ronnie Barker revealed a similar reluctance to speculate on the processes of comic performance:

> But performers involved in it tend not to get into discussions about Capital-A subjects, Art or Acting. Nobody in the business believes that comedy is easier, the people doing it are just as intent on achieving peak performances, but by and large, they get on with it.
>
> (1988: 143)

In the interviews, performers seemed more acceptant that the kind of reflection-in and on-action that is advocated in this book has some value. Su Pollard warned,

> Don't analyse – learn your craft ... Analysis comes after a few performances. Analyse then how you can improve things ... Instinct can be built on by experience and a few performances down ... Analysis ... not initially, but during a run.

Other performers were uncomfortable with the idea that there was any difference between performance approaches to comic and non-comic roles. Dolly Wells stated that 'perhaps it's dangerous to talk about "comic" and "serious" in this way? Every performance is a successful performance if it is true – truly comic or truly tragic'.

Advice on establishing truth

What emerged overwhelmingly from speaking with performers is the idea that comic performance has to be 'truthful'. As comedy actress Rebecca Front's recollected in a newspaper interview,

I remember being told, by a particularly scary teacher at drama school that although many people erroneously consider lying to be a central part of acting, in fact the opposite is true. Acting, my terrifying mentor drummed into us, 'is all about Truth'.

(2009: 36)

Front's recollection is reminiscent of George Burns' comic saw (about acting being about honesty and about good acting being faking honesty well). Finding and replicating a kind of truthful performance in comedy is perceived by practitioners as being crucial. As Vikki Michelle told me,

You have to keep the truth. You see how the writer sees the person, which accent ... how she speaks? Posh? Lower class? And the character evolves after that.

Most of the performers who attempted to elaborate on what they meant by establishing a 'comic truth' tended to agree that there was some difference between 'truth' and 'comic truth'. Some referred to an 'extra' factor that was required in comic performance. In his writings, the actor John Gielgud maintained that the actor 'may sometimes find a different kind of truth ... a solemn yet light kind for farce' (1965: 8), and this special form of interplay has also been defined by Alex Clayton as a sort of comic 'twinkle' and elsewhere as a comic 'brio' (Callow, 1991: 35) or, even, as an 'irrepressibility' (Goldman in Gruber, 1986: 189).

What, though, is actually meant by the term 'truth' in performance terms? Lee Strasberg suggests that:

The sense of truth is the last thing the actor develops ... the sense of truth is the sum total of all the experiences that the actor has had and can therefore develop only as a result of experience.

(Hethmon, 1966: 251)

How, though, is this process – the impression of truth – achieved in comic performance, which is, after all, an unrealistic and stylised form of representation? Perhaps, partly, through Robert McKee's 'theory of characterisation' which aims to 'find something admirable about the character' (in Wright, 2007: 308) – a fact corroborated in an interview with the actor Paul Beech, who continued his discussion of 'truth' with:

I mean, every character is serious to himself. If it happens to be a character who is funny, I go for the essence of the character ... if there is something about him that makes me cry – empathy – I wouldn't use the word 'truth' ... take when I did *The Rivals* ... Sir Anthony Absolute ... I discovered that the reason for his burst of temper is that he is passionate in the loss of his son and he becomes a sad man in a way as his son disappoints him ... but people still laugh.

This thought is in line with Theatre Workshop founder/director Joan Littlewood's advice to the actor Harry H. Corbett when he was playing Andrew Aguecheek in a production of Shakespeare's *Twelfth Night*: 'you're still behaving like a comic. Don't worry about being boring, play his own idea of himself, a real suitor' (Littlewood, 1994: 430).

Doing this may build rapport for the comic character by the audience. As Beryl Reid wrote,

> I have one or two theories about comedy, but it is impossible really to define. What I feel very strongly is that audiences must love the people before they can laugh at them ... the audience must feel affection for the person who is aiming to make them laugh. There has to be a great deal of affection going between the audience and the performers, whatever you're saying and however witty or clever you're being.
>
> (1985: 255)

INDIVIDUAL EXERCISE

Being

To find truthful 'being', you will use the Stanislavskian means to finding your character. This is an essential part of the process of preparing for any performance, comic or otherwise.

Stanislavski noted that 'all action in the theatre must have an inner justification, be logical, coherent and real' (2008: 46).

Apply the following Stanislavskian precepts – what he terms 'psychotechnique' to any character that you are working on:

1   Establish the 'given circumstances' of the play.
2   Find contact between your own life and your part. Use your imagination here. Ask 'what if' your character was placed in certain situations. How would he/she react?
3   Work out what your character's 'super objective' is. That is, what does he/she want most?
4   Break down the narrative into units, each with objectives.

(Continued)

(Continued)

In playing the part:

5   Maintain concentration of attention, both external and inner. Retain a sense of truth of actions.
6   Use emotional memory to explore inner motives and forces.
7   Retain observance and establish communion (interplay) with other characters (and with the audience). Adapt and adjust to one another.

(Taken from Stanislavski, Constantin (1936, 2008),
An Actor Prepares, London: Methuen)

Use these tips reflectively in a group situation. Compare your preparation (and subsequent playing) of the role with your fellow performers in order to discover what each character knows and perceives about each of the other characters that they meet in the play.

What does each character strive to show, what does each character wish and manage to hide in relation to other characters at any given time within the play?

Establishing interplay with the audience

Nearly half of the performers I spoke to mentioned some form of interplay with the audience as being necessary within comic performance. Performer/audience intercommunication seemed to delineate comic performance for them. This awareness, a kind of live, real-time evaluation and modification of performance in order to influence a desired response, is particularly germane to comic performance. Simon Callow refers to this interplay element of moderating the audience's response when he records that 'an element of control is always involved in the actor's relationship with the audience' (1984: 80–81).

Dolly Wells articulated the phenomenon of the interplay requirement in comic performance as being both a positive and negative factor, in that the necessary 'consciousness' of the audience response can lead the performer to worry that s/he is not completely absorbed in the role and 'in character' in a truly 'Stanislavskian' manner:

> There's an immediate response ... but a laugh is dangerous – it's a red herring ... there's an insecurity because you never know if you are doing your job only so far as you can gauge ... there's a feeling that I'm listening ... I've got to be 'in it' but how can I be if I'm listening out for the laugh? ... It leads to stress – you might indulge more in where it might lead you.

Arthur Bostrom, creator of the role of Crabtree in *'Allo, 'Allo* (BBC, 1982–1992), summed up the notion of interplay; how it takes a different form from working in non-comic forms of performance, and how it has to be carefully transmitted in order to be fully effective:

> Comedy is harder. But I don't find it hard in that there's more of a process. You listen to the audience's reaction for your timing. You are paying attention to the audience ... It's a fickle business with comedy performance. The audience reaction is of paramount importance to the performer's sense of satisfaction. With a straight play you are unaware. Comedy is constant feedback ... it is a strange checking that goes on and how it affects you as a performer. There is an exchange of energy. There is also with a serious play but you don't perceive it coming back in the same way. An audience rocking with laughter creates a vast energy, which is intoxicating. And the opposite ... I once had a note from David Croft in 'Allo, 'Allo – when I got the job, we didn't know if it would work till we were in front of the studio audience. It went a storm. I got cocky. David Croft said 'this time – don't come in knowing you are going to be funny'.

In interplay in comic performance, the performer is involved in a dual transmission with the audience in a specific way. As Armen Gregory told me:

> [There is a] buzz, which comes from making others' laugh. The immediacy of the response ... I have to consider the response of the audience ... comic performance is generous and sensitive to the audience.

While Paul Beech explained:

> I think because the audience reaction is instant. You are more aware when it doesn't work. It is a pleasure when it works but puts pressure on the performer.

For many performers, the interplay with the audience makes comedy more enjoyable to do. Eliza McClelland stated:

> [I get] more immediate satisfaction from potential audience response ...
> The audience teach you ... if ... the audience are with [you], the two-way energy can push the performance up a notch ... the contribution from the audience is more tangible and can be more easily used to feed your own imagination and energy. You can achieve more than you can on your own (on a good day!)

Michael Jayes reported:

> Because it relies more on technique and like maths, there is a right answer ... from the feedback of laughter – in theatre – on film you have to rely on feedback from the director ... in a successful comedy, like

when I did *Noises Off* [Michael Frayn, 1982], there was a buzz off of good comedy and rounds of applause – which audiences love.

In this way, as the playwright Friedrich Durrenmatt states, 'the audience of a comedy is a reality to be counted upon' (Corrigan, 1964: 268). Comic performance, as a system of communication, relies on interplay. This can be explicit – as in the case of the clown, where, as John Wright states, 'ignoring the fact that there are people watching you, especially if you're trying to be funny, isn't a choice that's going to take you very far' (2007: 63).

But how is this interplay actually achieved by performers in situations where no direct interplay is possible? The actress Athene Seyler describes it thus:

> When I talk of establishing direct contact with the audience I mean a subtle psychological bond, perhaps merely the subconscious acknowledgement that your job as a comedian is to point out something to the audience, and that the audience's reaction to this makes up an integral part of your job.
>
> (1943, 1990: 4)

As we have seen, this bond, once established, relies on you – the performer – reflecting in action to measure the success of your performance. It changes with every different audience. As the Edwardian comedian George Graves noted in his autobiography:

> In my own job I have learnt more by far from the audience than from any other source. In a way the comic's task is something like that of the author, for our actual past is usually a framework in which we build up our performance. And however satisfied I am at rehearsals with a joke, a bit of business or a situation, I have always tried to gather the reaction of the audience to it and to refashion my show in accordance with the public response.
>
> (1931: 148–149)

Later, in the same book, Graves talks of 'trying to sense the audience's mood' (ibid.: 184).

Despite this awareness of the audience's reaction, as the comic Dickie Henderson advised, 'the biggest trap you can fall into is listening to the audience's reaction instead of the other actors on the stage' (Cotes, 1989: 56). Similarly, expectation of a laugh can also become a pitfall for the comic performer:

> When the remembered response of the audience becomes the principal sensation of doing the play, and one starts unconsciously to engineer the repetition of that response – stops, in fact, playing the truth, the character, the situation: starts in a word to ACT IN THE PAST, to recreate

an effect. Then it stops being funny and one works harder and harder to bludgeon the audience into laughter.

(Callow, 1984: 169; emphases in the original)

Another actor, Michael Redgrave, expresses yet another danger inherent in performer/spectator interplay:

It is a fallacy to believe that the audience is *ipso facto* of assistance to the actor. It can force him to dominate their mood ... with force or tricks which are alien to the part he is playing.

(1995: 37)

The conception that the spectators 'collaborate' with the performer and are responsible, through the nature and quality of their response, for partially co-creating the comic performance was continued by Erika Poole when she played Gertrude in *The Underpants* (Sternheim/Martin) in 2006 who told me, 'I think the audience response allowed me to take the lid off Gertrude and have more of a look inside and explore her extremes more confidently'.

For others, the 'imagined' audience response still shapes their performance when they make the move from theatre to television. As Alex Woodhall confided after working on *Star Stories* (Channel 4, 2006–2008), 'I've realised that I don't need the audience so much to get to the point where I know what I am doing is good'.

Timing

The importance of timing was mentioned in over 40% of the conversations and interviews undertaken with performers about comic performance, while around 10% directly referred to 'rhythm' as being a constituent. Paul Cawley works on the premise that 'you have to be interested in the specifics of every moment ... with comic you have to attune your ear to rhythm for timing ... still truthful but looking for a different net result. In performance your ear is open'. Another respondent, Jerry Marwood, referred to 'the age-old question of timing'. He then defined mastery of timing as the way in which 'a line trips off the tongue in a certain way ... there is a magic there ... you know when it's really rocking'.

Here, rhythm connects to Theo Van Leeuwen's notion of 'the semiotic potential of tempo' that 'also derives from the meaning latent in the signifier, of the slow, medium or fast tempo itself. This then becomes more specific in context' (2005: 191). The actor and musician Michael Howcroft stressed the importance of an understanding of underlying comic rhythms in the context of interpreting comedy, 'in Moliere or well-written comedy you know where the laughs are ... sewn into the score of music of the script'.

In some instances, manipulations of rhythm contributed to utterance of comic text. As the late Stephen Howe expressed it, this can be in the delivery of lines and in the choice of specific words:

> In the first few days I feel the way and who you're going to work with – their timing ... If a gag doesn't suit you, to develop it so it is less uncomfortable, for example, the gag I do now goes, 'drink was the death of our dear devoted granny' – from 'father', then 'grandmother' to 'granny' – funnier. Same thing, 'fell on 'er 'ead' is funnier than 'fell on her head'.

Rhythm and timing can be physical. In an account of his performance as Jacob (the manservant) in an American production of *La Cage aux Folles* (Fierstein and Herman, 1983), the actor and dancer Miguel Angel put it like this:

> I became aware of pauses you needed to leave ... you get a rhythm for your speech, which is partly metered by audience reaction. I wouldn't change anything for another actor. By the second week I'd found my stride with the comic scene and when I hit a comic position, which I knew as a dancer, to changing the angle of my body ... I got a bigger laugh.

In the telling, Miguel demonstrated a physical pose which caused me, the interviewer, to laugh! Here, the physical demonstration of timing also exhibited mastery of performative skills (characterised here as 'expertise' or 'craft skills'), and in its suddenness, the gestural element manifested 'incongruity' which, in turn, duly prompted my laughter response.

A similar combination of interplay, timing and incongruity can be seen in operation in this piece of reflection-on-action taken from Martin Jarvis' published production diary of *By Jeeves* (Lloyd Webber and Ayckbourn, 1996):

> I may have found a new laugh. It's quite a good moment – after Bertie's 'Do you think that they're following it, this lot?' Intriguing how a tiny move can make all the difference: instead of having my eyes already fixed upon the house, I shifted my gaze crisply from John towards the audience as if to evaluate their intelligence. Big laugh. Then a firmer second laugh, as Jeeves decides, 'impossible to tell, sir'.
>
> (2003: 213)

As a component of comic performance, timing is one of the major 'acoustic elements of the linguistic sign [that] are an integral part of the vocal resources utilized by the actor' (Pavis, 1978: 4), while Theo Van Leewen refers to 'rhythm' as the 'segments ... the speech ... the action or the music' (2011: 169) which help provide the meaning behind the communicative event.

John Wright attempts to explain the phenomenon of timing in terms of a kind of innate, 'Multiple Intelligence' (Gardner, 1999), thus:

Most comic timing comes from the manipulation of external rhythm but most of the substance, the empathy, the depth of content, and the humanity in any interaction comes from the way we use internal rhythm ... Effective timing is more about inspiring instinctive reactions than executing accurate choreography.

(2007: 159)

Timing, as a conception of the performer's awareness and manipulation of a kind of intuitive musicality, is echoed by Oliver Double, who states that for stand-up comics timing is reliant upon 'an understanding of rhythm' (2005: 202).

In this way, many stand-up comedians use swearing as a kind of rhythmic tool within their routines. As Billy Connolly claims in an interview with David Pollock, 'it's like music ... three beats of silence before the offending word carries all the effect' (Pollock, 2009). In another interview (with Andrew Denton on Australian ABC's *Enough Rope* Programme), Connolly illustrated this effect:

There are times to swear and times not to swear and if you're ... see I swear but I'm very, very good at it and no animals were hurt while I was learning how to do it. And there's a rhythm to it. That's how you know when somebody's a good swearer. 'Why don't you go and take a fuck to yourself' [sings – laughter] 'I tell you what, why don't you fuck off?' [sings] But if you go 'oh you bloody bastard fuck' [laughter]. It doesn't work. So if you don't swear well, don't swear. Go and practise. Get a wee rhythm machine.

(*Enough Rope*, Episode 96, ABC, broadcast 20 February 2006)

Richard Boon catalogues the repetitions to be found in the routine of popular British comedian Eric Morecambe:

Morecambe's repertoire of catchphrases ('there's no answer to that', 'Oh yes, little Ern', 'This boy's a fool') insults to his partner ('short, fat, hairy legs'), or referring to Wise's imagined wig, 'you can't see the join' and visual gags (running his glasses up and down his leg or wearing them on the back of his head) were a vital and expected part of any show and a large part of the viewer's pleasure lay not simply in the inherent humour but also in the particular pleasure of watching craftsmen at work producing new laughs from old material.

(Milling and Banham, 2004: 187)

It could be argued that, to some extent, performers, in effect, control the audience and their responses though the use of the rhythms that they employ in comic practice. John Gielgud when playing John Worthing in *The Importance of Being Earnest* (Wilde, 1885) posited that:

It may sometimes be necessary to sacrifice laughs on certain witty lines in order that a big laugh may come at the end of a passage, rather than to extract two or three small ones in between, which may dissipate the sense and hold up the progress of the dialogue.

(1965: 81–82)

Comic principles and buttons

Comic principles (incongruity, superiority and relief) were seldom directly reported by performers but appeared indirectly in their discourse when they were reflecting on the constituents of comic performance. Incongruity, for example, emerged as a facet of comic performance in terms of the performer needing to have an awareness of the absurd – for example, as Armen Gregory stated, 'success in comic performance relies on several factors – timing, energy, lightness of touch, an appreciation of the absurdity of life'. Incongruity, too, was described through phenomena that were more easily describable as being demonstrably evident in the practice of other, expert practitioners. Michael Jayes spotted that:

> Some performers, for example, Roy Kinnear, can turn a concept on its head ... he consciously turned things on their head as a thought ... he made you believe that lines he was saying he was making up – even in the eighteenth century in *The Clandestine Marriage* ... he was both intuitive and aware.

Similarly, Roger Darrock told me:

> It takes some courage, I mean, opening waffling, or not on stage for five, ten minutes ... and Arthur Worsley, the vent act – he never spoke – his normal mouth and relaxed ... the dummy spoke ... Arthur Worsley only said 'yes' once in the act ... a lot of art.

Justin Giles gave a detailed description of an American performer called Frankie Kein whom he had seen performing in Las Vegas. Kein is an American-based Liza Minnelli impersonator. This impressionist clearly creates comic meaning through the use of layers of incongruity, not the least of which is that he is a non-famous male appearing as an internationally famous female:

> He embodies Lisa Minnelli so it is not a normal impersonation ... he makes the audience believe that he is Lisa Minnelli, even in the question and answer after the show ... it is something extraordinary ... an embodiment rather than impersonation. It is more comic accordingly ... it's extreme but not caricature ... real. He heightens her characteristics.

You could enjoy it even if you didn't know who Lisa Minnelli is ... a hundred per cent believable ... he does not come out of character ... affection for Lisa Minnelli, not taking the mickey.

Advice from two practitioners

Indirect references to comic buttons emerged in the advice that two practitioners I interviewed offered. The actors Andrew McDonald and Neil Stewart are both experienced practitioners of both comic and 'straight' acting. Each performer, individually, took up the theme of the importance of interplay with other actors (the ensemble). In the first piece of advice, both also indirectly mentioned the themes of superiority and playing 'truthfulness':

Recognising it is your scene

Andrew: It was a case of a group telling a story. I once did a version of *The Comedy of Errors* and the actor playing Adriana, the wife of Antipholus of Ephesus mistakes Antipholus of Syracuse for her husband and rails at him 'get yourself home' ... 'am I so ugly?', ranting and raving at her 'husband', with the payoff being him saying, 'fair dame, I know you not'.
For the joke to work the chorus has to be still. Out of the stillness, one actor had a tendency to jump up and down and say 'that's right' instead of quietly reacting. The physicality took away from the focus on Adriana. There were five people telling the story there was no need [for the actor] to create a moment and there was ample opportunity elsewhere to do so. The payoff was an earned gag between the two.

This is more about sensing the moment and reacting – giving focus appropriately.

Neil: In a play I was involved in there was a scene where one actor should have responded to a comic crescendo. Having been shouted at [by a stern sergeant-major] the performer on the receiving end should have been at the end of his tether for the comedy to make it crescendo. The actor concerned was outside looking in at that character and trying to do physical comedy rather than being the person in the situation.

Both Neil and Andrew also talked of the expertise skills being recreation of something recognisably truthful within the comic fiction and how judging the level of comic performance input is crucial.

Keep it real

Andrew: I remember doing a play reading with an eccentric actress (she must have been eccentric because she brought a dog along with her). In the reading she 'did' a comedy voice – she racked it up and got a bigger laugh – then more – now it has gone through the roof and we don't believe it any more. She'd gone through the ceiling of believability. This is another example of asking for a laugh. It was no longer grounded in believability. By the way, that reminds me – don't believe the rehearsal laughs that you get.

Neil: I remember playing in *Out of Order* at the Palace, Westcliff, and there was a great farce actor (Tony Jackson) whose timing of the laughs was amazing. I am intolerant of people milking laughs but he could put three minutes on to the play without sacrificing the truth of situation. He built the dilemma to the point where he could stop talking and just play the dilemma. We could see him thinking his own dilemma through. He was like a rat in trap but through his looks and gestures the audience would be held. He would think the thought and audience would be with him. It was ok for him to stop the show. He would listen for their reaction and once the moment had passed he would get on with the script and we'd all get on with it.

I guess he was doing it truthfully. He would hear the audience's response and he had put through a consecutive set of responses truthfully. He would feel a buzz and the correct endorphins released in his brain as it would in a real person. The audience would see him feeling it, compared with the leadenness [of non-interplay]. He would be catching the wave and it was all absolutely true.

Andrew: In a televised version of a play I recently did I was involved in a funny situation where the comedy was derived from something which I overhear, then the look I give in response as I leave the frame. The reaction look gives it the laugh. In the final filmed version, what sounds like canned laughter was put on because the joke did not work. The shot stayed on the speaker and so the shared laugh has been lost. The comedy, in this instance, came from the reaction not the speaker and this was missed.

Neil: In a play I was in, one actor did an embarassed look away. This look tells the audience 'I am a prick who is unsure of himself'. This simply conveys a lovely vulnerability and tells you all you need to know about the character.

Don't expect the laugh

Andrew: I was told a story by a director about Alfred Lunt and Lynn Fontanne – a golden couple in 1920s/1930s US acting. Every night she would ask for a cup of tea and she got a huge laugh on it. One night it didn't get a titter and she asked Lunt why. He said 'you didn't ask for a cup of tea, you asked for a laugh'. Don't play the 'comedy', play the situation.

Inappropriate laughter

Neil: Joan Littlewood apparently said 'any competent actor can make an audience laugh'. When you are in a play where the audience is permitted to release tension through laughter, actors with a reasonable degree of skill will release it truthfully. At first, they will be serious in front of an audience then when the play is well received, actors can get into a comfortable place. Everyone gets praise, there are laughs in this show, audience approval results. Because we want to be approved of as actors, if we delay this line or do this 'thing', it becomes a chase for laughs rather than a comedy. An actor likes to hear audiences laugh. Actor and playwright can become separated from each other. If a character gets approval, this can lead to bigger sweeps, to sit on it harder. The line gets a laugh and the actor thinks 'I have helped this play'. It might be that the comedy of the scene now has nothing to with the play. A mediocre laugh steals from a better laugh which the writer may have spent twenty pages trying to set up.

Advice from the cast of *Twelfth Night*

The following advice comes from actors who were involved in Principal Theatre's open-air version of Shakespeare's *Twelfth Night* in 2015.

In this interview with Alex Gilbert, who played Olivia, she talks about creating and playing the role. In the interview, Alex discusses the need for psychological, social and cultural knowledge of the character (i.e. who exactly was Olivia and how does she fit into the story?). Alex also mentions where and when Olivia leads the comic narrative and when she supports the comic story. She also muses on areas of interplay with the audience and considers the differences between approaching and playing comic roles as opposed to non-comic roles.

Interviewer: What kind of person is she?

Interesting ... So ... Olivia can be played straight or you can do it for laughs.

In the fact that ... the set-up is that she has lost her brother and her father and she is in mourning and then suddenly she falls in love. And this could be quite a tragic tale of someone trying to deal with grief and ... also form a good straight man to a lot of other funny business that's going on in the show. However I think she is quite funny.

The fact that the turn-around in the first act where she is completely in mourning – never wants to speak to anyone, never wants to, you know, even contemplate talking to Orsino let along marrying him and then within the space of a ten minute scene has completely turned the whole thing on its head and she's mad with desire, then is quite randy, I'd say, throughout the rest of the play ... she is fun to play in that way.

When is she being funny and when is she supporting the funny?

Supporting ... I feel in the scene with Malvolio, the stocking scene, you can't be ... she is the straight man, so to speak, in that, because she is completely in the dark as to what the hell is going on. He's dressed up for her, he's saying very suggestive things entirely against his character. It's very much like she has entered the asylum with that one. Then, in subsequent scenes, particularly with Viola/Cesario, there's ... and sadly this does happen with females playing comedy quite a lot, it comes down to a sexual thing ... but playing that sexual frustration and playing that desperation – you can 'up' it to the height of comedic satisfaction.

One of the biggest laughs in the show is when Olivia says 'most wonderful' on the reveal of the male/female twins – what do you think impels that laughter? What do the audience see that makes them go 'that's really funny'?

It's that, I think, for that split second it's like 'what's going to happen, what's going to happen, what's going to happen' when they see each other or whatever, and it just clicks into Olivia's story quickly – where it's like, 'oh, you know "two for the price of one, oh my God!"' I think it's a laugh at the realisation of her and her story. And, again, if you have built up the desperation and the sexual frustration to that point, to then be confronted with two of the objects of your desire – excellent stuff!

Do you have much interaction with the audience? Do you do anything straight out to the audience?

Yes. I think the main part of ... the first meeting of Cesario – is really the most important bit as far as the soliloquising, because it gives her a bit of humanity and I think that's important as with all ... you know, you are not going to laugh at a character, you're not going to or cry with a character unless you sympathise with what they are going through.

She engages with the audience saying 'Oh my God, my life has completely turned on its head and I've fallen madly in love with this steward/boy/person thing. What am I going to do?' But I'm going to enjoy this journey – come along and have fun.

Straight parts versus comic. Do you do anything differently if you are performing a comic part? Do you approach it differently? Does it come from the same place?

I'd say I approach it in the same way because you are not going to connect with theatre unless it's truthful. So you have to get to it at a truthful aspect first and then kind of build from there.

In some ways, comedy gives you freedom in certain areas and gives you less freedom in other areas. So, for instance ... particularly with the desperation [it] is funny [and] it becomes funnier the bigger it gets, so you have a little bit more leeway about how big you can be with that emotion – portraying it ... not big within you ... but showing it ... You see that in various comic parts – that sharing, I think ... but in other ways ... timing is far more strict with comedy. With classical shows you can kind of feel it and then you've got a bit more 'oh are the audience with me?' I can pause it a little bit longer – 'are they still listening?' Whereas with comedy there is a far more strict beat to it ... if it falls on the beat then its' funny, or even if it falls off the beat, then its' still funny but there's still got to be that music running under the scene to make it funny, I think.

How conscious are you of the ensemble moments? Do you find that there are bits where you think 'I'm retreating to the ensemble' and times where you think 'I'm at the forefront' and so, have to do something slightly different?

The ensemble is obviously very important and that comes out of the music question of the whole comedy. You have to be very aware of every-one else on stage the whole time. You do much with ... some actors play those trust games and the counting games and things like that where you have to feel the energy and it's like 'oh, it's my turn to move it onto the next step' ... and it is a group effort but it is a very ... if you are going to take that one step and lead the ensemble that little bit – you can never go off on your own because then the whole thing falls down – but if you want to take that one step, it's an awareness of, maybe you have the wink or the next line. For instance, where Viola and Sebastian meet and I do that kind of stare and pan out, that seems to be funny because then it moves the story along – because they've had that moment. Then if you break the physical line of the show and just stare out that seems to be funny and 'oh, now what's going to happen, we've had a resolution, what it is going to happen?'. And that's why that bit gets a bit of a giggle, I think.

Have you any other thoughts about performing comedy specifically?

What, is it harder?! I think there is the feeling you get, when, I think ... having people ... that instant ... people laughing, that instant ... gratifi-cation, if you like. 'Oh, I've made someone laugh'. It might be a kind of fast hit as opposed to ... you've gone through the whole *Crucible* and you get that applause at the end, you're absolutely knackered, you can't think and you've forgotten who you really are, and all that sort of thing. It is fun and ... you get an immense ... that laughter definitely gives me ... a kick of energy, more than anything that I don't think when you do more straight theatre ... it's very much laying out the table and laying your

Figure 7.2 Alex Gilbert as Olivia in *Twelfth Night*.

Photograph © Martha Geelan

heart on the table – not that I ... I quite enjoy doing that, don't get me wrong, it's quite cathartic in a lot of ways – it's a far more drawn out process to get the audience to come back, I guess.

The following interviews were with Michael Armstrong, Lawrence Russell and Will Gibson who played, respectively, Sir Toby Belch, Sir Andrew Aguecheek and Feste (playing an amalgamation of the characters of Feste and Fabian in the original version) in the same production of *Twelfth Night*. The scene under discussion was a devised moment developed by the actors along with the director Chris Geelan. Note in the discussion the themes of character preparation; Stanislavskian routes to preparing a role; the importance of the relationship with other characters; adjusting to other performers' character choices; superiority play between characters; working as an ensemble unit; interplay between characters in live action; interplay between the performer and the audience; the question of characters' functionality in a play; comic invention; and, crucially, the performer reflection-in and on-action that is displayed.

Interviewer: *I'm particularly interested in the comic scene that you have created. Tell me a little bit about each of your characters, that is, Feste, Sir Andrew Aguecheek and Sir Toby Belch.*

Will:	Feste is the clown … but what's interesting about Feste is that he is actually the shrewdest person on stage. He sort of oversees everything going on. That makes for a really interesting part to play.
	Has he any specific beliefs?
Will:	He basically has no religion within him whatsoever. Feste, in historical terms, is 'festival' so he's basically all the fun and no religion whatsoever which is why he doesn't get on with Malvolio. Because Malvolio is God-loving and doesn't like fun which makes for nice feud and a nice relationship between the two of them.
	What are his insecurities? What makes him insecure?
Will:	So, he puts on this façade the whole time. He puts on this whole show at all times but deep down I've discovered that actually he is a little bit of a showman and deep down he is a bit insecure and if somebody notices that, then that's what bugs him – which is what Malvolio does and hence why he agrees with Sir Toby to effectively torture him.
	Lawrence, tell me about Sir Andrew Aguecheek. What's he like?
Lawrence:	I think Sir Andrew is a bit of the stupid posh boy who often gets lead astray, frequently by Sir Toby, and also Feste. He means well and just wants to be loved really. He is constantly searching for Lady Olivia's affections and gets the interest of Sir Toby and that relationship is perpetuated 'cos he just wants attention and wants to be loved and wants to be with Olivia. That gets him into a lot of problems because Sir Toby realises that he's got a lot of money and so he can get something out of Sir Andrew, so constantly he is being put in difficult situations so that Sir Toby can keep getting money out of him. And cos', fortunately, Sir Andrew is a little bit slow and well-meaning, he just goes along with it … Being a Knight, I think he, sort of, has an idea of who he should be with and I suppose Lady Olivia is someone of his breed and standing and you get the idea maybe that his parents have told him to go and marry somebody but he's not very good at speaking to women and he constantly compares himself to others as well, like Cesario getting more attention than him and Orsino being the one who's going to woo her and he seems to fear other people's advances on his woman …
	The object of his desire! Mikey, tell me about Sir Toby Belch.
Michael:	Sir Toby is the life and soul of the party, he's the rambunctious, alcoholic sponge, he's the man that entertains everyone. He's the guy who just likes getting off his face pretty much, just living for today, living for present, and totally enjoying life as it comes at him, basically … He's a man of aristocracy, he's a 'Sir' but he doesn't act like one. He takes advantage of Sir Andrew but I

think that's more of a personal thing than a class thing. He definitely … yeah, he sees the likes of Malvolio … the well-behaved, the religious, the pompous, if you like, types of people, he definitely doesn't like to associate with and likes to, in fact, ridicule as much as possible.

Now you all created the 'Hangover Scene' in which you enter 'worse for wear'. You have created a comic moment – co-created it with the director, Chris Geelan. What goes into the moment from each of you – and then together? Technically what do you do?

Will: So, we're [going to be] mocking Malvolio. Feste is basically, as I said before, he's a clown but he's on it. He's pretty much the one that keeps it all together. I think if Feste wasn't there, then the two gents would … Malvolio would discover that they were there. So Feste is pretty much, like he is the whole way through, he's the brains of most operations, he's the one that keeps it …

Michael: The glue …

Will: The glue. He keeps it all together. The reason we did it as a hangover scene … it allows us to play all the lines … the words are quite long drawn out … well the words are quite long, so it allows us to get more into it and it works really well that way.

Does Feste lead that scene?

Will: He is like the orchestrator. Basically tells them to move where, what not to say, shuts them up where they're being too obnoxious and loud. So, yeah.

What comic business do you do? What props and stuff what do you use?

Will: Honestly, not a lot. The other two do a lot more than I do. Literally, I stand at the back and mediate it all. I think comedy lies in the stupidity of them mixed with the almost sincerity of me and they [the audience] can sort of relate, cause it's such a farce what's happening on stage and I often clock the audience, be like, 'this is a farce, look what I have to deal with, in my life, in my career' and yet, ironically, I am the clown I am the stupid one but of course I'm not, so yes, so to be the mediator to keep it all going, as Mikey said, the glue of the whole scene.

Lawrence: I think it has developed over the course of the shows and I like it to keep developing. I like to keep adding new things, if not to keep it fresh for me and to try to make the other guys on stage laugh and make myself look better by relation!

I think I started off just sipping the alka seltzer and looking a bit hungover and then I kind of thought, 'that's a bit boring,

I'm sure I could get more out of this'. Then I started playing around. There's a feather duster somewhere else in the scene. So I started playing around. Maybe I find that on me some-where. One day I put it down the front of my trousers and it looked like an erection – potentially coming out after the morning after the night before. That kind of works for 'morn-ing glory'. Once I had had that in there, I realised that I could rest my drink on it as well – so that's second joke Then pulling it out and finding it actually is a feather duster is a third joke. So I quite like adding to that.

It's good having these guys. Mikey pointed out that I needed to come further out so the joke was more visible to the audience. And then making sure that we know when the audience are watching each of us. So, like, if I get my bit done early on then the audience start watching Mikey when he goes onto his bit and then Will towards the end when he's doing the countdown to the drink and so they have a bit more of an interaction and, yeah, it kind of develops.

Mikey?

Michael: So I ... Sir Toby basically comes out and we all come out, as Lawrence said, we all come out as our actors, sorry, as our characters, trying to get the laughs before the real technical sides of things. So I come out with my top off and lots of pen drawn over me, you know, the '4-2' for the England game, noughts and crosses, 'I heart Malvolio' and then I neck an egg whole, I eat it, try and break it in a plastic cup. The plastic cup doesn't work so I throw the cup away and eat the egg ...

But just to relate back to what Will says it's nice that Feste is the person that is the glue who holds it all together. If it weren't for Feste then Sir Andrew's stupidness would get us caught, and Sir Toby's rage would also get us caught, so Feste is the glue that kind of keeps us all together but we still do ... we all go on our journeys. Just to emphasise the beginning bit again ... so, as we all come out as the actors we have all our individual bits that we do, which is more ourselves, and then we need to work as a team for the timing, for the listening to the cues, for the pulling down. So, to get the humour across, it's nice the two elements – of us personally being funny and, as Lawrence says, and developing our characters and our bits and pieces – but then as working as a team. It's equally as funny but in a different way. It's nice to have all the aspects.

Will: We do that the whole the way through. Before a comical scene we'll come on stage and something will be done. So, for example, for Sir Topas, Mikey hands me some sunglasses.

I look at the audience then look at the sunglasses and they'll have a laugh, 'oh this is going to be a comical scene'. So what that basically does is it gives the audience permission to laugh. The thing about *Twelfth Night* is it's serious/ funny, serious/ funny and it's hard to chop and change for the audience ... to be 'are we allowed to laugh?' I was just speaking to some guys after the show we did – a matinee – and they said it was really nice – we knew we were allowed to laugh and when we weren't and it's such an important thing in comedy to do because an audience can find it hysterical but if you haven't given them permission to laugh they won't laugh and it's frustrating. So, these little snippets we do at the start of every scene are so important ...

Michael: Setting the actors up ...

Will: We're going to do something funny now and you can laugh.
How conscious are you of the audience's laughter and how that affects how you do things, how you time things?

Michael: For me personally, it's funny, I don't actually notice the audience laughing through the scenes I'm involved in, because I'm so trying to focus on the timing and the interaction with my fellow actors. I mean, occasionally, when it's an absolutely bellow of a roar, yeah you kind of think 'oh well, we've obviously done a good job there' but I notice the other actors when I don't necessarily have so much to do on stage and that's where I really notice the audience. But for myself I'm too focused into the scene, or just trying to make it comical – so for the audience, I don't necessarily hear the audience.
Would you say the same?

Will: No, I always used to be told 'it's 90% scene/ 10% audience', so I feel it's important to have an ear out for how the audience are finding it. For example, there's a joke that I make at the start of Act Two about a church. It's quite a play on words and it's a very complex joke but I knew I could make it funny and then for the first couple of weeks I wasn't getting the laugh and I was like 'ok, ok, I'm going to try it a different way'. I didn't get the laugh, I tried it a different way, I didn't get the laugh, the third way I tried it – now I get a laugh at every show, because I listen out for it *[mimics listening]* 'no ... no ... no ...'. I think it's something that you do?

Lawrence: Yes, definitely. I think you have to be aware of what the audience are doing ... 'cos I've endeavoured to do a lot of clown-based workshops and stuff and that is very much focussing on what the audience are giving you and responding to that and knowing what's funny so that you can do it again.

And if that doesn't work then try something new. So I think being aware of what the audience are doing is something ... I think there's bit of vanity too – I want to make sure the audience are laughing as much as they can possibly get out of it, so I keep changing things until I get the most consistent laughs. And that's how I work but sometimes I forget about that but I need to constantly be aware of what the audience are laughing at and then do more of that.

You mentioned earlier something about doing more directly to the audience which seemed to make it funnier?

Lawrence: I forgot that, which was stupid really. At the beginning of the run I wasn't looking at the audience enough and suddenly, yes, I suddenly started thinking 'I need to incorporate that a bit more' and then just looking at the audience more and looking ... clocking them and opening things out to them a little more ... I suppose its eye contact. It gives them that contact and you are doing something to them as opposed to just doing it out to the air and perhaps they don't feel connected to you then but if you're connecting directly with them it's like you're affecting them in the same way as you would affect another character on stage.

Will: I think it's important to know your part in the play, so in the rehearsal process I was 'I'm not getting any jokes, I'm not getting any laughs, I'm not really getting it', but actually you need to take a step back and go 'actually, Feste is not there to be a comical character he's there to be the sort of eyes and ears of everyone else, he's there to keep it going, to be the glue in most scenes which he is, to keep it going. But Sir Andrew is there to be funny and so is Sir Toby' ... well he's more of an in-awe sort of character ... but if I tried to make Feste as funny as, you know, Sir Toby, it would just fall flat on its face so I think it's always important in comedy to know where your role lies in the overall perspective of the play.

Is there anything about comedy you would like to observe? Is it different? Do you approach and execute it differently? Or is it the same processes?

Michael: It's nice to keep it fresh. You know? I add bits, keep progressing, throw bits in – it can be a bit naughty at times – but it makes the comedy real and it makes it truthful when people are laughing onstage if you're allowed to laugh [as the character]. It makes it enjoyable for not just the actors but also for the audience watching it. It's very easy to be stifled and to do things exactly the same and it becomes mechanical and although it might be, you know, amusing to the audience it can

Will:

be a lot more comical if things are always fresh and people are kept on their toes and stuff, in my opinion.

I think it's important in comedy – but more with regards to open air theatre – to be aware that the audience are outside – and this is where comedy can lie – so, for example, one show it started raining so I was onstage and I was like 'don't worry it's not going to rain, it's not going to rain' then it started to rain. So, before my monologue I came on and I apologised to the audience which obviously got a big laugh and they were 'oh that's fine, so he's noticed it'. It ups the ante a little bit. And the scene where we hide behind the desk and I go, 'he's found it' and their hands go up and they go 'yeah!' In the rehearsal room, obviously the director could hear me, but outside where you've got 200 people and cars going past you can't hear it, so I have to poke my head up, look, and go 'he's found it', then I go down, then their hands come up. So it's important to always be aware that the audience are not always in a nice black box studio …

Michael: Adapt, as well, be flexible.

Will: Yeah adapt to it.

Figure 7.3 Lawrence Russell as Sir Andrew Aguecheek and Michael Armstrong as Sir Toby Belch in *Twelfth Night*.

Photograph © Martha Geelan

Figure 7.4 Michael Armstrong as Sir Toby Belch and Will Gibson as Feste in *Twelfth Night.*
Photograph © Martha Geelan.

INDIVIDUAL EXERCISE

Observing others

Watch comic performers who you admire working live and reflect on what they
do to create their effects. How does the performer create a sense of truth,
establish interplay, press the comic buttons and demonstrate expertise skills?

Suggested further study

Reading

Some actors consider the processes of performing:

Callow, Simon (1984) *Being an Actor*, London: Methuen
Gielgud, John (1965) *Stage Directions*, London: Mercury
Stanislavski, Constantin (1936, 2008) *An Actor Prepares*, London: Methuen

---

Audio visual

Type in your favourite comic performers to study how they do what they do.

For example, 'Charlie Chaplin, Buster Keaton, Laurel and Hardy, The Marx brothers, Jacques Tati, Sid Field, Joyce Grenfell, Peter Sellers, Terry-Thomas, Alastair Sim, Walter Matthau, Jack Lemmon, Mary Wickes, Madeleine Kahn, Cloris Leachman, Kenneth Connor, Robin Williams, Steve Martin, John Lithgow, David Hyde Pierce, Megan Mullally, Kristen Wiig, Any Schumer, Melissa McCarthy, Rowan Atkinson, Catherine Tate, Tamsin Greig, Jessica Hynes, Bob Newhart, Lisa Kudrow, Jennifer Aniston, Will Ferrell, Jim Carrey' etc.

Example

From Stanislavski:

> Try always to begin by working from the inside, both on the factual and imaginary parts of a play and its setting. Put life into all the imagined circumstances and actions until you have completely satisfied your *sense of truth*, and until you have awakened a *sense of faith* in the reality of your sensations ... You will need a great deal of attention and concentration to aid the proper growth of your sense of truth and to fortify it. Avoid falseness ... do not let the reeds choke the tender flow of truth. Be merciless in rooting out of yourself all tendency to exaggerated, mechanical acting ... To me, as a spectator, what was going on inside of you was of much greater interest. Those feelings, drawn from our actual experience, and transferred to our part, are what give life to the play.
>
> (1936, 2008: 129, 162; 164, italics in original)

Chapter 8

The happy ending

The age-old barometer of theatrical merit: the audience. Did we think it funny? Well, did the audience laugh?

(David Mamet, 1998: 126)

To conclude with a list of skillset ingredients of comic performance:

- interplay with the audience;
- interplay with the rest of the ensemble;
- effective use of rhythm and timing;
- having an awareness of the comic buttons (i.e. how the comic principles work);
- the ability to find truthfulness within the comic world that is on show in the text;
- constantly and consistently being a reflective practitioner.

In order to review and reapply your performance work, it is worth becoming a reflective practitioner. Reviewing your practice on your own and in tandem with your fellow performers will help you to ensure that your overall performance remains as skilled, crafted and fit-for-purpose as it can possibly be.

The interplay that comic performance demands – between each person in the ensemble, individually and jointly with the audience – means that you are required to be consciously aware of each different audience's ongoing response of laughter as it arises (or not) within live theatrical situations. John Cleese expresses it thus:

Every single night you learn something more about the psychology of audiences ... The function of laughter is, of course, to be the total arbiter of what is funny. It's so simple: if they don't laugh, there's something wrong and you've got to fix it.

(Khan, 2015: 52)

Crucially, too, interplay requires awareness of where the truly ensemble nature of the comedy is created through the interactions that you are jointly presenting. In its most basic form, this joint interplay might take the form of awareness that the audience's laughter might be prompted equally from the originator of the line as from them seeing the hearer's response to it – or, more likely, it will require both performers' performance skill sets to be firmly in place to make such a comic moment work. In recorded forms of comic acting, interplay requires anticipating where and how the laugh is likely to occur in advance of the taping. This necessity for the performer's awareness and expectation of laughter means that performing comedy is, by its very nature, a much more interactive and intercommunicative, audience-dependent form of theatrical experience. In his consideration of the 1970s' 'Living Theatre' company, Pierre Biner notes the importance that the audience plays in creating and shaping the live event:

> Even today's psychoanalytical and phenomenological approaches cannot uncover the meaning of a theatrical experienced conceived as a real event. The vibrations that emanate from the stage to the audience are still considered to be beyond the reach of analysis. The reactions evoked in the audience, however, raise the only real questions for critical interpretation.

> (1972: 168)

To meet the needs of that intercommunicative activity – what Michael Chekhov terms to 'radiate' and 'receive' (2002: 20) – 'the audience enter[s] into a pact with the actors to balance what is happening. It's a matter of faith' (Phyllida Lloyd in Giannachi and Luckhurst, 1999: 55). The interplay of audience approval is both an immediate and inevitable component in shaping the comedy occurring, as Robert Provine suggests in *Laughter: A Scientific Investigation*, when 'the brain of the speaker and audience are in a dual processing mode' (2000: 38). Only then can the conditions for what another director and actor, Simon McBurney, terms 'collective imagining' (1999: 71) occur.

Developing and honing your performance skills through practice with the ensemble, and in front of live audiences, is necessary. As Brett Mills states, 'performers respond to the ways in which audiences react to the comedy which is performed for them, and this is more than simply allowing them time to laugh' (2005: 89). Here is where the full extent of the craft or expertise skills of the comic performer comes to the fore. The audience receives everything that you convey to them in performance and that includes the 'leakage' of any insecurity. As Patrice Pavis notes in the *Semiotics of the Theatre*, 'the smallest natural gesture of the actor is transformed into an element of a codified system, since it has to be understood correctly by the public' (1978: 9). It is therefore important that what 'leaks' are the insecurities of the character and not your own anxieties about yourself or your performance! Practice, therefore, makes perfect.

Your comic performance skill set requires the use of interplay, while the effectiveness of the comic character that you play relies on a sort of truth being present. As we have seen, the comic world is, in and of itself, not, generally speaking, entirely truthful! Comedy tends to take place in a less psychologically recognisable, less plausibly balanced world, in which coincidences, incongruities and stereotypical characters might humorously clash

before harmony is restored with a happy resolution. In non-comic theatrical representations, effects are dependent, generally speaking, on the expression and representation of the feelings inherent in human behaviour as channelled through some recognisably plausible conflict – even where supernatural occurrences may be the catalysts which affect the psychological reactions of the protagonists. The truth that is shown is more dependent on the performers' expression of a personalised presentation of a realistic simulation of internalised feeling as stimulated through some personal catastrophe or struggle. Comic truth, however, is an even more subtle and nuanced construct in as much as it must be possible for an audience to read realistic depictions of internalised and externalised being, feeling and reacting within the world of comedy's heightened and more inherently implausible realities.

Comic characters themselves often have a license to challenge (but not ultimately to overthrow) the hegemonic order. There can be the possibility of subversion of the established status quo in comedy. As with Barthes' wrestlers, whose pantomimic behaviours often result in a kind of 'final charivari … a triumphant disorder' (1957, 2009: 12), comic characters' activities might take the form of the sort of Bakhtinian 'carnivaleque' expression of reversal of normality and celebration of misrule – as in scenes of Falstaffian revelry or the trouser-dropping denouement of a modern farce. To some extent, comic characters may operate as the 'anarchic tricksters of myth' (Southworth, 2003: 8). Sometimes, too, the wrestler figure is much like the comic character as the 'outsider' comic interlocutor or commentator figure that operates from without the societal norm:

> What then is a 'bastard' for this audience composed in part, we are told, of people who are themselves outside the rules of society? Essentially someone unstable, who accepts the rules only when they are useful to him and transgresses the formal continuity of attitudes. He is unpredictable, therefore asocial.
>
> (Barthes, 1957, 2009: 13)

In essence, as Geoff King notes of comic truth:

> Comedy has the potential to be both subversive, questioning the norms from which it departs and affirmative, reconfirming that which it recognises through the act of departure; or a mixture of the two. Two different conceptions of comedy are often combined: comedy in the sense of laughter, anarchy and disruption of harmony, and comedy in the sense of a movement *towards* harmony, integration and the happy ending.
>
> (2006: 8)

Working within this heightened form of truth means that you, as the performer, must find ways to perform your own truths within the false premise represented. What you signify must be realistic and credible, despite any broader inconsistencies that may abound. These fictive anomalies will be automatically overlooked by the audience that will be prepared to buy into the falsehood being presented if your performance of the role is skilled enough. For example, by way of illustrating how the audience will be complicit in accepting the fiction being presented, Christian Metz notes, 'in the theater, one laughs if a stage prop collapses but, not at the sight of a "parlor" with only three sides' (1974: 12). Audiences will accept unlikely or exaggerated characters if your comic performative expertise carries them through the presentation of such without jarring or registering as false:

> Characters are comic through a carefully structured culmination of incoherences: their behaviour is not commensurate with their (constructed) motivation; other characters' responses are not in measure within the intended effects; all their signification is inappropriate; and this incites the Audience to notice the disjuncture between the 'presentation' and 'representation' of the text.
>
> (Purdie, 1993: 81)

So, in preparation for a comic role, mine the text for clues. What are the comic buttons that can release audience laughter? Do these rely on comic principles of superiority or incongruity acting as mechanisms to impel the comedy? Throughout the narrative, what is likely to give rise to the smaller laughs; where are the peak laughs and how are these best co-created in the actual performance? What clues do the rhythms in the text give you to your character, to the way they think and how they express themselves? How rhythmically does the comic impetus build to a big comic moment?

In terms of expertise, three invaluable nuggets of advice come from the great Michael Chekhov, one acting theorist who was prepared to attempt to identify constituents of comic performance. These may seem superficial, even self-evident, but the advice goes deep. Apply them to your practice, and your performance of comedy will only bloom:

1   [Find] one predominant psychological feature which the character requires ... [an] outstanding quality.
2   [Comedy] must be performed with utmost inner truth and without even the slightest attempt to be funny in order to get big laughs.
3   A comedy character always reacts naturally, so to speak, no matter how peculiar the character and the situation might be.

(2002: 127, 129)

Remember, to achieve great performance in comedy, this may often mean that you find ways to subvert the stereotype. If you create your character from within – by following a Stanislavskian journey to creating truthful comic performance – this will mean that you are already operating as a reflective practitioner:

> Any accomplished comic practitioner will tell you that without the real honest or serious dedication to circumstances, a performance threatens to lose an essential comic integrity.
>
> (Weitz, 2009: 119)

Donald Schön sums up how reflection can inform the performer's practice. To communicate in performance, Schön wrote, 'he must discover the meaning ... enact decisions, correct errors ... [and] so the performer makes his ephemeral, temporally unfolding artefact' (1987: 175). Bear in mind that as a performer, you are part of a 'community of practice'. That is to say that you are not, most likely, working alone, but will be working together as part of a community with your fellow practitioners and director to create comedy that emanates through the ensemble presentation of a script. Learn, therefore, from those comic performers who you admire. Study how they achieve their effects:

> All the time (Glenn Melvyn) was teaching me. It was hardly a conscious process, one wasn't sitting there with a notebook, I'm sure this happens in a lot of trades and professions – a youngster admires an older, experienced colleague, wanting to emulate him.
>
> (Ronnie Barker, 1988: 47)

Keep a live journal of what works and what does not. Share your discoveries within the process with your fellow performers. This will keep the comedy that you co-create fresh, fully informed and valuably reimagined for each and every performance. To gain the ultimate laughter of release, as Charles Marowitz writes, 'comedy may be predicated on truth, is often suffused with insights that reveal the inner workings of social and psychological mechanisms, but great comedy is ... an extension of what most of us take to be apparent' (1996: 29). This is a difficult trick to pull off, to make the comedy seem as organic, effortless and inevitable as possible. Like anything that seems easy, it actually requires an awful lot of hard work, preparation and a joint will to succeed! Work together as an ensemble – but the work should take the form of play. Do not lose sight of performance and comedy's close relation to childhood in relation to how we learn. As Susan Purdie notes, 'joking of some kind appears as a necessary exercise for all language-users to test and confirm their control in the Symbolic Order' (1993: 54). So, have purposeful fun, do the exercises and learn through play with each other and, in live situations, with the audience. Trust your instincts and never forget, despite any amount of theorising that

comedy is 'basically anything that's funny' (Franklin, 1979: 10) and, ultimately, when everything is said and done, if ever in doubt, 'funny is funny'
(Dave Spikey cited by Hall, 2006: 20).

Happy comedy making and I hope to be able to see your work some day!

Audio visual

Type in 'Etienne Wenger' for 'community of practice' and 'reflective
practice' for ideas about how to do, apply, review and reapply your
performance of comedy.

Suggested further study

Reading

Chekhov, Michael (2002) *To the Actor*, London: Routledge. A practitioner considers some approaches to performing comedy.

Pavis, Patrice (1978) 'The Semiotics of Theatre', Versus, No. 21, 1978, trans. Tjaart
Potgieter. Accessed online at: http://archive.lib.msu.edu/DMC/African%20
Journals/pdfs/Critical%20Arts/cajv1n3/caj001003002.pdf. Pavis offers a useful
discourse about how we read theatrical significations.

Purdie, Susan (1993) *Comedy: The Mastery of Discourse*, Herts: Harvester Wheatsheaf. Purdie's theorising on the constituents of comedy is very useful for the performer.

Sciama, Lidia (ed.) (2016) *Humour, Comedy and Laughter: Obscenities, Paradoxes, Insights and the Renewal of Life*, Oxford: Berghahn Books. This book contains new, international, perspectives on the theories of comedy within culture and society.

Example

An example of all the proposed constituents of comic performance working together might be seen in the following extract. Here, a performer discusses another performer to illustrate comic expertise and the story is, perhaps significantly, located in an early, formative exchange. The spectator/performer account is taken from Alec Guinness' autobiographical recollection of his experience of watching the comedienne Nellie Wallace perform in a variety show at the Coliseum when he was aged six or seven. In this account, it is possible to see interplay, timing, expertise, superiority, incongruity and comic truth in operation. Nellie Wallace is described here by Guinness as being likeable to the point of 'love'; and her act clearly effected release in the impressionable young spectator:

> I don't believe I laughed at Miss Wallace on her first appearance. Truth to tell, I was a little scared, she looked so witch-like with her parrot-beak nose and shiny black hair screwed tightly into a little hard bun. She wore a loud tweed jacket and skirt, an Alpine hat with an enormous, bent pheasant's feather, and dark woollen stockings, which ended in neat, absurd, twinkling button boots. Her voice was hoarse and scratchy, her walk swift and aggressive; she appeared to be always bent forward from the waist, as if looking for someone to punch. She was very small. Having reached centre stage she plunged into a stream of patter, not one word of which did I understand, but I am sure it was full of outrageous innuendoes. The audience fell about laughing but no laughter came from me. I was in love with her.
>
> Later in the afternoon she turned up in a bright green, shiny and much too tight evening gown. She kept dropping things – bag, fan, handkerchief, a hairbrush – and every time she bent to retrieve them the orchestra made rude sounds on their wind instruments, as if she had ripped her dress or farted. Her look of frozen indignation at this pleased me enormously, but my companion clearly thought the whole act very vulgar … I laughed a lot but didn't fall out of my seat until Nellie's next act, in which she appeared in a nurse's uniform ready to assist a surgeon at an operation. The patient, covered with a sheet, was wheeled on stage and the surgeon immediately set about him with a huge carving knife. Nellie stood by, looking very prim, but every now

and then would dive under the sheet and extract with glee and a shout of triumph quite impossible articles – a hotwater bottle, a live chicken, a flat-iron, and so on. Finally, she inserted, with many wicked looks, a long rubber tube which she blew down. The body inflated rapidly to huge proportions and then, covered in its sheet, slowly took to the air. Nellie made desperate attempts to catch it, twinkling her boots as she hopped surprisingly high, but all in vain. The orchestra gave a tremendous blast as she made her last leap; and that is when I fell off my plush seat and felt faintly sick.

(1985: 9–10)

Guinness describes interplay in Wallace's 'centre-stage' address to the audience and her use of 'wicked looks'. He also attempts to conjure Wallace's use of timing in her sudden 'dives' 'under the sheets' while depicting her expertise in her 'twinkling' comic leaps. Superiority is evident in her 'aggressive' style and the potential loss of face signalled in the mock-farting sequence. Incongruity is present in the performer's costume and the improbable items that are removed from the 'patient'. Finally, there is comic 'truth' discernible in what Guinness describes as the 'seriousness' with which Wallace goes about her comic business.

NELLIE WALLACE.

Appendices

As Gareth White notes:

> Post-hoc reflection on an aesthetic experience is always an important – perhaps the most important – element of how it becomes meaningful to us ... choices are the material that need to be reflected on.
>
> (2013: 78)

The following practice exercises are designed to help you become a reflective practitioner to improve your practice of comic performance. They involve employing Stanislavskian ways to create 'character from within' while also using Brechtian methods to directly affect the audience. The checklists are intended as tools to help you to evaluate the 'doing' and 'applying' of comic performance within the world of the play. They will ask you to consider concepts such as character; building truth to yourself and to the other characters; finding ways to subvert the stereotype; ensemble working; and presenting a consolidated appearance of comic truth for the audience.

You should use the checklists as a cycle, from (1) preparing your own role; through (2) sharing in your fellow actors' preparation of their characters and how this affects your character's motivations and playing intentions; through (3) presenting your role in front of an audience and seeing what worked; to (4) evaluating the whole ensemble process in front of a live audience and how this, in relation, might change some of your performance choices. Re-evaluating your performance in the light of your own discoveries about what worked and did not; reviewing this in relation to what your co-performers discovered and what, if anything, they will be altering in the light of their own discoveries from the audiences' reaction; and then reapplying these findings as a result of these reflections will ensure that you keep the comic performance fresh, polished, coherent and true.

You can use the final two checklists to maintain a consistent and ongoing reflective review of the process, using them in collaboration with your community of practice.

The model of this reflective process looks like this:

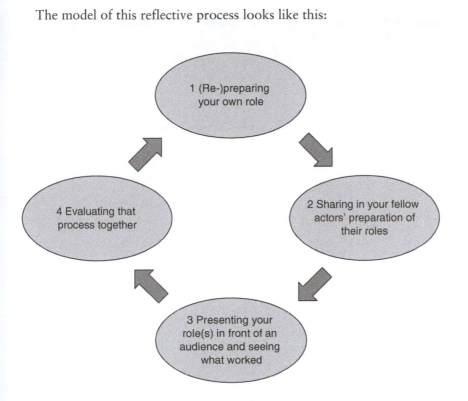

Reflective checklist 1: Preparing your own role: individual self-reflection on-action

In preparing you own character, ask yourself the basic questions – who is, or was, she (or he)? What was her society like? What aspects of society might have shaped her? What class does she belong to? What would her clothes be like and why would she have chosen what she is wearing? How were her attitudes, beliefs, prejudices, securities and insecurities formed?

Also, how does she express herself? Where was her language and speaking formulated?

What clues are there in the text to answer the above questions?

Finally, to explore the character more deeply and to begin to subvert any stereotype, ask yourself 'what do you know about the character's fantasy of herself?'

What do you *not* know about the character's fantasy of herself?

Can you effectively subvert any stereotype while still remaining true to the authors' intention or sacrificing any of the comic effect?

Finding truth in the text: What is your character's main motivation in this play? What does he/she most want?

What are his/her other motivations/intentions at other points in the play?

Describe your character. What is he/she like? How shaped by his/her environment is he/she?

What does he/she like to show?

What does his/her essential 'being' look like at key moments in the text?

What does he/she not like to show? Why? What are his/her insecurities that may 'leak' out?

Are there any textual clues to how your character speaks or reacts (timing and rhythm).

Comic principles: What are the main comic buttons in this piece?

Interplay: Are there any obvious moments of audience interplay?

Ensemble: Are you at the forefront of creating particular comic moments?

Is your reaction central to creating any comic moments?

Are you supporting the comic moment by giving focus at any point(s)?

Reflective checklist 2: Reviewing your performance in relation to others: sharing in group reflection on-action

In collaboration with the rest of the ensemble and the director, share your own reflections on your role from Checklist 1 with the rest of the group. What are their opinions, thoughts and ideas about how your interpretation of the process fits in with the piece as a whole? How do your decisions correspond and complement their intended performance choices? If differences arise, how might a compromise be reached that works for the unity, truth and overall comic message of the piece?

Rehearse the scenes in the light of this community of practice reflection.

Finding truth in the text: What are your characters' main motivations in this play? What do they most want?

What are their other motivations/intentions at other points in the play?

Each to describe your character. What is he/she like? How shaped by his/her environment is he/she?

What does he/she like to show? How does this affect other characters in the play? How aware are they of these characteristics?

What does his/her essential 'being' look like at key moments in the text? How does this affect other characters in the play?

What does he/she not like to show? Why? What are his/her insecurities that may 'leak' out? How aware are the other characters of these 'hidden' tendencies?

Are there any textual clues to how your character speaks or reacts (timing and rhythm)? How does this affect other characters' actions and responses?

Comic principles: What are the main comic buttons in this piece? Does everyone agree that these are the key comic peaks in the text?

Interplay: Are there any obvious moments of audience interplay? Again, does everyone agree?

Ensemble: Are you at the forefront of creating particular comic moments? Each to explain where you expect this to be the case.

Is your reaction central to creating any comic moments? Again, each to explain where you expect this to be the case.

Are you supporting the comic moment by giving focus at any point(s)? Again, each to explain where you expect this to be the case.

Reflective checklist 3: Reviewing your performance: post-performance individual reflection in- and on-action

Once the play has been performed in front of audiences, review – from your own perspective – what worked and what did not and assess the possible causes of this. Ask yourself if there is anything you will try differently next time and, in turn, subsequently reflect on what result the application of these changes had on the effectiveness of your performance.

Truth and interplay: Has your perception of what your character is like been altered in any way by the audience's reception to him/her?

Have you successfully subverted any stereotypical aspects of your character while still remaining true to the author's intention?

Have you discovered any moments of possible audience interplay?

Comic principles: Has your sense of what the main comic buttons in the play are changed in any way as a result of performing the play in front of a live audience?

Have you found any moments where your reaction aids the comic flow or where you can support the comic message without stealing focus?

Have you made any other discoveries that you want to put into practice?

Have you found something not working that you think should? What is it?

Have you any positive observations to offer your community of practice about how they might possibly strengthen the truth of their character and deepen the overall comic message of the play?

Reflective checklist 4: Reviewing your performance: post-performance group reflection in- and on-action

Working as a community of practice, jointly evaluate what you have achieved. Reflect together on how the audience's reactions affected or will affect your performance. Evaluate any changes that each performer would like to try and assess how this might affect anyone else's performance within the play. Is there anything that, as an ensemble, you will do differently? Are there any changes that you, jointly, will agree to try, based on an awareness of how this might affect the motivations and intentions of the other performers in relation to their own characters and their journeys through the narrative?

Truth and interplay: Has your perception of what your characters are like been altered in any way by the audience's reception to him/her?

Have you successfully subverted any stereotypical aspects of your characters while still remaining true to the author's intention?

Have you each discovered any moments of possible audience interplay?

Comic principles: Has your sense of what the main comic buttons in the play are changed in any way as a result of performing the play in front of a live audience?

Have you found any moments where your reaction aids the comic flow or where you can support the comic message without stealing focus?

Have you each made any other discoveries that you want to put into practice?

Have you each found something not working that you think should? What is it?

Have you each got any positive observations to offer your community of practice about how they might possibly strengthen the truth of their character and deepen the overall comic message of the play?

References

Abbott, Chris (2012) *Putting on the Panto to Pay for the Pinter*, Salisbury: The Hobnob Press.

Abraham, F. Murray (2005) *Actors on Shakespeare: A Midsummer Night's Dream*, London: Faber & Faber.

Achard, Marcel (1958) 'Introduction to Feydeau'. In Bentley, Eric (ed.) *Let's Get a Divorce! And Other Plays*, New York: Albany.

Adams, Guy (2009) 'Irresistible rise of the "mockumentary"'. Article in *The Independent* Newspaper, 20/04/2009.

Aitken, Maria (1996) *Style: Acting in High Comedy*, London: Applause.

Akbar, Arifa (2007) 'What Salvador Dali saw in the cinema'. Article in *The Independent* Newspaper, 19/01/2007.

Akbar, Arifa (2010) 'Fry's new show scripted by his Twitter fans'. Article in *The Independent* Newspaper, 13/08/2010.

Allen, Robert C. (ed.) (1987) *Channels of Discourse: Television and Contemporary Criticism*, London: Methuen.

Aristotle (1997) *Poetics*, London: Dover.

Aristotle (2007) 'Rhetoric III', Accessed online at: http://ebooks.adelaide.edu.au/a/aristotle/a8rh/.

Aston, Elaine and Savona, George (1991) *Theatre as Sign-System: A Semiotics of Text and Performance*, London: Routledge.

Auden, W. H. (1963) *The Dyer's Hand*, London: Faber & Faber.

Auslander, Philip (2008) *Liveness: Performance in a Mediatized Culture*, London: Routledge.

Bakhtin, Mikhail (1941, 1965) *Rabelais and His World*, trans. Hélène Iswolsky, Bloomington: Indiana University Press, 1993.

Banks, R. A. (1998) *Drama and Theatre Arts*, London: Hodder & Stoughton.

Barker, Ronnie (1988) *It's Hello from Him!*, Kent: New English Library.

Barthes, Roland (1957, 2009) *Mythologies*, London: Vintage Books.

Bean, Richard (2011) *One Man, Two Guvnors*, London: Oberon Books.

Beckerman, Bernard (1990) *Theatrical Presentation: Performer, Audience and Act*, London: Routledge.

Beckett, Samuel (1956) *Waiting for Godot*, London: Faber & Faber.

Bennett, Alan (1985) *Forty Years on and Other Plays*, London: Faber & Faber.

Bentley, Eric (ed.) (1958) *The Theory of the Modern Stage*, Harmondsworth: Penguin.

Bergson, Henri (1900) *Laughter*. In Sypher, Wylie (1994) *Comedy*, London: Johns Hopkins University Press. Also in Morreall, John (ed.) (1987) *The Philosophy of Laughter and Humor*, New York: Albany. Also in Enck, John J., Forter, Elizabeth T. and Whitley, Alvin (eds) (1960) *The Comic in Theory and Practice*, New York: Appleton-Century Crofts.

Biner, Pierre (1972) *The Living Theatre*, New York: Avon.

Boal, Augusto (2002) *Games for Actors and Non-Actors*, London: Routledge.

Bock, Paula (2005) 'Infant science: a UW couple leads our new thinking about babies' amazing minds'. Article on Meltzoff and Kuhl in *The Seattle Times*. Accessed online at: http://community.seattletimes.nwsource.com/archive/?date=20050306&slug=pacific-pbaby06.

Boon, Richard (2004) 'The Democratic Comedy of Morecambe and Wise', in Milling, Jane and Banham, Martin (eds) *Extraordinary Actors: Essays on Popular Performers*, Exeter: University of Exeter Press.

Bownass, Helen (2008) 'It's no joke, the Web is hilarious'. Article in *The London Paper*, 22/07/2008.

Bradbrook, M. C. (1963) *The Growth and Structure of Elizabethan Comedy*, Harmondsworth: Peregrine.

Brecht, Bertold (1949, 1968) 'The Street Scene: A Basic Model for an Epic Theatre', trans. John Willett. In Bentley, Eric (ed.) *The Theory of the Modern Stage*, Harmondsworth: Penguin.

Brecht, Bertold (1994) *Collected Plays*, London: Methuen.

Bridie, James (1931) *The Anatomist*, London: Constable.

Brockbank, Philip (ed.) (1988) *Players of Shakespeare 1*, Cambridge: Cambridge University Press.

Brook, Peter (1968) *The Empty Space*, Harmondsworth: Penguin.

Brooke, Michael (2005) 'Funny peculiar'. Article on Alistair Sim in *Sight and Sound Magazine*, July 2005. London: BFI.

Brown, Janet (1986) *Prime Mimicker: The Autobiography of Janet Brown*, Sevenoaks: New English Library.

Brown, Jonathan (2010) 'Revealed: the YouTube rich list'. Article in *The Independent* Newspaper, 26/08/2010.

Bruce, Frank (2000) *Scottish Showbusiness: Music Hall, Variety and Pantomime*, Edinburgh: NMS.

Bull, Peter (1985) *Bull's Eyes*, London: Robin Clark.

Burrell, Ian (2007) 'A funny old business'. Article in *The Independent* Newspaper, 13/08/2007.

Burrell, Ian (2010a) 'Funny business'. Article in *The Independent* Newspaper, 08/07/2010.

Burrell, Ian (2010b) 'Heard the one about Channel 4?' Article in *The Independent* Newspaper, 29/10/2010.

Byrne, John (1987) *Cuttin' a Rug: The Slab Boys Trilogy*, Harmondsworth: Penguin.

Callery, Dymphna (2001) *Through the Body*, London: Nick Hern Books.

Callow, Simon (1984) *Being an Actor*, London: Methuen.

Callow, Simon (1991) *Acting in Restoration Comedy*, New York: Applause Theatre Books.

Callow, Simon (1992) *Shooting the Actor*, London: Vantage.

Carnovsky, Morris (1961) 'Design for acting: the quest of technique', *Tulane Drama Review*, 5(3). In Corrigan, Robert W. and Rosenberg, James L. (eds) (1964) *The Context and Craft of Drama*, San Francisco: Chandler.

Carr, Jimmy and Greeves, Lucy (2006) *The Naked Jape*, London: Michael Joseph.

Casey, Bernadette; Casey, Neil; Calvert, Ben; French Liam and Lewis, Justin (2008) *Television Studies: Key Concepts*, London: Routledge.

Chapman, Graham; Cleese, John; Gilliam, Terry; Idle, Eric; Jones, Terry and Palin Michael (1989) *Monty Python's Flying Circus: Just the Words Volume Two*, London: Guild.

Chekhov, Anton (1970) *Plays*, Harmondsworth: Penguin Classics.

Chekhov, Michael (2002) *To the Actor*, London: Routledge.

Cleese, John and Booth, Connie (1988) *The Complete Fawlty Towers*, London: Methuen.

Cook, William (1994) *Ha Bloody Ha: Comedians Talking*, London: Fourth Estate.

Cooper, Lane (1943) *Fifteen Greek Plays*, New York: Oxford University Press.

Corrigan, Robert W. and Rosenberg, James L. (eds) (1964) *The Context and Craft of Drama*, San Francisco: Chandler.

Cotes, Peter (ed.) (1989) *Sincerely Dickie: A Dickie Henderson Collection*, London: Robert Hale.

Coward, Noel (1989) *Collected Plays*, London: Bloomsbury.

Craig, Nicholas (1989) *I, an Actor*, London: Pan.

Critchley, Simon (2002) *On Humour*, London: Routledge.

Csikszentmihalyi, Mihaly (1990) *Flow: The Psychology of Optimal Experience*, New York: Harper & Row.

Dardis, Tom (1979) *Keaton: The Man Who Wouldn't Lie Down*, London: Andre Deutsch.

Darwin, Charles (1872, 1904) *The Expression of the Emotions in Man and Animals*, London: John Murray. In Enck, John J., Forter, Elizabeth T. and Whitley, Alvin (eds) (1960) *The Comic in Theory and Practice*, New York: Appleton-Century Crofts. In Greig, J. Y. T. (1969) *The Psychology of Laughter and Comedy*, New York: Cooper Square.

Davies, Russell (ed.) (1994) *The Kenneth Williams Diaries*, London: HarperCollins.

Double, Oliver (1997) *Stand-up: On Being a Comedian*, London: Methuen.

Double, Oliver (2005) *Getting the Joke*, London: Methuen.

Draper, R. P. (2000) *Shakespeare: The Comedies*, Basingstoke: Macmillan Press.

Durgnat, Raymond (1971) *A Mirror for England: British Movies from Austerity to Affluence*, London: Faber & Faber.

Durrenmatt, Friedrich (1958) 'Problems of the Theatre'. In Corrigan, Robert W. and Rosenberg, James L. (eds) (1964) *The Context and Craft of Drama*, San Francisco: Chandler.

Dyce, Alexander (1860) *Kemps Nine Daies Wonder: Performed in a Daunce*, London: John Bowyer Nichols and Son.

Eddershaw, Margaret (1994) 'Actors on Brecht'. In Thomson, Peter and Sacks, Glendyr (eds) *The Cambridge Companion to Brecht*, Cambridge: Cambridge University Press.

Edmondson, Ade (1989) On *Tommy Cooper: Just Like That!* Channel 4 Television Video: PVC 4063A, Directed Jeff Perks.

Elam, Keir (1994) *The Semiotics of Theatre and Drama*, London: Routledge.

Eliot, T. S. (1923) From *Marie Lloyd*, in Hayward, John (ed.) (1953) *Selected Prose*, Harmondsworth: Penguin.

Enck, John J.; Forter, Elizabeth T. and Whitley, Alvin (eds) (1960) *The Comic in Theory and Practice*, New York: Appleton-Century Crofts.

Everitt, David (2001) *King of the Half Hour: Nat Hiken and the Golden Age of TV Comedy*, New York: Syracuse University Press.

Fielding, Henry (1742) Author's preface to 1948 edition of *Joseph Andrews*, New York: Rinehart & Co. Inc.

Finlayson, Iain (1987) *The Scots*, London: Constable.

Fisher, John (2007) *Tommy Cooper: Always Leave Them Laughing*, Leicester: W. F. Howes.

Flanagan, Bud (1961) *My Crazy Life*, London: Frederick Muller.

Franklin, Joe (1979) *Joe Franklin's Encyclopedia of Comedians*, Secaucus, NJ: Citadel Press.

Freud, Sigmund (1905, 1964) *Jokes and Their Relation to the Unconscious*, London: Hogarth Press. Also in Morreall, John (ed.) (1987) *The Philosophy of Laughter and Humor*, New York: Albany. In Enck, John J., Forter, Elizabeth T. and Whitley, Alvin (eds) (1960) *The Comic in Theory and Practice*, New York: Appleton-Century Crofts.

Front, Rebecca (2009) 'Days like these'. Article in *The Independent* Newspaper, 26/01/2009.

Fry, Stephen (2010) *The Fry Chronicles: An Autobiography*, London: Michael Joseph.

Frye, Northrop (1957) *Anatomy of Criticism*, Princeton, NJ: Princeton University Press. In Enck, John J., Forter, Elizabeth T. and Whitley, Alvin (eds) (1960) *The Comic in Theory and Practice*, New York: Appleton-Century Crofts.

Fulton, Rikki (1999) *Is That the Time Already?* Glasgow: BW.

Gablik, Suzi (1992) *Magritte*, London: Thames & Hudson.

Gardner, Howard (1999) *Intelligence Reframed: Multiple Intelligences for the 21st Century*, New York: Basic Books.

Gay, Penny (2008) *The Cambridge Introduction to Shakespeare's Comedies*, Cambridge: Cambridge University Press.

Gellatly, Andrew (1999) 'Steve McQueen', in *Frieze* magazine, Issue 46, May 1999. Accessed online at: http://www.frieze.com/issue/review/steve_mcqueen/.

Giannachi, Gabriella and Luckhurst, Mary (1999) *On Directing: Interviews with Directors*, Basingstoke: Palgrave MacMillan.

Gielgud, John (1965) *Stage Directions*, London: Mercury.

Gilbert, Gerard (2009) Review of 'This is Spinal Tap'. *The Independent* Newspaper, 30/03/2009.

Gilbert, Gerard (2011) 'Critic's Choice', Review of 'Not Going Out', *The Independent* Newspaper, 06/01/11.

Gillett, John (2007) 'No madness in the method?' Article in *Equity Journal*, Winter, 2007.

Godber, John (2001) *Plays: 1*, London: Methuen.

Goffman, Erving (1959) *The Presentation of Self in Everyday Life*, New York: Anchor Books.

Goldman, Michael (1975) *The Actor's Freedom: Towards a Theory of Drama*, New York: Viking Press. In Gruber, William (1986) *Comic Theaters*, Athens: University of Georgia.

Goodwin, C. (1986) 'Audience Diversity, Participation and Interpretation', *Text*, 6(3), 283–316. In McIlvenny, Mettovaara and Tapio (1993) '*I Really Wanna Make You Laugh: Stand-up Comedy and Audience Response*'. In Suojanen, Matti K. and Kulkki-Nieminen (eds) (1992) *Folia, Femistica & Linguistica: Proceedings of the Annual Finnish Linguistics Symposium*, May 1992, Tampere University Finnish and General Linguistics Department Publications 16. Accessed online at: http://paul-server.hum.aau.dk/research/cv/Pubs/stand-up93.pdf.

Gorman, Dave (2014) *Too Much Information…or can everyone just SHUT UP for a MOMENT. SOME of us are TRYING TO THINK*, London: Ebury Press.

Graves, George (1931) *Gaieties and Gravities: The Autobiography of a Comedian*, London: Hutchison & Co.

Graves, Lawrence (2004) *Samuel Beckett: Waiting for Godot*, Cambridge: Cambridge University Press.

Gray, Adam (2013) *Brilliant Social Media: How to Start, Refine and Improve Your Social Media Business Strategy*, Harlow: Pearson.

Gray, Simon (2006) *The Year of the Jouncer*, London: Granta Books.

Greig, J. Y. T. (1969) *The Psychology of Laughter and Comedy*, New York: Cooper Square.

Griffin, Stephen (2005) *Ken Dodd: The Biography*, London: Michael O'Mara Books.

Gruber, William (1986) *Comic Theaters*, Athens: University of Georgia.

Guinness, Alec (1985) *Blessings in Disguise*, London: Hamish Hamilton.

Hall, Julian (2006) *The Rough Guide to British Cult Comedy*, London: Rough Guides.

Hall, Julian (2008) 'The Nutty Professor'. Interview with Chris Addison in *The Independent* Newspaper, 10/07/2008.

Hall, Julian (2009) 'Short and tweet'. Article in *The Independent* Newspaper, 20/06/2009.

Hallam, Susan (2006) *Music Psychology in Education*, London: IOE Publications.

Halliwell, Leslie (1987) *Double Take and Fade Away*, London: Grafton Books.

Halpern, Charna and Close, Del (2001) *Truth in Comedy*, Colorado: Meriwether.

Hankinson, Andrew (2011) 'New king of angry comedy'. Article in *The Independent* Newspaper, 11/02/2011.

Hanks, Robert (2011) 'We've tired of this relentless cynicism'. Review in *The Independent* Newspaper, 24/01/11.

Hartley, Anthony F. (1982) *Linguistics for Language Learners*, London: The Macmillan Press.

Hasan, Ruqaiya (1989) *Linguistics, Language and Verbal Art*, Oxford: Oxford University Press.

Havel, Vaclav (1965) *The Memorandum*, London: Jonathan Cape.

Hawkes, Terence (1997) *Structuralism and Semiotics*, London: Routledge.

Hawthorne, Nigel (2002) *Straight Face*, London: Sceptre.

Hay, Ian (1938) *Housemaster*, London: Samuel French.

Hayward, Anthony and Hayward, Deborah (1993) *TV Unforgettables: Over 250 Legends of the Small Screen*, London: Guinness Publishing.

Hazlitt, William (1885) From '*Lectures on the English Comic Writers*', London: George Bell. In Morreall, John (ed.) (1987) *The Philosophy of Laughter and Humor*, New York: Albany.

Heggie, Iain (1988) *A Wholly Healthy Glasgow*, London: Methuen.

Hethmon, Robert (1966) *Strasberg at the Actors Studio*, London: Jonathan Cape.

Hobbes, Thomas (1839) From '*Leviathan*', Part 1, Ch. 6, in *English Works*, Vol. 3, ed. Molesworth, London: Bohn. In Morreall, John (ed.) (1987) *The Philosophy of Laughter and Humor*, New York: Albany. Also in McKellar, Peter (1968) *Experience and Behaviour*, Harmondsworth: Penguin.

Hoggart, Richard (1960) *The Uses of Literacy*, Harmondsworth: Pelican.

Holt, John (1976) *How Children Learn*, Harmondsworth: Penguin.

Hordern, Michael with England, Patricia (1993) *A World Elsewhere: The Autobiography of Sir Michael Hordern*, London: Michael O'Mara Books.

Houston, Renee (1974) *Don't Fence Me In*, London: Pan.

Hudd, Roy (1993) *Roy Hudd's Book of Music-Hall, Variety and Showbiz Anecdotes*, London: Robson.

Humes, Walter M. (1983) 'Science, Religion and Education: A Study in Cultural Interaction'. In Humes, Walter M. and Paterson, Hamish M. (eds) (1983) *Scottish Culture and Education 1800–1980*, Edinburgh: John Donald.

Iannucci, Armando (2009) 'I don't despise politicians'. Interview with Christina Patterson in *The Independent* Newspaper, 14/08/2009.

Ionesco, Eugene (1960) Interview in *L'Express*, 29/01/1960. In Bevis, Matthew (2013) *Comedy: A Very Short Introduction*, Oxford: Oxford University Press.

Ionesco, Eugene (1967) *Three Plays*, Harmondsworth: Penguin.

Jacobson, Howard (2013) 'Stand-up and sitcom: even with Stephen Fry on hand, this is no way to treat "Twelfth Night"'. Article in *The Independent* Newspaper, 08/02/2013.

Janko, Richard (2002) *Aristotle on Comedy: Towards a Reconstruction of Poetics II*, London: Duckworth.

Jarvis, Martin (1999) *Acting Strangely: A Funny Kind of Life*, London: Methuen.

Jarvis, Martin (2003) *Broadway Jeeves? The Diary of a Theatrical Adventure*, London: Methuen.

Jennings, Charles (2001) *Faintheart*, London: Little, Brown.

Johnson, Samuel (1751) *Rambler*, No 125, in *British Essayists*, Vol. XXI, May 28, 1751. London.

Johnston, Chris (2012) *Drama Games for Those Who Like to Say No*, London: Nick Hern Books.

Jones, Alice (2015) 'Reasons to be fearful'. Article on Dan Swimer in *The Independent* Newspaper, 08/01/2015.

Kant, Immanuel (1892) *Critique of Judgment*, London: Macmillan.

Kawasaki, Guy and Fitzpatrick, Peg (2014) *The Art of Social Media: Power Tips for Power Users*, London: Penguin Random House.

Kerr, Walter (1980) *The Silent Clowns*, New York: Da Capo.

Khan, Jemima (2015) 'Finding the laugh the hard way'. Interview with John Cleese in *New Statesman*, 19/12/2014.

Kierkegaard, Soren (1941) '*Concluding Unscientific Postscript*', trans. David. F. Swenson, Princeton: Princeton University Press. In Morreall, John (ed.) (1987) *The Philosophy of Laughter and Humor*, New York: Albany.

King, Geoff (2006) *Film Comedy*, London: Wallflower.

Kitto, H. D. F. (1971) *Form and Meaning in Drama*, London: Methuen.

Knight, Naomi K. (2011) 'The Interpersonal Semiotics of Having a Laugh'. In Dreyfus, Shoshana, Hood, Susan and Stenglin, Maree (eds) *Semiotic Margins: Meanings in Multimodalities*, London: Continuum.

Koss, Richard (1997) Foreword to *Aristotle's Poetics*, London: Dover.

Kunze, Peter (ed.) (2016) *Comedy Studies: Online and Digital Edition*, 6(1).

Langer, Susanne (1953) *Feeling and Form*, New York: Charles Scribner's Sons. In Enck, John J., Forter, Elizabeth T. and Whitley, Alvin (eds) (1960) *The Comic in Theory and Practice*, New York: Appleton-Century Crofts.

Lau, I. (1998) 'Besides Fists and Blood: Hong Kong Comedy and Its Master of the Eighties', *Cinema Journal*, 37(2), 18–34.

Lauder, Harry (1919, 2008) *Between You and Me*, Tutis Digital Publishing.

Leno, Dan (1968) *Dan Leno Hys Booke*, London: Hugh Evelyn.

Levinson, Stephen C. (1983) *Pragmatics*, Cambridge: Cambridge University Press.

Lewis, Roger (2001) *Charles Hawtrey, 1914–1988: The Man Who was Private Widdle*, London: Faber & Faber.

Lichtenberg, Georg Christoph. In Mare, M. L. and Quarrell, W. H. (1938) *Lichtenberg's Visits to England*, Oxford: Clarendon Press. In Thomson, Peter (2000) *On Actors and Acting*, Exeter: University of Exeter, p. 105.

Lister, Martin; Dovey, Jim; Giddings, Seth; Grant, Iain and Kelly, Kieran (2009) *New Media: A Critical Introduction*, London: Routledge.

Littlewood, Joan (1994) *Joan's Book: Joan Littlewood's Peculiar History as She Tells It*, London: Minerva.

Luckhurst, Mary and Veltman, Chloe (2001) *On Acting*, London: Faber & Faber.

McBurney, Simon in Giannachi, Gabriella and Luckhurst, Mary (1999) *On Directing: Interviews with Directors*, Basingstoke: Palgrave Macmillan.

McCabe, Bob (2005) *The Rough Guide to Comedy Movies*, London: Rough Guides.

McCabe, John (1966) *Mr. Laurel and Mr. Hardy*, New York: Signet.

McKellar, Peter (1968) *Experience and Behaviour*, Harmondsworth: Penguin.

Mackie, Albert D. (1973) *The Scotch Comedians: From the Music Hall to TV*, Edinburgh: Ramsay Head.

McIlvenny, Paul; Mettovaara, Sari and Tapio, Ritva (1993) 'I Really Wanna Make You Laugh: Stand-up Comedy and Audience Response'. In Suojanen, Matti K. and Kulkki-Nieminen (eds) (1993) *Folia, Femistica & Linguistica: Proceedings of the Annual Finnish Linguistics Symposium*, May 1992, Tampere University Finnish and General Linguistics Department Publications 16. Accessed online at: http://paul-server.hum.aau.dk/research/cv/Pubs/stand-up93.pdf.

McLuhan, Marshall (1962) *The Gutenberg Galaxy: The Making of Typographic Man*, Toronto: University of Toronto Press.

Mamet, David (1998) *True and False: Heresy and Common Sense for the Actor*, London: Faber & Faber.

Marc, David (1996) *Democratic Vistas: Television in American Culture*, Philadelphia: University of Pennsylvania Press. In Mills, Brett (2005) *Television Sitcom*, London: BFI Publishing.

Marowitz, Charles (1996) *Alarums and Excursions*, New York: Applause.

Marshall, Jill and Werndly, Angela (2002) *The Language of Television*, London: Routledge.

Martin, Sylvia (2006) *Video Art*, Koln: Taschen.

Mawer, Irene (1932) *The Art of Mime*, London: Methuen.

Mead, Margaret (1963) *Growing Up in New Guinea: A Study of Adolescence and Sex in Primitive Societies*, Harmondsworth: Penguin.

Medhurst, Andy (2003) *A National Joke: Popular Comedy and English Identities*, London: Routledge.

Mellencamp, Patricia (1986) 'Situation Comedy, Feminism and Freud: Discourses of Gracie and Lucy'. In Modleski, Tania (ed.) *Studies in Entertainment: Critical Approaches to Mass Culture*, Indiana: Indiana University Press.

Merchant, Moelwyn (1972) *Comedy*, London: Methuen.

Merlin, Bella (2010) *Acting: The Basics*, London: Routledge.

Metz, Christian (1974) *Film Language: A Semiotics of the Cinema*, New York: Oxford University Press.

Meyer-Dinkgrafe, Daniel (2001) *Approaches to Acting Past and Present*, London: Continuum.

Miles-Brown, John (2006) *Acting: A Drama Studio Source Book*, London: Peter Owen.

Milligan, Spike (1973) *The Goon Show Scripts*, London: Sphere.

Milling, Jane and Banham, Martin (eds) (2004) *Extraordinary Actors: Essays on Popular Performers*, Exeter: University of Exeter Press.

Mills, Brett (2005) *Television Sitcom*, London: BFI Publishing.

Mills, Brett (2010) 'Contemporary Comedy Performance in British Sitcom'. In Cornea, Christine (ed.), *Genre and Performance: Film and Theatre*, Manchester: Manchester University Press.

Mintz, Lawrence (2008) 'Humor and Popular Culture'. In Raskin, Victor (ed.) *The Primer of Humor Research*, New York: Mouton de Gruyter.

Monkhouse, Bob (1993) *Crying with Laughter*, London: Century.

Monkhouse, Bob (1998) *Over the Limit: My Secret Diaries 1993–8*, London: Century.

Moore, Sonia (1974) *The Stanislavski System: The Professional Training of an Actor*, New York: Viking Press.

Morreall, John (ed.) (1987) *The Philosophy of Laughter and Humor*, New York: Albany.

Muir, Edwin (1935) *Scottish Journey*, London: Heinemann. In Finlayson, Iain (1987) *The Scots*, London: Constable.

Muir, Frank and Brett, Simon (eds) (1992) *The Penguin Book of Comedy Sketches*, Harmondsworth: Penguin.

Mulkay, Michael (1988) *On Humour*, Oxford: Basil Blackwell.

Munro, Michael (1999) *The Complete Patter*, Edinburgh: Canongate.

O'Brien, Mike (2006) *The Best Stand-up Comedy Routines*, London: Constable and Robinson.

O'Casey, Sean (1963) *Three Plays*, London: MacMillan and Co.

O'Gorman, Brian (1998) *Laughter in the Roar: Reminiscences of Variety and Pantomime*, Weybridge: Badger Press.

Olsen, Christopher (ed.) (2015) *Acting Comedy*, London: Routledge.

Owen, Maureen (1986) *The Crazy Gang*, London: Weidenfeld & Nicolson.

Palmer, Jerry (1987) *The Logic of the Absurd: On Film and Television Comedy*, London: BFI Publishing.

Palmer, Jerry (1994) *Taking Humour Seriously*, London: Routledge.

Parsons, Nicholas (1994) *The Straight Man: My Life in Comedy*, London: Weidenfeld & Nicolson.

Patterson, Christina (2009) Untitled interview with Armando Iannucci. *The Independent* Newspaper, 14/08/2009.

Pavis, Patrice (1978) '*The Semiotics of Theatre*', Versus, No 21, 1978, trans. Tjaart Potgieter. Accessed online at: http://archive.lib.msu.edu/DMC/African%20Journals/pdfs/Critical%20Arts/cajv1n3/caj001003002.pdf.

Pease, Allan and Pease, Barbara (2004) *The Definitive Book of Body Language*, London: Orion.

Pertwee, Michael (1974) *Name Dropping*, London: Leslie Frewin.

Pertwee, Michael and Davies, Jack (1950) '*Laughter in Paradise*', Shooting Script, tentative title *The Joker*, dated 2 August 1950. © London: BFI Archive.

Pinker, Steven (1994) *The Language Instinct*, Harmondsworth: Penguin.

Pirandello, Luigi (1985) *Three Plays*, London: Methuen.

Plato, *Republic* 388e. *Philebus* 48–50. In Morreall, John (ed.) (1987) *The Philosophy of Laughter and Humor*, New York: Albany.

Plautus (1968) *Three Plays by Plautus*, New York: Mentor Books.

Pollock, David (2009) 'Back on the bill and on top form'. Article and interview with Billy Connolly in *The Independent* Newspaper, 21/09/2009.

Pollock, David (2015) 'Bringing it all back home'. Article on the Edinburgh Royal Lyceum's Production of *Waiting for Godot*, *The Independent Radar* Newspaper, 19/09/2015.

Powers, Mala (2002) in Chekhov, Michael (ed.) *To the Actor*, London: Routledge.

Priestley, J. B. (1976) *English Humour*, London: Heinemann.

Provine, Robert R. (2000) *Laughter: A Scientific Investigation*, London: Faber & Faber.

Purdie, Susan (1993) *Comedy: The Mastery of Discourse*, Herts: Harvester Wheatsheaf.

Quinlan, David (1992) *Quinlan's Illustrated Directory of Film Comedy Stars*, London: B. T. Batsford.

Raskin, Victor (ed.) (2008) *The Primer of Humor Research*, New York: Mouton de Gruyter.

Redgrave, Michael (1995) *The Actor's Ways and Means*, London: Nick Hern Books.

Reed, Christopher (2003) 'Obituary of Charles Douglass'. *The Guardian* Newspaper, 01/05/2003. Accessed online at: http://www.guardian.co.uk/media/2003/may/01/broadcasting.guardianobituaries.

Reid, Beryl (1985) *So Much Love: An Autobiography*, London: Routledge.

Ritchie, Chris (2006) *The Idler and the Dandy in Stage Comedy*, London: Edwin Mellen.

Ritchie, Chris (2012) *Performing Live Comedy*, London: Methuen.

Robinson, Fred Miller (1993) *The Man in the Bowler Hat: His History and Iconography*, London: University of North Carolina Press.

Rogers, Carl (1956) *Client-Centered Therapy: Its Current Practice, Implications and Theory* (3rd ed.), Boston: Houghton-Mifflin.

Russell Brown, John (1993) *Shakespeare's Plays in Performance*, New York: Applause Theatre Books.

Rutherford, Margaret (1972) *Margaret Rutherford: An Autobiography*, London: W. H. Allen.

Santayana, George (1896) 'The Sense of Beauty', New York: Scribner's. In Morreall, John (ed.) (1987) *The Philosophy of Laughter and Humor*, New York: Albany.

Sante, Luc and Holbrook Pierson, Melissa (1999) *O.K. You Mugs: Writers on Movie Actors*, New York: Pantheon Books.

Sartre, Jean Paul (1957) *Being and Nothingness*, trans. H. E. Barnes, London: Methuen.

Schechter, Joel (1994) *Brecht's Clowns: 'Man is Man' and After*. In Thomson, Peter and Sacks, Glendyr (eds) (1994) *The Cambridge Companion to Brecht*, Cambridge: Cambridge University Press, pp. 68–78.

Scheuer, Steven H. (ed.) (1992) *Movies on TV and Videocassette*, New York: Bantam.

Schön, Donald (1987) *Educating the Reflective Practitioner*, San Francisco: Jossey-Bass.

Schopenhauer, Arthur (1907) *The World as Will and Idea*, trans. Haldane, R. B. and Kemp, John, 6th edition. London: Routledge and Kegan Paul. In Morreall, John (ed.) (1987) *The Philosophy of Laughter and Humor*, New York: Albany.

Sciama, Lidia (ed.) (2016) *Humour, Comedy and Laughter: Obscenities, Paradoxes, Insights and the Renewal of Life*, Oxford: Berghahn Books.

Sclater, Ian (2015) 'The world's first superstar'. Accessed online at: http://www.eurograduate.com/lifestyle/article.asp?id=21&pid=5.

Scollon, Ron and Scollon, Suzie Wong (2003) *Discourses in Place: Language in the Material World*, London: Routledge.

Scott, Sophie (2006) 'Research project at University College London'. Accessed online at: http://www.wellcome.ac.uk/News/2006/News/WTX034943.htm.

Seyler, Athene (1943, 1990) *The Craft of Comedy*, London: Nick Hern Books.

Shakespeare, William (2005) *The Oxford Shakespeare: The Complete Works* (eds. Stanley Wells *et al.*) (2nd ed.). Oxford: Oxford University Press.

Sher, Antony (2015) *Year of the Fat Knight: The Falstaff Diaries*, London: Nick Hern Books.

Silvers, Phil (1973) *This Laugh is On Me*, New Jersey: Prentice Hall.

Simon, Neil (1966, 1994) *The Odd Couple*, London: Samuel French.

Sinden, Donald (1985) *Laughter in the Second Act*, London: Futura.

Sinden, Donald (1988) 'Malvolio in *Twelfth Night*', in Brockbank, Philip (ed.) *Players of Shakespeare 1*, Cambridge: Cambridge University Press.

Southworth, John (2003) *Fools and Jesters at the English Court*, Stroud: Sutton.

Stanislavski, Constantin (1936, 1986) *An Actor Prepares*, London: Methuen.

Stoppard, Tom (1968) *The Real Inspector Hound*, London: Samuel French.

Sturges, Fiona (2015) 'Why the sound of silence is always worth listening to'. Article on Evelyn Glennie in *The Independent* Newspaper, 30/07/2015.

Styan, J. L. (1975) *Drama, Stage and Audience*, Cambridge: Cambridge University Press.

Sutcliffe, Tom (2010) 'Television review of *The Persuasionists*'. Article in *The Independent* Newspaper, 14/01/2010.

Sutcliffe, Tom (2011) 'Comic timing's no laughing matter'. Article in *The Independent* Newspaper, 28/10/2011.

Sykes, Eric (2005) *If I Don't Write It, Nobody Else Will*, London: Fourth Estate.

Sypher, Wylie (ed.) (1994) *Comedy*, London: Johns Hopkins University Press.

Tafuri, Johannella (2008) *Infant Musicality: New Research for Educators and Parents*, trans. Hawkins, Elizabeth. Farnham: Ashgate.

Taylor, Malcom (1994) *The Actor and the Camera*, London: A & C Black.

Terence (1976) *The Comedies*, London: Penguin.

Thompson, Ben (2004) *Sunshine on Putty: The Golden Age of British Comedy, from Vic Reeves to the Office*, London: Harper Perennial.

Thomson, Peter (2000) *On Actors and Acting*, Exeter: University of Exeter.

Thomson, Peter (2002) 'The Comic Actor and Shakespeare'. In Wells, Stanley and Stanton, Sarah (eds) *The Cambridge Companion to Shakespeare on Stage*, Cambridge: Cambridge University Press.

Thomson, Peter and Sacks, Glendyr (eds) (1994) *The Cambridge Companion to Brecht*, Cambridge: Cambridge University Press.

Triezenberg, Katrina E. (2008) 'Humor in Literature'. In Raskin, Victor (ed.) *The Primer of Humor Research*, New York: Mouton de Gruyter.

Tucker, Patrick (2015) *Secrets of Screen Acting Abingdon* (3rd ed.). London: Routledge.

Unwin, Stephen (2005) *A Guide to the Plays of Bertold Brecht*, London: Methuen.

Van Leeuwen, Theo (2005) *Introducing Social Semiotics*, London: Routledge.

Van Leeuwen, Theo (2011) 'Rhythm and Multimodal Semiosis'. In Dreyfus, Shoshana, Hood, Susan and Stenglin, Maree (eds) *Semiotic Margins: Meanings in Multimodalities*, London: Continuum.

Walker, Tim (2009) 'Cowell's reality circus espouses British talent for eccentricity'. Article in *The Independent* Newspaper, 26/05/2009.

Walker, Tim (2011) 'And now, back to the studio...'. Article in *The Independent* Newspaper, 02/02/2011.

Wall, Max (1975) *The Fool on the Hill*, London: Quartet.

Walsh, Brian (2013) 'New directions: audience engagement and the genres of *Richard III*', in Connolly, Annaliese (ed.) *Richard III: A Critical Reader*, London: Bloomsbury.

Walsh, John (2015) 'Tour de Frances'. Article on Frances de la Tour in *The Independent* Magazine, 23/05/2015.

Watts, Peter (2011) 'This vintage satire leaves a sharp taste'. Article in *The Independent* Newspaper, 05/01/2011.

Weir, Molly (1979) *Walking into the Lyons' Den*, London: Arrow.

Weitz, Eric (2009) *The Cambridge Introduction to Comedy*, Cambridge: Cambridge University Press.

Welford, Heather (1999) *Ready, Steady, Baby: A Guide to Pregnancy, Birth and Early Parenthood*, Edinburgh: Health Education Board for Scotland.

White, Gareth (2013) *Audience Participation in the Theatre: Aesthetics of the Invitation*, Basingstoke: Palgrave Macmillan.

Whitehouse, David (2009) 'Ricky Gervais takes on Englishness'. Article in *The Shortlist* Magazine, 23/04/2009.

Whitfield, June (2000) *...And June Whitfield*, London: Bantam Press.

Wilde, Oscar (1974) *Plays*, Harmondsworth: Penguin.

Wilkie, Ian and Saxton, Matthew (2010) 'The Origins of Comic Performance in Adult–Child Interaction', *Comedy Studies*, 1(1), 21–32.

Williams, Kenneth (1993) *The Kenneth Williams Diaries*, London: HarperCollins.

Williams, Kevin (2003) *Understanding Media Theory*, London: Arnold.

Wilmut, Roger (1989) *Kindly Leave the Stage: The Story of Variety 1919–1960*, London: Methuen.

Wood, John Christopher (1977, 1999) *Elsie and Norm's 'Macbeth'*, London: Samuel French.

Worsley, T. C. (1952) *The Fugitive Art: Dramatic Commentaries 1947–1951*, London: John Lehmann.

Wright, John (2007) *Why Is That So Funny?* New York: Limelight.

Yacowar, Maurice (1982) *The Comic Art of Mel Brooks*, London: W. H. Allen.

Index